DREAM NATION

LATINIDAD

Transnational Cultures in the United States

This series publishes books that deepen and expand our knowledge and understanding of the various Latina/o populations in the United States in the context of their transnational relationships with cultures of the broader Americas. The focus is on the history and analysis of Latino cultural systems and practices in national and transnational spheres of influence from the nineteenth century to the present. The series is open to scholarship in political science, economics, anthropology, linguistics, history, cinema and television, literary and cultural studies, and popular culture and encourages interdisciplinary approaches, methods, and theories. The series grew out of discussions with faculty at the School of Transborder Studies at Arizona State University, where an interdisciplinary emphasis is being placed on transborder and transnational dynamics.

MATTHEW GARCIA, *Series Editor, School of Historical, Philosophical, and Religious Studies; and Director of Comparative Border Studies*

María Acosta Cruz, *Dream Nation: Puerto Rican Culture and the Fictions of Independence*

Rodolfo F. Acuña, *In the Trenches of Academe: The Making of Chicana/o Studies*

Adriana Cruz-Manjarrez, *Zapotecs on the Move: Cultural, Social, and Political Processes in Transnational Perspective*

Marivel T. Danielson, *Homecoming Queers: Desire and Difference in Chicana Latina Cultural Production*

Rudy P. Guevarra Jr., *Becoming Mexipino: Multiethnic Identities and Communities in San Diego*

Lisa Jarvinen, *The Rise of Spanish-Language Filmmaking: Out from Hollywood's Shadow, 1929–1939*

Regina M. Marchi, *Day of the Dead in the USA: The Migration and Transformation of a Cultural Phenomenon*

Desirée A. Martín, *Borderlands Saints: Secular Sanctity in Chicano/a and Mexican Culture*

Marci R. McMahon, *Domestic Negotiations: Gender, Nation, and Self-Fashioning in US Mexicana and Chicana Literature and Art*

A. Gabriel Melendez, *Hidden Chicano Cinema: Film Dramas in the Borderlands*

Priscilla Peña Ovalle, *Dance and the Hollywood Latina: Race, Sex, and Stardom*

Luis F. B. Plascencia, *Disenchanting Citizenship: Mexican Migrants and the Boundaries of Belonging*

Cecilia M. Rivas, *Salvadoran Imaginaries: Mediated Identities and Cultures of Consumption*

Maya Socolovsky, *Troubling Nationhood in U.S. Latina Literature: Explorations of Place and Belonging*

Dream Nation

Puerto Rican Culture
and the Fictions of Independence

MARÍA ACOSTA CRUZ

Rutgers University Press
NEW BRUNSWICK, NEW JERSEY, AND LONDON

LIBRARY OF CONGRESS CATALOGING-IN-PUBLICATION DATA

Acosta Cruz, María, 1956–
  Dream nation : Puerto Rican culture and the fictions of independence / María Acosta Cruz.
      pages cm. — (Latinidad: Transnational Cultures in the United States) (American Literatures Initiative)
  Includes bibliographical references and index.
  ISBN 978-0-8135-6547-7 (hardcover : alk. paper)
  ISBN 978-0-8135-6546-0 (pbk. : alk. paper)
  ISBN 978-0-8135-6548-4 (e-book)
    1. Puerto Rican literature—History and criticism. 2. National characteristics, Puerto Rican. 3. Puerto Rico—Civilization. 4. Puerto Rico—History—Autonomy and independence movements. I. Title.
  PQ7421.A27   2014
  860.9'97295—dc23

                                                          2013021948

A British Cataloging-in-Publication record for this book is available from the British Library.

Copyright © 2014 by María Acosta Cruz

All rights reserved

No part of this book may be reproduced or utilized in any form or by any means, electronic or mechanical, or by any information storage and retrieval system, without written permission from the publisher. Please contact Rutgers University Press, 106 Somerset Street, New Brunswick, NJ 08901. The only exception to this prohibition is "fair use" as defined by U.S. copyright law.

Visit our website: http://rutgerspress.rutgers.edu

Manufactured in the United States of America

A book in the American Literatures Initiative (ALI), a collaborative publishing project of NYU Press, Fordham University Press, Rutgers University Press, Temple University Press, and the University of Virginia Press. The Initiative is supported by The Andrew W. Mellon Foundation. For more information, please visit www.americanliteratures.org.

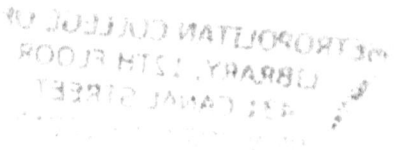

To my children, Daniel and Amanda Cesarano

Contents

	Preface	ix
	Acknowledgments	xi
	Introduction	1
1	Literary Tradition and the Canon of Independence	46
2	Breaking Tradition	80
3	From the Lush Land to the Traffic Jam	110
4	Dream History, Dream Nation	132
5	Dreaming in Spanglish	156
	Conclusion	176
	Biographical Appendix	179
	Notes	183
	Works Cited	187
	Index	201

Preface

On a cool night in April 2010, *Crime against Humanity*—a play about "Puerto Rican political prisoners"—was staged at my home institution, Clark University. Written, performed, and produced by the National Boricua Human Rights Network (Chicago Chapter), it offered a hero-worshipping view of Puerto Rico's "lucha por la independencia" (struggle for independence). The play's emphasis on heroic patriots was backed up by the presence, in the Q&A that followed, of self-proclaimed political prisoners who were identified as having "struggled for independence and fought colonialism."

Three of these freedom fighters—a term they embraced within hours of being apprehended, if one of the websites that champions them is to be believed—were there: Ricardo Jiménez, Alicia Rodríguez, and Adolfo Matos, members of the radical pro-independence group Los Macheteros who had served time after being convicted, in 1983, of robbing a Wells Fargo office. They explicitly and earnestly cast the Puerto Rican *people* as unwavering in the struggle for liberty. This fictional representation, to put it kindly, flies in the face of political reality since both the majority of islanders as well as Puerto Ricans in the United States reject independence for the island.

That night a mix of students, professors (including this specialist in Puerto Rican literature), and members of the Worcester, Massachusetts, community acquiesced mutely, timidly, to that illusory (if not delusional) picture of Puerto Rico as a land that wants, yearns for, fights for freedom.

Why did no one point out in the Q&A that for more than fifty years the overwhelming majority of the island has voted against independence? Or that despite the media attention paid in the 1970s to the Young Lords' ¡*Palante siempre palante!* activism for national sovereignty, Puerto Ricans in the United States also mirror island preferences and favor ties to the United States over independence? Carlos Vargas-Ramos notes that 54 percent favor commonwealth; 39 percent, statehood; 4 percent, independence; and 3 percent, some other status (151). Furthermore, he writes, "the longer a migrant sojourned abroad, the greater the preference for Puerto Rico becoming a state" (152). But that night we let it slide and did not question the fantastical notion that *la lucha* lives on in Puerto Rican hearts and minds. Maybe we were being polite. Or perhaps the public was there because it felt the cultural allure of independence, the *je ne sais quoi* that still makes independence heroes, symbols, and stories ineffably aspirational: dreams that conjure up a Puerto Rico of the imagination, a beloved *dream nation*. Despite (or perhaps because of) its political ineffectiveness, *independentismo* has created compelling fictions in significant and widely read works of Puerto Rican literature (and other forms of culture). What the "*la lucha* lives on" notion does *not* do is correspond to reality. We, the public, on that cool night in 2010, did not want to burst the bubble of the play's dream nation, a verdant land in which a unified people fight for independence.

With this book, I want to do what I didn't do then. Speak up.

Acknowledgments

I've wanted to write this book since I was sixteen, and it would not have been possible without the people who sustained and blessed me with their help. *¡Gracias, mi gente!*

My dad, Ing. Aníbal Acosta Ayala bravely read the entire manuscript in record time. The book has an introduction thanks to the impressive editing skills and dedication of my boyfriend, the Honorable William H. Abrashkin. My daughter, Amanda Cesarano, cheered me on throughout. The book proposal would not have seen the light of day without my dear friend (once student) Dr. Jessica Jiménez.

Clark University has nurtured and supported my entire career. Two provosts, Fred Greenaway and David Angel (who is now Clark's extraordinary president) gave me their steadfast support and academic guidance. My thinking has been profoundly impacted by the work of Clark's Higgins School of Humanities, which, under the leadership of Sarah Buie and Amy Richter, encourages a broad community of dialogue. Our wonderful librarians, Irene Walch, Mary Hartman, Holly Howes, and Rachael Shea, succored my research more times than I can say. Clark's information technology crew, especially Gregory Geiger and Cheryl Elwell Turner, saw to it that all possible tech support and tools were at my disposal.

The Foreign Languages & Literatures Department, particularly Alice Valentine, Robert D. Tobin, Marvin D'Lugo, and Juan Pablo Rivera, helped me develop the guiding ideas about nationhood at the heart of the book. I could not have been chair of the department and written the book at the same time without Dilma Lucena, our fearless department manager, who kept me on track, kept me sane.

My ideas and readings grew and expanded through interactions with my students in the "Caribbean Literatures" and "The National Imagination" courses, among others. With their happy curiosity, dogged search for meaning, and their patience with a professor prone to wild tangents, they made our shared discoveries and love of culture all the more productive and enjoyable.

Leslie Mitchner and Lisa Boyajian of Rutgers University Press and Tim Roberts and Susan Murray of the American Literatures Initiative shepherded and steered the book to the final product. Alison Russo heroically indexed its contents.

And finally, to my Facebook friends, family, and colleagues, thanks for keeping me up to date on life in our beloved island.

My love and gratitude to you all.

Note on Text

All translations in this book are my own. I have included the Spanish originals of works of creative writing for the enjoyment of bilingual readers.

Dream Nation

Introduction

In a world in which Chechen, Catalan, Scottish, and Sri Lankan nationalists, among others, command significant attention calling for national liberation, Puerto Ricans have perplexingly rejected political independence.[1] Puerto Rican independence (through political action or by force of arms) is an anachronism, a relic buried under more than a half century of electoral rejection.[2]

Given that political reality, why are themes of independence still so powerful in Puerto Rican culture? Why do many Puerto Rican writers on the island and in the United States cling to this ideal? Who among them has opposed this established position? Why has cultural independence succeeded whereas political independence failed? How does the dream nation enhance what being a Puerto Rican *means*?

This book explores these questions in relation to how independence has become a *symbolic aspiration*, a grand gesture of love, a refuge for national pride, and an intellectual fantasy that sustains how Puerto Rican culture imagines the nation (its heroes, its allegories, its significant stories). Puerto Rican culture has, until recently, hardly explored the two other status options, commonwealth and statehood. And yet it is these two that represent the political will of the people. Like Puerto Rico and Puerto Ricans themselves, the issue of sovereignty is fraught with the push and pull of wishes, yearnings, dashed aspirations, and hoped-for dreams.

The paradoxes that this book grapples with are mostly absent from discussions in Puerto Rican cultural studies because for the most part, culture critics have favored independence, and as a result, the disconnect between culture and daily reality has largely remained on the sidelines. There are some specialists in Puerto Rican cultural studies who have critiqued the dream of independence, but they have done so in academic articles and scholarly books that are not widely read. The present book aims to remedy that by being clear, forthright, and jargon-free.

The people who produce and criticize high-end cultural products have themselves had discussions and conflicts on the matter, as the spat between Rosario Ferré and the literary establishment in the 1990s proves (see chapter 2). And it must not be forgotten that the dream of independence also remains strong in popular culture, for instance in rap music, where its long-standing pose of defiance against The Man as well as expressions of powerful self-regard (or national self-esteem) are extremely appealing.

At the outset, I want to state clearly that I do not view independence as a viable political alternative *nor* as the sole lodestar of Puerto Rican literature and culture. I am fully aware that nothing is a monolith; that is certainly the case for a broad political movement such as *independentismo*, which has many shades.[3] Neither do I believe that any one book can be comprehensive about Puerto Rican culture.

This book aims to sample a variety of cultural artifacts, history, and politics to scrutinize the paradoxical impulses of independence/dependence in Puerto Rico. Some of the central concepts explained in later chapters spring from the intricacies of Puerto Rico's political status in relationship to the United States, especially the historical context of the island's 1898 annexation by the United States. I explore how stories, symbols, and fictions of achieving sovereignty have often depended on nostalgia linked to a premodern lost Lush Land paradise. Another issue I consider important is how a sense of shame shapes the reactions of a dependent country. As the book progresses, I stress the rift between cultural/literary ideas of independence and the realities of daily dependence, as well as point out how more complex concepts of the nation arise in contemporary cultural production, and, finally, how the ambivalent love/hate relationship to Puerto Rico plays out in Latino writers.

Embedded in Puerto Rican culture is a deep longing for the stories, themes, and symbols of independence which are woven into the DNA of the culture's highbrow as well as popular modes. The independence ideal exerts the fascination of a cultural meme that therapeutically processes the failed project of political independence as a national wrong that was never made right—and provides a shared tragedy (or at least melodrama).[4]

The people, however, have rejected the practical burdens of independent nationhood. Why? Among the reasons for the voting patterns are that, initially, the island consciously hitched its wagon to a rising star in the 1940s and 1950s, when the American Century was in full swing and when islanders decided on the present political status, the commonwealth, or ELA. Nowadays, after consumer culture has taken root, it may be difficult for people to risk losing their intricate web of connections to the United States and, more importantly, their hard-earned social benefits and instead choose the radical changes and the austerity that sovereignty would bring. So that like a recurring stubborn dream, Puerto Rican independence remains a deeply significant part of the island's cultural unconscious: unreal, unattainable, yet constantly resurfacing.

At the polls, ordinary Puerto Ricans rebuff independence, but many of the people who produce culture (as well as the outnumbered *independentista* voters) can't resist its appeal. Yet the siren song of the fight for liberty doesn't surface only in highbrow culture, such as in the works of the poets allied to the literary journal *Guajana* or in the films of Jacobo Morales; it shows up in popular and mass culture as well. Calle 13, arguably the most famous Puerto Rican musical group of the early twenty-first century, is a good example. This superstar hip-hop and alternative-reggaeton group's pro-independence political stylings have endeared them to the literary establishment, for whom their songs are "tirades against state power" (Negrón-Muntaner and Rivera 39). The band is noteworthy for its continued public support for independence. During his 2011 performance at the Latin Grammy ceremony (where his group received a whopping nine Grammys), René Pérez (a.k.a. Residente) sported a T-shirt with the message "una sola estrella libre" (only one free star), a well-known motto of independence that contrasts Puerto Rico's one-star flag with the U.S. multistar flag. Juan Flores says that "the 'one-star flag' (la monoestrellada) is the most venerated singular emblem of the Puerto Rican nationality" (*Bomba* 31). Because of Calle 13's pro-independence stance, Pérez has been lionized by the nationalist[5] cultural establishment. For instance, he appeared in 2009 alongside the novelist Mayra Montero and the playwright Lin-Manuel Miranda at the fifth gala dinner of the pro-independence flagship newspaper *Claridad*. Moreover, the leftist credentials awarded by his support for Puerto Rico's independence led to his meeting with the president of Argentina, Cristina Fernández de Kirchner, in 2012. On the other hand, the centrist contrarian Edgardo Rodríguez Juliá has reviled him.[6]

One can see the logic of pronouncements for independence in the 1960s and 1970s Nueva Trova singer-songwriters, like Roy Brown for example, because that was the height of Cuban-inspired leftism, but why the activism of Calle 13? Not to discount real feelings on the part of its members, but in the video *Querido F.B.I.* they exaggeratedly portray the entire country, all 3.5 million (at the time), as wielding rebel machetes! Moreover, Calle 13 is not the only hip-hop/rap group or artist to embrace the cause. Tego Calderón, a rap star, caught the attention of an NPR reporter (in 2013) not only because he is representative of Latin hip-hop, but more distinctly because he is also "vocal about Puerto Rican independence" (Garsd). Calderón vividly uses the full pantheon of independence heroes (Lolita Lebrón, Pedro Albizu Campos, José Antonio Corretjer, Juan Mari Brás, Filiberto Ojeda Ríos) in his video *Cosas que pasan*. He does so because independence heroes are still popular beyond the reach of their political effectiveness.

The feelings of power and solidarity that come from independence heroes have deep roots. And for rap stars a pro-independence posture has the added bonus of being confrontational to the government and the bourgeoisie. The political stance therefore enhances their attitude of braggadocio and of (mostly) manly rebelliousness against the establishment in general. In addition, there is the seduction of independence's continuing connection to what is regarded as a more authentic form of national identity. Independence in sum, teases out a long-standing countercultural cachet, which is *cool*.

The Rican Nation and Heroes

Inarguably, Puerto Rican independence has been defeated at the polls, which is partially the appeal of its heroes, who never achieved their vision and who populate Puerto Rican culture in significant and enduring ways. Few, actually, *no* political movement in Puerto Rico rivals the centrality of independence in begetting heroes. Martinican critic Édouard Glissant speaks of the *need* for heroes in the Caribbean: "One can go so far as to argue that *the defeats of heroes* are necessary to the solidarity of communities" (68; my italics).

Another appeal of heroes can be the loftiness of their rhetoric. Pedro Albizu Campos, himself a tragic, fearless public figure, spoke soaringly about independence heroism. In Albizu's grandiose, old-fashioned rhetorical style, the dream of national freedom becomes the quasi-religious path to the nation's redemption: "Se busca en las grandes figuras de la historia el secreto de su poder, de su heroísmo, de su sacrificio, el secreto de su sabiduría. Para quien la muerte no existe, es la hora de la humildad, es la hora de desafiar todas las fuerzas terrenales. Se levanta el heroísmo con una sonrisa que es el amanecer de gloria" ("Discurso en Utuado," 23 Feb. 1950, in Rodríguez Vázquez 221; In the great figures of history one searches for the secret of their power, their heroism, their sacrifice, the secret of their wisdom. For whom death does not exist, it is the hour of humility, it is the hour to defy all earthly forces. Heroism rises with a smile that is the dawn of glory). José Rodríguez Vázquez says that in effect Albizu's brand of nationalism was "obsessed with the cult of heroes" (429) and that hero worship is one of the building blocks of Puerto Rican nationalism, or specifically, "Albuizuist" nation-building culture: "Albuizuism shaped its moralizing project for public life by exalting heroism" (216). John Pervolaris says that rhetoric outlived Albizu's political aims: "'La patria es valor y sacrificio,' Albizu famously proclaimed, and these virtues have tended to function as a cathartic end in themselves rather than an effective means to independence" (694).

This continuing appeal of heroes for the nationalist (i.e., *independentista*) cause proved much more culturally effective and exercises a far more tenacious hold on the literary and popular imagination than the political facet of the nationalist political movement, which was ground down under the sad reality (for Albizu) of government repression. The quintessential martyrdom connected to heroes like Albizu results in hero worshipping that ripples in popular culture beyond politics. Pervolaris describes some of the complexities of the cult of Albizu as "anachronism and self-sacrificing futility, as well as undeniable courage and integrity" (693).

In significant cultural circles, Albizu's star has dimmed; later we will examine what José Luis González, famous dissenter of standard *independentismo*, had to say about him. Historians, for instance, are inclined to look at Albizu's legacy with a jaundiced eye. An example is Luis Ángel Ferrao's *Pedro Albizu Campos y el nacionalismo puertorriqueño 1930–1939*, which documents Albizu's tendency to authoritarianism as well as the power grabs within his political party. But the appeal of his image of courage and defiance continues into the twenty-first century, and certainly his face has not faded from popular graphic arts.

6 / INTRODUCTION

FIGURE 1. Albizu on a billboard, 2012. (Photo by María Acosta Cruz)

The legend is aided by the ubiquitousness of the *independentista* leader's image. The striking photos of a fiery Albizu in midspeech, for instance, are so well known and have become so commercialized (since they are not copyrighted) that in 2012 his face and his motto "Despierta boricua" (Wake up, Puerto Rican) appeared on billboards hawking a cell-phone provider. Despite such craven marketing of the dead leader's image, there is still much heartfelt affection for him and for other *independentista* figures regarded as martyrs. For instance, Filiberto Ojeda Ríos, a Machetero (an extremist wing of nationalist activism), killed during an FBI assault in 2005, was featured in Calle 13's video *Querido F.B.I.*, which accuses the federal agency of ambushing the nationalist hero.

Another, more immediate and perhaps more earnest sign of the popular devotion to nationalist figures was the outburst of obituaries and tributes by the intelligentsia, pro-independence politicians, and everyday bloggers in the wake of Lolita Lebrón's death. She was both freedom fighter and *mater dolorosa,* a heroine of Puerto Rican independence who has inspired devotion since the 1950s. When Lebrón died in August 2010, there was a flood of media and Internet obituaries, tributes, and expressions of mourning from cultural figures, *independentista* stalwarts, and social media, highlighting how important a *woman* hero can be. Lebrón's actions during the 1954 nationalist attack on the U.S. Congress—she shouted, *¡Viva Puerto Rico libre!* the die-hard slogan of independence—made her a star of the movement and of *nonpolitical* sympathizers, and they were legion. A press release from the Nationalist Party (a party in name only as it is not registered for elections) highlighted the "military" significance of her most famous action. Though she later hedged on the need for violence,[7] according to the *Washington Post,* the attack on Congress gave her international cachet comparable to Latin American freedom fighters such as Che Guevara and Pancho Villa (Brown). The fact that she and her three companions fired between twenty-nine and thirty pistol shots into a group of people (hitting five, one congressman in the chest) is not only glossed over by most admirers but, as in *Claridad*'s obituary, turned around to *her* intended martyrdom since Lebrón and her fellow shooters expected to be killed: "On one occasion, the nationalist leader stated that the attack on the U.S. Congress did not intend to cause the death of any congressman and, on the contrary, members of the command intended to sacrifice themselves, because they thought they would die in action" (*Claridad* obituary, 2 Aug. 2010).[8]

Lebrón's image is also commonplace in both highbrow and popular iconography, particularly the famous photo taken when she was apprehended after the attack on Congress, showing her beautifully defiant.

Her long-term activism—at eighty-one years of age she was arrested during a Vieques protest—ensured that she remained a hero in the public eye, particularly as she was adamant about the need for sovereignty and devoted her life to its pursuit. The tenor of the pro-independence obits hailed her as a true Puerto Rican. Her gender assured the devotion of Young Turk postfeminist writers such as Ana María Fuster Lavin, who described a saddened, energized but tiny *independentista* crowd at her memorial chanting the Puerto Rican revolutionary anthem and shouting, "Lolita Lebrón! Example of valor!" and "Lolita Libre!" (forwarded through Fuster's Yahoo group).The mourning of the symbolic body of independence was enacted to a lesser extent when Juan Mari Brás, founder of the Partido Socialista Puertorriqueño (Puerto Rican Socialist Party), died a few weeks later. *Independentistas* gathered to see the body of the leader whom *Claridad* (the *independentista* newspaper which he cofounded) proclaimed as "the most important Puerto Rican independence leader of the second half of the twentieth century" (obituary, 10 Sept. 2010).

Sadly for enthusiasts, the heroes of independence are passing away. And, given the lack of recent popular heroes from the political sphere (due to the shortcomings and incompetence of recent governments in Puerto Rico), it is no accident that Lebrón—political crusader, feminist icon, and defender of human rights—would mean so many things to so many people (Romero-Cesareo). Very few national figures today outside of media celebrities command the feverish hyperbole evident when the longtime head of the PIP, Rubén Berrios, exalted her as "the most eternal of the women in our history," stating further (with the customary religious overtones of old-time *independentismo*) that she became "a mystic of patriotism" (PIP press communiqué, 1 Aug. 2010).

FIGURE 2. Lolita Lebrón's arrest in 1954.

Part of the fanatical devotion that dead nationalist heroes like Lebrón and Pedro Albizu Campos can still inspire arises from their identification with *La Gran Familia Puertorriqueña*, the widespread attachment of political movements (everywhere) to the Family = Nation allegory. Lebrón was venerated as a living symbol of the struggle for freedom because of the maternal representation of her particular mythology. María de Lourdes Santiago, senator for the PIP, succinctly said that "Lolita was the mother of the independence movement. This is an insurmountable loss" (Associated Press). Revealing hidden depths of gender stereotyping, Albizu is commonly called "Maestro" (Teacher), although he is also revered as a "father" of the cause. The depiction of Lebrón's death as "insurmountable" isn't only a politician's predictable histrionics; instead, it responds to the power of the allegory of family linked to the dream nation. Undoubtedly, a mother figure packs an emotional significance that *is* irreplaceable.

Lest anyone forget the link that defenders of independence make between the island's quest for sovereignty and Puerto Rican identity, at Lebrón's funeral Josean Santiago, the mayor of the town of Comerío and president of the association of mayors, declared, "Today we can celebrate our national identity, our Puerto Rican race" ("Último adiós a Lolita Lebrón," *El Nuevo Día* 2 Aug. 2010).

In sum, the independence movement's cadre of activist heroes gave it the upper *symbolic* hand over all the other political parties on the island for a long time. Only one figure from an opposing party had as much fame and left a significant literary and cultural imprint: Luis Muñoz Marín, founder of the middle-of-the-road, ELA-option party, the Partido Popular Democrático (PPD).[9] And he started out as an *independentista!*

The Francophone Islands: A Comparison

Given that the cultural identity of the island has in the past decades became more entwined with its Caribbean context, it is curious that most discussions of status matters overlook the road taken by the Caribbean French islands, or DOMs (Départements d'Outre-Mer), which are official departments of France, including Guadeloupe and Martinique.[10] These neighboring island nations willingly chose to incorporate in their powerful *métropole*, a relationship that has been increasingly fraught with difficulties. The Council on Hemispheric Affairs (COHA), an independent research and information organization, offered a summary of the colonial and neocolonial conditions that led to widespread unrest in Guadeloupe during 2009: "France decided to launch its assimilation process through a system called '*départementalisation*.' The *République* wanted to generously offer to those territories what they had been fighting to achieve for decades: their full recognition and integration as part of France. Yet, in the middle of the process, independence movements began to gain credence in Guadeloupe, particularly during the 1960s" ("Guadeloupe: Out of Sight").

Puerto Rico and the DOMs are similar because they never achieved the formal status of sovereign states. Yet the DOMs made the decision to incorporate and thus rarely figure in the cultural discussions of Puerto Rico's status (one exception is the critic Ramón Grosfoguel). One reason given by culture critics for the distance between the areas is, as expected, that colonialism keeps Puerto Rico apart from other regions (Santiago Caraballo).

There are, however, significant differences between the current day-to-day situations of Puerto Rico and the DOMS; the chief divergence is that the DOMs, now as part of France, vote in French presidential elections and are members of the National Assembly and the Senate, whereas Puerto Ricans have no say in presidential or congressional elections. Nevertheless, in the 1970s, both the DOMs and Puerto Rico experienced a similar resurgence of independence-minded factions. The *Encyclopedia of Contemporary French Culture* notes the political climate of the French islands at that time: "In Martinique and French Guiana, and especially in Guadeloupe and Reunion, there was considerable *indépendantiste* activity in the 1970s, but thereafter it diminished markedly because of government crackdowns on militant extraparliamentary protests, the administrative decentralization of the 1980s, and the waning of the radical views with which pro-independence positions were linked" (414). Another similarity in both regions was that during that crucial period in literary history (the 1960s and 1970s), a powerful group of talented writers gave their support to the cause.

So, how do *independentistas* explain the people's inclination to *dependence*? As I mentioned before, the most common justification is that the colonial condition itself has alienated Puerto Ricans, who are therefore incapable of making an informed decision on the matter. This portrayal of the people as victims and/or dupes, however, alienates the very people who need to be swayed if the independence-minded activists and writers are to achieve their dream. The belief that Puerto Ricans have allowed themselves to be bamboozled has been fuelled by one of the most fruitful (and contentious) cultural depictions of the national character: the docile Puerto Rican. Carlos Gil, a critic who talks about a crisis of *independentismo*, explains how the dubious concept of docility has worked: "After five hundred years of colonialism, the docile Puerto Rican would be incapacitated and unable to act responsibly and consciously in regards to its own future" (98). The image of a docile Puerto Rican has been debated since influential essays such as Antonio S. Pedreira's *Insularismo* (1934) and René Marqués's notorious "The Docile Puerto Rican" (1966), which characterized the colonial condition as a sickness suffered by the Puerto Rican people. Luis Rafael Sánchez remains the staunchest foe of the idea of Puerto Rican docility, which he tears apart in *Abecé indócil* (Un-docile abc).

This notion, however, has been retrodden into hard-core *political* pro-independence thinking that has sometimes held that Puerto Ricans have become, through colonialist misuse, weak-willed and *incapable* of deciding for sovereignty. Rafael Cancel Miranda—who served twenty-eight years in U.S. federal prison because of his participation in the nationalist attack on the House of Representatives in 1954—summarizes this reasoning: Puerto Rico's residents are disempowered and victimized by their colonial status. In addition, he believes repressive entities such as the CIA and the FBI control the mass media. Finally, Cancel Miranda categorically rejects the legitimacy of any island electoral process since "it is not possible to have democratic elections in a colony" (Rodríguez, "Rafael Cancel Miranda").

1990s Turn-Around: Voices of Dissent

There is a consequential minority of scholarly critics who point out that the time for independence has passed irretrievably. Nonetheless, their message has not been more widely read outside academia because it has, for the most part, been couched in the dense jargon of cultural criticism. For instance, in 1997, in the introduction to *Puerto Rican Jam*, Frances Negrón-Muntaner and Ramón Grosfoguel declare themselves beyond mere taking of sides: "We are not necessarily suggesting a new 'content' for a national project (under the guise, for example, of a new revolutionary subject). On the contrary, we are posing a set of questions that propose that the resistance to a nation-state project by the majority of Puerto Ricans partly speaks to a discursive terrain of heterogeneity that is alien to nationalism as a political strategy leading to the founding of a state" (2–3). Given the thickly theoretical language of the book, it is not a surprise that their questioning of conventional pro-independence thinking as well as their positing alternate ways of conceiving the nation have not become more popular outside of academic circles. Further proof that Puerto Rican culture is not a monolith behind independence, Carlos Pabón's book-length broadside *Nación postmortem* (2002) was an assault on old-fashioned "one-language" nationalism and touched off a brawl with "neo-nationalist" as well as old-guard *independentistas* who accused Pabón and his ilk of being postmodern and/or nihilistic.[11]

As we will see, although a contingent of cultural critics has questioned the dream nation in the past few decades, few major writers (or other so-called culture producers) in Puerto Rico have stepped away from the dream and almost none identify themselves as belonging to the political parties that favor statehood or the ELA, so that prominent exceptions like the major writer Rosario Ferré stand out all the more. We'll look at the exceptions carefully in chapter 2, "Breaking Tradition." Most contemporary writers skirt the matter of status altogether. On the other hand, some notable stateside Puerto Rican writers, such

Esmeralda Santiago, write from within pro-independence ideology (see chapter 5).

The heroic faces of figures such as Albizu and Lebrón represent the *patria*, but there are equally important events that help build its stories. Ernst Renan, the venerable theorist of nationhood, speaks of how memory (and forgetting) of past events is a contributing factor of national formation. In Puerto Rico there are solemn memories of traumatic moments in history when independence *held center stage* that are regarded as central to the dream nation. The Grito de Lares and the Ponce Massacre are fateful events featured frequently as scenes of national meaning.

Two stories by pro-independence writer Ana Lydia Vega serve to illustrate how heroic events play out in literature. In "Un domingo de Lilliane" (Lilliane's Sunday), the Ponce Massacre is seen from three different points of view (from characters who are also from different social strata). At least one of the characters, Carlos, a newspaper photographer, is witness to the scene of the nationalist protestors mowed down by the police: "vio a los nacionalistas en atención con sus rifles de palo; vio, detrás, a las mujeres todas vestidas de blanco. Vio también la fila de ametralladoras Thompson como una oscura frontera entra la vida y la muerte, como un río congelado. —Mira eso, es una encerronada, —dijo" (119; he saw the nationalists at attention with their wooden rifles; he saw behind them the women all dressed in white. He also saw the row of Thompson machine guns like a dark frontier between life and death, like a frozen river. —Look at that, it's an ambush, —he said). Like shock waves, the effects of the deadly incident of that Sunday transform all the characters' lives, even those who were not direct witnesses to the event.

Another of Vega's stories, "Sobre héroes y tumbas" (On heroes and tombs), wades into the historical fray to discuss the importance of the other iconic event, the Grito de Lares. It bears noting that the story is divided into past and present: the unsung dead of the Grito and, in the present, the modern-day upholders of the torch, three hapless, would-be historians. The story is a postmodern 1980s fun/serious take on hero worship, with the Grito and its heroes sought by the present-day quixotic rescuers of the event: a historian, a feminist, and a patriot. Connecting to the heroes directly, the story starts with Don Virgilio, the elderly patriot, whose quest for historical truth and redemptive patriotism drives the narration, having a dream of Albizu as a spiritual guide (*Pasión de historia* 99). Don Virgilio's passion for history ensnares the two youngsters in the search for the tombs of the nationalist heroes.

The Grito de Lares is at the center of the story, but there are allusions to the Ponce Massacre also. The young historian's sensationalist thesis is that murder is the unifying element in Puerto Rican colonial history. He is researching eyewitness accounts to the Grito de Lares but also accounts of yet another traumatic event, the Cerro Maravilla ambush of young *independentistas* by government forces. The *signal* moments of independence are what the story calls "la Intra-Historia, la épica oculta, la canción de gesta de los supuestamente derrotados" (103; Intra-History, the hidden epic, the epic song of the supposedly vanquished). In other words, it is the hidden story of the losing side, which the young historian believes ties the meaning of the nation all together.

Through Guiomar, the young feminist, Vega highlights a different set of values through heroines: Mariana Bracetti, Doris Torresola, Ana Roqué de Duprey, and Luisa Capetillo, a patriotic heroine/writer who was herself "rescued by history" in the late twentieth century. The search for the dead heroes is an offshoot of frustrated nationalism; Virgilio thinks all his physical ills have to do with the crime against Grito nationalists that remains hidden to history, crimes that refuse to die down, that will not be forgotten, that carry the weight of their symbolism to the younger generation when the older one dies. Don Virgilio's solemn letter (before the postmodern devil-may-care false ending) cuts across the story's blithe sarcasm as he entrusts the ten volumes of the history he's been writing, called *Guerrillas del recuerdo* (Guerrillas of memory), to the young patriots (138). The story, published in 1987, has the usual marks of postmodernism: it mixes high and low culture, has multiple narrators and inner story lines, and mocks—in the funny, self-reflexive manner of the times—all ideologies *except*, that is, the heroism of independence.

These two stories show how unsuccessful attempts at armed revolution left a storytelling legacy disproportionate to their small size. The Grito de Lares, which was a small rebellion in the town of Lares in the nineteenth century, is still regarded as a cultural landmark central to the story of Puerto Rico.

Part of the role of culture for *independentistas* is that literature, film, music, or the other arts can invent fiction where history lagged behind. For instance, since the real-life results from the resistance to the Americans in 1898 were lackluster, the writer Luis López Nieves invented an entire *town* that resisted the invasion *to the death* in his novella *Seva* (see chapter 4).

However, as I mentioned earlier, a recent contingent of culture critics has reassessed the dream of independence and its reliance on heroism as the binding glue of the national story. Many of these critical voices live in the United States since challenging the orthodoxy on the island can be dicey. Prominent Stateside cultural theorists such as Juan Flores, Ramón Grosfoguel, and Frances Negrón-Muntaner have followed the trail blazed by the exiled writer José Luis González in voicing criticism of rote adherence to independence. Juan Flores speaks of this rupture: "Puerto Rican identity is described by the newer critics as multiple, nomadic, diasporic, and disengaged (in the theoretical language of the 1990s) from the categorical moorings of hoped-for independent nation. The undermining of the primacy of the concept of nation (as sovereign nation) has gone so far as to lead some [. . .] to abandon the 'heavy,' totalizing, propagandistic nationalism of earlier years in favor of what is termed 'la independencia lite'" (*Bomba* 34).

The first decade of the twenty-first century, however, brought us works by thinkers who signal renewed support of independence such as Rafael Bernabe's *Manual para organizar velorios* (2003) and José R. Rodríguez Vázquez's *El sueño que no cesa* (2004). The historian Ángel Collado Schwarz led (prior to the 2012 elections) cohorts in the Instituto Soberanista Puertorriqueño (Puerto Rican Sovereignty Institute, or ISP) around the island giving PowerPoint presentations about how to lead the island to a sovereign status.

The strategic alliances between nationalist activists and repressed minorities regarded as *heroic* has been strong in the culture industries since the 1970s, when women writers found a spiritual home under the umbrella provided by the independence outlets. This kind of connection between *independentismo* and excluded minorities is still going strong; for instance, the *independentista* flagship newspaper *Claridad* makes common cause with the LGBT movement in its "En Rojo" culture section. The swirl of creativity and controversy evident on display around the rights of marginalized people and the responses by independence activists are a reason that *la lucha* remains a vital presence on the island's culture scene.

So culture, with its eagerness for strong heroic story lines, has been one of the most successful instruments for Puerto Rican nationalism. Heroism enhances the dignity of *cultural* nationalism, which has powerful pull and is embraced equally by commonwealth and statehood supporters for whom it saves face in light of continued political and economic dependence. So pervasive is the force that, as Mario Ramos Méndez says, there is a long-standing tradition of Puerto Rican statehooders who regard statehood as a form of independence. The notion of states' rights is, as Ramos Méndez's *Posesión del ayer* specifies, key to statehooders' emphasis on national dignity, which is commonly linked to sovereignty. He quotes Luis A. Ferré, founder of the pro-statehood party (PNP), in rapprochement with nationalist champions: "So I am sympathetic to fierce *independentistas:* because we are fused with the supreme aspiration. They want sovereignty apart [...] we ask for the same sovereignty within the American Union" (99). Both factions, as a matter of fact, usually agree on their disdain for the party in the middle, the PPD. The PNP has also used the phrase "estadidad jíbara" (*jíbaro* statehood) to connect to cultural nationalism through the *jíbaro*, that iconic symbol of Puerto Ricanness.[12]

In fact, the emotional appeal of national sovereignty of any sort is used by *all* political factions in Puerto Rico. The Partido Popular, the pro-commonwealth PPD, is equally adamant in its defense of Puerto Rico's autonomy, which it claims will (when perfected) be the political equal of sovereignty. The *populares* profess equal love to *la patria,* as is obvious in their old motto "pan, tierra y libertad" (bread, land, and liberty). And it was they who pushed the *jíbaro* as a national cultural emblem.[13] Proof of the effectiveness of this kind of patriotic use of stereotypes is how assiduously all political parties (not just nationalists)—as well as corporations—have pursued identification with the landscape. For example, the statehood party, the PNP, appropriated the majestic royal palm tree as its logo.

All parties want to own symbols of Puerto Ricanness because "the possession of a national culture has become one of the standard marks of nationhood within the world system" ("Literature and Nationalism," *Encyclopedia of Nationalism*). Literature and the arts are taken to express, in almost Romantic terms, the valiant uniqueness of the people (the *Volk*) separating them from other nations.

Independentistas, perhaps more than any other cultural agent, had a strong hand in creating that culture of nationhood. Arlene Dávila asserts that they had a significant role in the rise of the prominent Instituto de Cultura Puertorriqueña (ICP, Institute of Puerto Rican Culture) founded in 1956 and they comprised many of its top administrators, "including its first two directors as well as the artistic core of the institution" (42).

In fact, the *cultural* definition of the nation—and the links between literature and independence—allow Papo Coss, a "hostosiano,"[14] to declare victory on behalf of the *independentista* struggle in the twenty-first century: "the independence movement, Puerto Rican culture workers and Puerto Rican athletes have been pivotal in the defense of Puerto

Ricanness. [...] In this cultural trench *we've conquered* all attempts at assimilation" ("La renovación del independentismo 2009" [The Renovation of Independentismo 2009]). Coss strategically mixes *independentistas* with personalities such as sports figures and other nonspecific "culture workers" who he believes have won the fight for the *cultural* delimitation of the Puerto Rican nation against assimilation by the United States and its powerful culture. He thinks the fight for the nation was waged and *won* in the culture trenches, where literature and the arts remain crucial for the dream nation despite political defeat.

Zilkia Janer, in *Puerto Rican Nation-Building Literature*, on the other hand, says that "colonial nationalism" implies giving up on politics, de facto validating colonialism (2). She speaks of a Puerto Ricanness that lives on only in cultural artifacts and commodities—where the flag on a T-shirt is enough proof of Puerto Ricanness. Furthermore, she adds, "In the case of Puerto Rico, cultural nationalism has been an end in itself [...] its power to eventually challenge colonial rule has been neutralized" (3). As Janer points out, culture alone (separate from the political, legal, and economic realms) cannot change the island's status. What it *can* do is avoid the shame of dependency and sustain the dream nation.

National symbols, which are resonant with dreams of sovereignty, have become part of the Puerto Rican brand. The selling of the nation is done by many kinds of commercial interests. An opportunistic market sells sentimental or kitschy *tchotchkes* featuring national icons associated with the Land and its most iconic human representations: the *jíbaros* and the Taínos. These two human icons are featured alongside the Puerto Rican flag or maps of the island, along with cutesy national symbols such as the indigenous frog called *coquí*, palm trees, the *pava* hat, etc., items inevitably manufactured in Asian economies. In the end, independence also has worked to sell the dream nation brand.

As Arlene M. Dávila and other critics have documented, corporate interests frequently co-opt Puerto Rican nationalist cultural symbols. Dávila summarizes this process: "Culture is certainly fashionable in Puerto Rico. In addition to the hundreds of cultural festivals that are celebrated every year on the island, transnational corporations, well aware that culture sells, are drawing on images of Puerto Rican folklore and popular culture to advertise beer, cigarettes, and other products" (1). Dávila speaks of the culture wars that have raged in island institutions since the 1950s and that have resulted in the present ascendancy of cultural nationalism and its marketable symbols, and she ties many of these symbols to pro-independence groups: "Once limited and associated with pro-independence sectors of society, manifestations of cultural identity are now widespread: musicians sing nationalist songs on prime-time television, and nationalist symbols, such as the Puerto Rican flag, decorate advertisements and private dwellings alike" (1).

In response to the question, How can Puerto Ricans celebrate their national cultural difference and yet want ever-closer ties with the United States?, Ángel R. Oquendo lays blame on the two successful political parties (the pro-commonwealth PPD and the pro-statehood PNP), which he says have manipulated public opinion into accepting the coexistence of cultural nationalism and close ties with the United States. Beneath the surface of one cultural nation, two impulses move paradoxically in tandem: the popular acquiescence to political dependency along with cultural images of independence (aided by the cultural silence bordering on censorship about its rejection by the voters).

Vieques, a Victory for *La Lucha*

"El grito de Vieques," as Juan Manuel García Passalacqua called it (Ramos Méndez 13)—the battle won in 2003 against the U.S. military in Vieques through protests and good publicity—gave renewed energy and visibility to the heroic bent of nationalism and its supporters. As I mentioned previously, the cause for national freedom has at one time or another been seen as allied with other, more popular social campaigns. For instance, independence supporters usually identify with an anti-U.S. military stance. Such has been the case of pro-independence students at the University of Puerto Rico, Río Piedras campus (UPR-RP), who have fought, from the 1960s to the present day, against the presence of the ROTC on their campus.

With the protests in Vieques, *independentistas* successfully collaborated with other social activists (and many high-profile outsiders) to end the Navy's long-standing presence on this tiny island off the eastern coast of Puerto Rico. The main figures associated with political nationalism found common cause with other political factions, staged protests, and gained international attention until they dislodged the U.S. Navy from the town island, a considerable victory. José E. Rivera Santana (of the Movimiento Independentista Nacional Hostosiano, MINH) hopes the triumph in Vieques ushers in a new cycle in the fight for independence; "in the Baby Island [Vieques] Puerto Ricans opened the new century with a *magnificent victory* that showed how much we can do when we unite as a people" (Rivera Santana; my italics). Vieques is the movement's most triumphant and effective achievement as a political force and gave new hope for their activism.

As in all things about the cause for independence, contradictions abound. The success in Vieques has to be measured against the constant voluntary participation of ordinary Puerto Ricans in the U.S. Armed Forces; most of them do so primarily for the job opportunities and educational benefits. Ironically, the island's economic conditions that drive people to seek work in the U.S. military are also the result of United States control over the island economy. But it appears that with Vieques the dream nation got its twenty-first-century *collective* hero, an epic that involved pacifist resistance achieved through coalitions to defeat what is known in independence-speak as the Empire. What fictions will that create?

It seems clear that the forces of independence have engendered real-life heroes and martyrs and events that continue to inspire awe and affection and that aid the story and the images of the dream nation. They validate the better side of the nation's self-image and hide the shame of dependency. And so the heroic component feeds the dream nation, as constantly effective and enduring figures of nationalism—like Albizu and Lebrón, as well as heroic events, the Grito de Lares, the Ponce Massacre, Vieques—light up the inner life of the dream nation.

One could argue that the stubbornness of the dream nation in popular culture is due to the contributions that the ideal makes to a robust sociopolitical debate on the island. Except there usually isn't much of one, at least not in the sense of real dialogue between opposing political viewpoints listening to and learning from one another. Nevertheless, political alliances are sometimes successful, as was the case in Vieques, and the coalitions that helped elect Carmen Yulín Cruz to the mayoralty of San Juan in 2012. The across-the-board demonstrations for the release of Oscar López Rivera are another visible instance.

A not-so-hidden secret of the dream nation's appeal is the righteous indignation and other strong emotions it can inspire which, as much as love or desire, get one's blood pumping. Finally, Puerto Rican culture highlights independence because influential groups of culture producers inspire and cheer one another in an echo chamber of hope and defiance.

What Is a Nation?

How does a *dependent* territory become a *nation*? Ernst Renan's venerable question, "What is a nation?" takes on renewed significance with the island's situation. In reality, the Puerto Rican *nation* itself has never been in doubt among the residents of Puerto Rico or among islanders in the United States. Puerto Ricans don't have to be free in order to feel like they are a nation because the island is a firmly established *cultural* nation. The distinction between *cultural* and *political* nationalism explains how a sense of national identity flourished among Puerto Ricans. According to the *Encyclopedia of Nationalism*, "The major goal of most political nationalists is the creation of an independent state," while "[c]ultural nationalists, on the other hand, are less interested in a separate state per se, as much as they are in the protection and preservation of a distinct historical tradition." As far as culture is concerned, the writers and artists who brought about the Puerto Rican literary canon, for instance, most of whom advocated for sovereignty, helped create that *cultural nation* despite the island's dependent status because most Puerto Ricans do not identify as Americans, despite the passport they carry. Puerto Ricans in the United States do not use a denomination such as Puerto Rican American like Cuban Americans use.

Modernity proved crucial to Puerto Rico's definition as a nation. Modernity is a term so contentious and ubiquitous nowadays that Frederick Luis Aldama calls it "today's academic piñata" (299). Most dictionaries define it as a historical period of significant social changes, especially in Europe, beginning around 1800 and continuing to the mid-twentieth century. I use it in its common acceptance referring to the shift into rapid technological advances, industrialization, and urbanization in Puerto Rico during the span of the twentieth century. Nonetheless, even in our times the idea of a nation is overwhelmingly linked to a revolutionary phase that, in the liberal definition used in the West, conceives the nation as central to "resistance [usually armed] and mobilization against the existing order" (Rodríguez Vázquez 19). That is something Puerto Rico can only dream of.

The concept of nationhood itself is a primordial cause for the longevity of the dream nation. In the twenty-first century, "love of country" is still an organizing principle as powerful as religious faith. Even in an increasingly globalized world,[15] the nation persists as a force that most everyone assumes will *naturally* move people to fight, to struggle, and even to die in order to achieve sovereignty. If the modern state system is regarded as coming out of the 1648 Peace of Westphalia, few territories can be thought of as always (or almost always) having been dependent (that is to say, having few or no significant independent moments). We can think of Western Sahara, Abkhazia, Somaliland, and Palestine. In a few other cases, they have partial recognition, such as Kosovo. Puerto Rico, as we shall see, is part of that small number.

Benedict Anderson himself states that the nation is imagined as sovereign (6). Commenting on Anderson, Kenneth Hodges reinforces the primacy of independent national status in how nations imagine themselves: "Sovereignty is crucial not just because it distinguishes nations from other imagined communities but also because the question of sovereignty helps shape the ways communities are imagined" (558). For instance, the dream of national sovereignty, though it hasn't come close to having a real-life political effect, has heavily influenced the Puerto Rican national imagination, that is to say, how Puerto Rico imagines itself (through its culture, both highbrow as well as popular) and how it is imagined to be by many outsiders.

"Imaginary," "imagined," and "imagination" are words that swirl around the concept of the nation and that, for the purposes of this book, center around the repetitive, deep forms of national meaning that the culture of a nation produces or, better yet, that produce the dream nation. At my home institution, Clark University, we teach a comparative literature course called "The National Imagination," which studies how cultural artifacts, values, stories, and myths create, process, and question what and how the Nation constitutes or "imagines" itself. We are humanists, but the social sciences also use the term "imaginary" to refer to the values, institutions, laws, and symbols common to particular social groups and/or societies.

Giving wings to the imagined independent Puerto Rico are recent examples of resurgent nations arising, phoenix-like, to claim their sovereignty. After the fall of the Soviet Union, many formerly dependent regions that had agitated for freedom achieved their dream. Scotland and Cataluña are, as of this writing, calling for freedom. This process of *dependent* territories—not, for example, the independent nations involved in the Arab Spring—striving for sovereignty fits the usual model of how nations are created by the will of "the people" who either vote or fight for independence from foreign subjugation.

The Puerto Rican rejection of independence is therefore baffling to those who consider that nations grow "organically" because Puerto Rico is viewed (and views itself) as a nation. Nevertheless, by assuming Puerto Ricans must want their freedom, many outsiders ignore the reality of Puerto Rico. An event like the rousting of the United States in Vieques—in which independence leaders had a high profile—reaffirmed that outside perception and, for example, led critic Ed Morales to say (in

2002) that there is "growing nationalism in Puerto Rico" (*Living* 208); his remarks are in glaring contradiction to the voting trends of the same time frame.

How, then, did the dream of sovereignty remain strong in Puerto Rican culture despite its popular rejection as a political goal? The dream became ingrained in overt and symbolic ways in canonical (classic) works of Puerto Rican culture because the cultural establishment of the island, until late in the twentieth century, presented a solid block in support of the cause. In part, this is because the venues for publication on the island have never been very numerous, and many hold in their ranks people devoted to the traditional ideas of independence. For instance, "En Rojo," the literature and culture wing of *Claridad*, is regarded as "an obligatory space of literary culture in Puerto Rico" (Gómez Beras in Bobes, Valdéz, and Gómez Beras 193).

Nation building, says Jean Franco, has been one of the missions of Latin American literature since its inception so that, particularly in the nineteenth century when the Latin American republics were created, writers wanted "to create original national literatures" (47). By "original," read "independent" too. Franco singles out Hostos's *La peregrinación de Bayoán*, whose hero is "the spirit of Caribbean Independence incarnate" (61).

Late-nineteenth- to early-twentieth-century literary luminaries such as José Gautier Benítez, Eugenio María de Hostos, Ramón E. Betances, Lola Rodríguez de Tió, Pachín Marín, Manuel Zeno Gandía, José de Diego, Luis Lloréns Torres, and others all maintained a steadfast devotion to attaining Puerto Rico's national sovereignty. They wrote the nation-affirming canon of Puerto Rican literature that is taught in schools and universities. Puerto Rican writers in the United States, particularly the prominent Nuyorican Poets Café in the 1970s (which featured such writers as Miguel Algarín, Miguel Piñero, Sandra María Esteves, Pedro Pietri, Victor Tato Laviera, and Piri Thomas), include in their works themes and images that replicate orthodox Puerto Rican nationalism. Currently one of the most successful Puerto Rican writers in the United States, Esmeralda Santiago, very explicitly represents the island as being pro-independence.

Puerto Rican literature had its first homegrown coherent literary movement during the 1930s (roughly), when, coincidentally, nationalism (a word synonymous with *independentismo*) became most radicalized on the island. In talking about that group of writers, known as the Generación del 30, who were devoted to creating nation-building works of literature, Magali Roy-Féquière states that they were fascinated by the conundrum of Puerto Rican identity, its "character and personality" (1). From roughly the 1930s to the 1950s, Puerto Rico grappled with the upheaval caused by a fiery nationalist minority that was being actively repressed by the government. Another driving cultural force of the twentieth century was their rejection of the island's brand of modernity, which became a bone of contention for nationalist culture producers. Writers such as Antonio S. Pedreira, Tomás Blanco, Emilio S. Belaval, Nilita Vientós Gastón, Julia de Burgos, Juan Antonio Corretjer and *their works* set the templates for much fiction and many tropes to follow, a literature imprinted by nationalism and its dream nation.

Despite a few confrontations and opposition from writers and critics starting around the 1980s (José Luis González, Rosario Ferré, and Edgardo Rodríguez Juliá, for instance), in terms of literature, independence retains a visible hold on important writers and critics because many still vital famous writers came of age during the 1960s and 1970s, a period of resurgent political and literary nationalism. Literature and culture at large can be a front for nationalism because culture becomes the only place for fulfilling the dream. Luis Rafael Sánchez is illustrative; he is one of the most important Puerto Rican writers who defines literature as a necessary countercurrent to the harsh reality of the island's dependency and colonial situation, saying that a "caricaturesque" reality is asking to be forgotten anyway: "Un arte a feliz contracorriente de la realidad, a veces tan caricaturesca e insidiosa en su despliegue que convida a abandonarla" ("Preguntas con ton y con son"; An art which happily counters a reality that is so caricaturesque and insidious that it invites one to abandon it). The logic of this use of culture, I argue, provides a systemic counterbalance to the defeat of political nationalism.

Whatever the causes, Puerto Rican culture has usually been largely defined by a left-leaning Puerto Rican intelligentsia—that is to say, most of it—for whom independence remains the quintessentially patriotic cause. Assimilation to the United States is anathema to the large majority of culture producers and consequently almost absent from cultural representations.

Historical Overview

Since Columbus came to town, Puerto Rico has been a dependent possession of two successive empires, first Spain and then, starting in 1898, the United States. In a 1951 referendum, Puerto Ricans voted overwhelmingly for U.S. nonincorporated commonwealth status, calling it the Estado Libre Asociado (freely associated state, or ELA; the word *libre* cannot have been chosen by happenstance since it resonates so profoundly with the dream nation). The following year, Puerto Rico's constitution was adopted. It established what the Puerto Rican government's website defines paradoxically, vexingly, as "a self-governing commonwealth in association with the United States." Richard Brookhiser put it succinctly, after Puerto Rico ceased being a U.S. territory, "the designation, though not the substance, was changed to 'commonwealth.'" In many significant ways the island is still a dependent territory. For example, U.S. courts and statutes determine many legal and economic issues; also, Puerto Ricans, although they have had American citizenship since 1917, cannot vote in U.S. congressional or presidential elections. The conspicuous lack of substance to claims of self-governance is apparent in the government's website, which states that Puerto Rican institutions are in charge of internal affairs "unless U.S. law is involved." The site notes that the United States controls, among other things, trade, customs, immigration, citizenship, all military affairs and "legal procedures," communications, Social Security, and, tellingly, "air, land, and sea" (http://welcome.topuertorico.org/government.shtml).

The writer Edgardo Rodríguez Juliá sums up Puerto Rico's situation under federal jurisdiction: "The fundamental law that governs this country, "the law of the land," is the federal constitution and the laws passed by the U.S. Congress" ("No culpable"). This state of colonial nonbeing contributes, for instance, to novelist Eduardo Lalo's notion of the invisibility of Puerto Rico.

The Voting Panorama

Given its state of dependency, one would expect the people of Puerto Rico to clamor for freedom. Yet the overwhelming majority of Puerto Rican voters have rejected that option in all plebiscites and elections. Luis Raúl Cámara Fuertes summarizes the big picture of the voting/status landscape in the twenty-first century: "The main political cleavage in Puerto Rico is not the liberal-conservative continuum as in the United States or the left-right continuum as in other countries. Rather, it revolves around the so-called 'status debate'" (17).

The official independence party, the Partido Independentista Puertorriqueño (PIP, founded in 1946) had its best showing in its second try at the polls in 1952, capturing a total of 19 percent of the vote. Since then, its electoral potency has spiraled downward. Rubén Ríos Ávila—with black humor—has called it, "an *independentista* party that has dedicated itself almost vocationally and professionally to losing elections" ("Queer Nation" 294).

In the 2012 election, despite an appealingly smart, young, hip, and tattooed gubernatorial candidate, the PIP again had a dismal performance (2.53 percent of the vote). Its failure has become so entrenched that in the last few election cycles the party has struggled to remain a legally registered party. By contrast, the winning Partido Popular Democrático (PPD, favoring the ELA, or status quo) got 47.85 percent and the contending Partido Nuevo Progresista (PNP, favoring statehood), 47.04 percent. There were three other so-called emerging parties; one, the Partido del Pueblo Trabajador (PPT, .96 percent), had a platform that went beyond the status issue and advocated a "depoliticized" government around labor issues and social inclusivity. Two even smaller poststatus parties fared worse, the Movimiento Unión Soberanista (MUS, .56 percent) and the Partido Puertorriqueños por Puerto Rico (PPR, .35 percent).

Could these last three new alternatives signal that the island has entered a poststatus phase in its politics? The PPT, whose platform is dedicated to denouncing the island's failed economy (which it claims is due to the island's tax-exemption policy) did not even call for a status change.[16] Its platform specifically stated that it is open to "statehooders, autonomists, and *independentistas* who are willing to work together [. . .] for a democratic, united and sustainable Puerto Rico." To prove they meant it, one of its mayoral candidates (for the town of Arroyo) was pro-statehood. Cámara Fuertes tells of a recent reorientation in the political process toward "candidate-centered campaigns" (120) and therefore away from status affinities.

Are elections every four years an exact measure of the Puerto Rican people's support for any of the three status options? No. Elections continue to hinge on party machines and candidate performances and appeal. Carlos Vargas-Ramos says the prevailing political party system since 1972 "has been characterized by a highly competitive system, with the two leading parties alternating power" (134). In the general elections since 1972, the competition has been won alternatively by either the party representing the commonwealth (PPD) or the pro-statehood party (PNP). Independence always came in dead last at the polls. In some sense, the independence movement has a voice but no vote (ironically, just like the ELA, which has no vote in the U.S. political system).

Puerto Rican elections are more like a national pastime in which masses of people participate with carnavalesque joy; Cámara Fuertes cites three scholarly sources who describe the island's voting environment this way. The critic Ed Morales says Election Day on the island is a mix "between Super Bowl Sunday and Mardi Gras."[17] Elections every four years in Puerto Rico are not about pristine dreams like sovereignty or statehood or even about sentimental attachments to the commonwealth; overwhelmingly they are decided by the scandals, issues, and concerns of their specific time.

Fernando Bayrón Toro's monumental tome about the island's electoral history, *Elecciones y partidos políticos de Puerto Rico 1809–2000*, is laden with examples of the kinds of election shenanigans offering real-life narrative twists that would tax the imagination of even the most inventive novelist. Bayrón Toro examines each Puerto Rican election in light of the day-to-day events that fascinated Puerto Ricans at the time and were breathlessly reported by the sensationalist media. Politicians' escapades always prove decisive at the polls, with the fate of political parties at any given time subject to the latest scandal. Furthermore, some successful politicians thrive by being difficult and quarrelsome and therefore attention getting. For example, Carlos Romero Barceló, who was governor with the pro-statehood PNP, was a notoriously contentious and divisive figure, so much so that he ran a separate campaign *from his own party* in the primaries of 1988. A statehooder, he also famously said that if Puerto Rico were not granted statehood, then he would favor independence (!) (Bayrón Toro 329), thus proving that José Luis González was right when he said that "el anexionismo y el independentismo son, históricamente hablando, los hermanos mellizos que la misma madre separatista alumbró en el siglo pasado" (*Nueva visita* 185; annexionism and independence are, historically speaking, fraternal twins to which the same separatist mother gave birth last century).

Far from being decisive about significant matters like the island's status, elections offer proof of the centrifugal forces of local politics and of the clout of power brokers that result in a political climate which is definitely divisive, to say the least. Ángel Israel Rivera describes the strident political climate in cringe-worthy terms as a "climate of harsh criticism among Puerto Ricans, of promoting distrust, of mutual accusations, of concentrating political discourse in notions of 'guilt' and punishment and of bestowing the worst intentions or psychological traits on the political opponent" (41).

A further complication is that the island participates in a subordinate way in the U.S. political system; even though Puerto Ricans cannot vote for U.S. president or members of Congress, Puerto Rican politicians are often registered with the U.S. Republican or Democratic Parties and vote in their primaries. This dual allegiance is another factor that churns up the local political scene. Likewise, regional and sectarian interests, such as the influential mayors' federation and a number of powerful churches, affect voting outcomes.[18] In fact, though Puerto Rico is a secular society, the national conversation is sometimes manouvered by religious organizations; for instance, a coalition of Pentecostal and Catholic leaders have led the movement against marriage equality and LGBT adoption rights. So powerful are they that in 2013 a protest march of between 150,000 and 200,000 people demonstrated against these twin causes.

Alas, Puerto Rican elections are also shaped by people's fears. Because of entrenched patronage systems, the citizenry considers the state its largest employer and entitlement distributor so that elections have real-life consequences: if you vote for a particular party, your sister or your cousin gets to keep her job at city hall.

Intraparty politics also are implicated in the failure of the nationalist movement to persuade its fellow citizens to vote (or fight) for the cause. Bayrón Toro says the dream of independence has always had to contend with "the perennial division and sparring among Puerto Rican separatists, who are active in dozens of political organizations" (330). *Independentistas* are sometimes epically quarrelsome among themselves; for example, Juan Mari Brás, the socialist stalwart, recalled how during the Second Pro-Independence Congress at the Ateneo Puertorriqueño (in the early 1940s), there was an internal revolt against Gilberto Concepción de Gracia (then leader of the PIP). Leaving the session, Mari Brás and five others went to the lobby of the Ateneo, where they founded *another* pro-independence party (Marrero-García and Rodríguez). In effect, pro-independence activists have long been prone to internal splintering; in 1972, for example, independence was represented by three parties: the long-standing PIP; the Partido Unión Puertorriqueño (Puerto Rican Union Party); and the Partido Auténtico Soberanista (Authentic Sovereignty Party) (Bayrón Toro 255).

Perhaps because of their very fractiousness, elections hold Puerto Ricans in thrall. Even though they bemoan a downward trend in voter turnout, Puerto Ricans take passionate delight in the political process (79 percent participation in 2008, 77 percent in 2012). *Slate.com* says of voter turnout, "Puerto Rico's culture of engagement is all the starker when juxtaposed against voter apathy in the United States. Throughout the late twentieth century, turnout for Puerto Rico's quadrennial elections was 50 percent higher than it was for presidential contests in the 50 states" ("The Mystery of the Puerto Rican Voter," 27 Jan. 2012). Even fake elections elicit voter interest; on November 5, 2011, a news organization (Notiuno 630) held an electoral simulacrum that drew more than thirty thousand people.

Given this scenario, it seems that the pro-sovereignty parties (mainly the PIP but also the other fleeting registered political parties) offer a necessary outlet, a steam valve for the discontent of those voters who are sick of having what is basically a two-party system. Even though ultimate victory is elusive, nay, impossible, *independentistas* who stick with the PIP can sometimes vote for a few influential senators and representatives and thus agitate about other items on the party's agenda. As Vargas-Ramos notes, the political effectiveness of the PIP has evolved from being on a regime-changing quest to being an alternative political agent that is "less election-centered and more focused on community organizing," where, he says, they agitate through "protest marches, demonstrations, strikes, sit-ins; boycotting the electoral process; and even the use of deadly force" (134). A new spin on political independence is the recent rebranding of the dream of independence into calls for *soberanía* (sovereignty), instead of independence in entities such as Soberanía Para Puerto Rico (Sovereignty for Puerto Rico).[19]

Aren't plebiscites—not elections—supposed to resolve the matter of the island's status? In the ones held so far, the majority of voters have voted for either statehood or the commonwealth. The plebiscite of 1997 was eye-catching because the voters proved to be weary of the entire issue of status and preferred the option "none of the above." The election of 2012 was supposed to help make the matter easier since the pro-statehood party (which was in power) favored a status decision and the U.S. House had passed a bill supporting a plebiscite. In the end, the ballot initiative of 2012 proved indecisive because, for one thing, too many blank ballots were cast. Pushing the matter forward in a very real sense, President Obama proposed in April 2013 that the island hold a definitive plebiscite (or two) so the matter can be resolved.

When President Obama visited the island in 2011, he promised, "to stand by Puerto Rico no matter what residents decide about its future; statehood, independence, or a continuation of the status quo" (Cooper). But the catch was that there must be a "clear mandate" for one or another status option, a highly unlikely outcome (Delgado, "En ocho minutos").

In any case, the U.S. Congress would be the one to grant the new status so that, if Puerto Rican voters were to miraculously embrace independence at some point, Congress would, one presumes, have to grapple with the mechanics and complications of granting sovereignty to the island.

What Do Puerto Ricans Want?

Political scientists and researchers conclude that no systematic attempt has been made to discern or document what ordinary folks think or want in order to resolve the status issue. Luis Raúl Cámara-Fuertes and Olga I. Rosas Cintrón state that "[s]tudies (at least publicly available) using survey data are virtually nonexistent" (150); their own study uses data from 1991, when the Cold War threat of communism was still an important factor in keeping people attached to the United States. Cámara-Fuertes and Rosas Cintrón state that the traditional view is that supporters of continuing association with the United States are worried about security issues (geopolitical or economic) versus an emphasis on national *pride* for supporters of independence. They quote Ángel Israel Rivera on how Puerto Ricans adhere to the status quo because it bolsters security by keeping the island within the United States' (then) strong economy yet allows a feeling of independence. Other sources of information about what Puerto Ricans want to do regarding the status are sparse; the media do only partial, small, man-on-the-street opinion polls during electoral years. Political parties in turn hire consultants to slant the news their way.

I want to stress that despite how colorful the political picture is, this whole convulsive political system caught up in carnavalesque elections is almost wholly absent from literary representations or cultural discussions, which on the other hand feature expansive symbols, repetitive themes, and consequential fictions long associated with the unfulfilled, independence-yearning dream nation.

For instance, armed struggle—the other option to achieving liberty—has a history of doomed, scattered attempts in Puerto Rico, the most culturally significant of which was the Grito de Lares in 1868. In general, such endeavors (including also events in the 1930s and 1950s) failed because (*a*) the United States and the local government brutally suppressed the nationalist factions, and (*b*) the people, fearing a destabilizing crisis, did not rise up in arms. Yet the legacy of armed struggle has had huge cultural impact, particularly in generating heroic stories and iconography, which we will look at in chapter 4, "Dream History, Dream Nation."

A cynic might say that Puerto Ricans want to have their cake and eat it too; keeping their Spanish-language culture and a semblance of sovereignty while receiving the protection and support of the strongest nation in the hemisphere. As Ángel R. Oquendo says, the seeming contradiction between the consumerist lifestyle and ideals has long been *intellectually* resolved: "though Puerto Ricans almost unanimously take an immense pride in their national culture and in their distinctness from the United States, they overwhelmingly support keeping Puerto Rico part of the United States" (2).

The intelligentsia, on the other hand, has vociferously called for Puerto Rico's freedom, or at least autonomy, from foreign overlords (both Spain and the United States) since the 1800s, when the island was under Spanish control. Puerto Rico's literary luminaries were, until recently, nearly all sympathizers of the oldest independence political party, the PIP, a stalwart of leftist radicalism that also has been well represented in like-minded causes such as racial and gender equality and workers' rights. As affiliated literary stars embraced the central place of independence in the dream nation, the aims of the party remained, for a long time, their aims. The majority of writers, artists, critics, and intellectuals have followed a leftist, *independentista* creed—particularly those affiliated with the influential University of Puerto Rico, Río Piedras campus, where most of the top writers have been educated and/or, at one time or another, have taught. In the 1960s and 1970s, Puerto Rican intellectuals replicated the general leftist cultural mood of Latin America. Later at the turn of the century, part of the PIP's appeal to the intelligentsia were common causes such as minority and women's and gender rights.

What pro-independence enthusiasts have typically failed to note, to discuss or debate in a *central* way, was the increasing distance between themselves and the people at large on the matter of national sovereignty.

The view that the arts serve the dream of a free nation has held strong because the symbiosis between the PIP and Puerto Rican culture is ongoing. For instance, a 2009 press release from the PIP regarding government cuts in the arts states that these and the cause for independence are linked. María de Lourdes Santiago Negrón, the party's vice president, says "In a country such as ours, threatened on so many fronts, artistic expression has special meaning. Our artists have been the first line of resistance against a project of assimilation" ("PIP se solidariza con la clase artística del País" [PIP solidarizes with the country's artistic class]).

Further fuelling the link of culture to independence has been the Puerto Rican intellectual sector's identification with Latin American intellectual trends, long distrusting of or outright hostile to the United States since at least José Martí's "Nuestra América" in the late 1880s. Since Puerto Rico shares a language and cultural history with Latin America, however, Puerto Ricans' continued reluctance to support political sovereignty is also paradoxically at variance with Latin American history.

Given this pro-independence cultural landscape, it is no surprise that large parcels of Puerto Rican canonical nineteenth- and twentieth-century literature—the kind taught in schools—contain either direct calls for independence or metaphorical uses of that ideal. One cannot escape the calls for freedom in works by nineteenth-century luminaries Eugenio María de Hostos, Alejandro Tapia y Rivera, Lola Rodríguez de Tió, José de Diego, Manuel Zeno Gandía, José Gautier Benítez, and others. Many paid a high price for their beliefs since Spain brutally repressed all nationalist movements in its colonies and many of those intellectuals were forced into exile. When the United States took over the island in 1898 as part of the agreement with Spain at the end of the Spanish-American War, the early part of the twentieth century saw a period of cultural transition, as Puerto Ricans and their culture adapted to their new masters.

From the 1930s to the 1950s, there was enough unrest and discontent with the economic, cultural, and political alliance with the United States that real political action toward independence in Puerto Rico seemed possible. Yet the push for freedom failed to gain a popular and effective foothold for many reasons. One important reason was the harassment and repression of the Puerto Rican Nationalist Party, led by iconic Pedro Albizu Campos (or Albizu, as he is affectionately known), the most famous nationalist leader. The level and quantity of harassment is staggering; in 1992, the Puerto Rican Supreme Court ordered the release of 135,000 files (called *carpetas*) on people and groups considered subversive (Bayrón Toro 348). In keeping with the heating up of the Cold War, in 1948 a new law, Ley 53, or Ley de la Mordaza (Law of the Muzzle), made the expression of nationalist or socialist ideas punishable. The 1978 Cerro Maravilla ambush and killing of two young *independentistas* by government police forces is an infamous example of the violence visited upon independence sympathizers.

The real-life climate of fear and intimidation was carried out not just by outside forces, specifically the FBI, but also with the complicity of the Puerto Rican government, according to José Anazagasty Rodríguez, who states that "the cooperation of local authorities with federal authorities was habitual. [. . .] Many Puerto Ricans consented to the *carpeteo*." How has this climate of repression of nationalism affected culture? Fascinatingly, critic José Ángel Rosado's *El cuerpo del delito* (The body of evidence) posits the theory that Puerto Rico's modernity in its totality, and specifically the political harassment of *independentismo*, led in many cases to the deployment of detective fiction in Puerto Rican literature. He says these novels make creative use of the climate of vigilance and state repression and particularly the persecution of *independentismo*. He studies detective novels by famous (and lesser-known) writers such as Edgardo Rodríguez Juliá, Mayra Santos Febres, Rafael Acevedo, and Wilfredo Mattos Cintrón and traces how they directly and indirectly relate to the repressive political atmosphere including "the bureaucratic legal operation of surveillance, the world of drugs, police corruption, the contradictions of the state, conspiracies and political assassination" (266).

Mario Cancel Sepúlveda says that the climate of repression in those decades led to Pedro Albizu Campos's desperate calls for violence. That time period (the 1940s and 1950s) also saw the rise of the Popular Democratic Party, which instituted the ELA and became popular with the voters, who embraced its message of modernization. Ramón Grosfoguel agrees that throughout the twentieth century there was also an attendant "campaign to misinform and instill a fear of independence" (*Colonial Subjects* 44).

This brief historical summary confirms what the nineteenth-century independence luminary Eugenio María de Hostos saw coming (in 1900): that the Puerto Rican people would be "una masa difícil de mover que es necesario poner en movimiento" ("Carta 15 de octubre de 1900," López-Baralt, *Antología* 13; a hard-to-move mass which it is necessary to set in motion). He stated this when the island had just been transferred as a prize of war to the United States. As Hostos foresaw, getting the people to follow the cause for national freedom was easier said than done; in fact, over the course of the twentieth century, popular momentum turned into a stampede away from sovereignty, which Hostos, an ardent *independentista*, hoped for. The voting public has fled from independence into the two other status options, both of which favor ties to the United States. The political parties representing these two options have alternated in the island's governance since 1968. The independence party has never come close to controlling the government or making its dream come true.

Why? Why Not? A Spate of Theories

How to give solace over the invariable rejection of sovereignty at the polls? Electoral repudiation is easy to dismiss (if one is so inclined) by the simple device of questioning the validity of so-called colonial elections in general. Albizu Campos himself called elections a trap: "Las inscripciones y las elecciones es [sic] la trampa para que los puertorriqueños sigan dándole la vuelta a la noria" (Marrero-García and Rodríguez, chapter 3; Registrations and elections are the trap so that Puerto Ricans will continue going around in circles). Juan Mari Brás, founder of the Partido Socialista, dismissed voting in "colonial elections" (Marrero-García and Rodríguez, chapter 4).

A related theory states that Puerto Ricans are "alienated" by long exposure to colonialism. For instance, the *independentista* prisoner Rafael Cancel Miranda speaks of a "syndrome of dependency" that stifles self-determination (quoted by Colón Solá). It seems entirely possible, however, that this type of nationalist explanation for voters' rejection of sovereignty has negatively impacted nationalist political effectiveness. Why? Because calling people victims and dupes of colonialism will not get many of them on your side.

On the other hand, heroic tales have been spun out of whole cloth depicting Puerto Rican defense of liberty by arms. Culture invents heroic acts where they never succeeded or even happened perhaps because, despite René Marqués's charge of docility as a national trait, Puerto Ricans never gave themselves over en masse to armed carnage in defense of national sovereignty because they cannot help noticing the bloody and costly toll of most armed revolutions in the history of the world. There are few exceptions even in recent times; the 2011 independence of South Sudan resulted in two thousand killed and three hundred thousand displaced in that one year alone.[20] Is dread of slaughtering one's fellow citizens "docility"?

There is no lack of theories to explain why the Puerto Rican people reject fighting for national freedom. Juan Antonio Corretjer, the iconic nationalist poet, theorized that Puerto Rico is gripped by contrary impulses: one he called the autochthonous (i.e., homegrown and therefore "natural") tendency to revolution, which leads to independence; the other is an imported tendency to reformism, which he regarded as an accomodationist stance of anyone not bold enough to change history by means of revolution. Boring reformism dulls national feeling, according to the poet (*La lucha por la independencia* 5–12). He, of course, favored revolutionary action (and served time for it). In the same vein as Albizu Campos, he dismisses all electoral processes on the island because they are "colonial" and therefore "enslaving," a commonly held opinion among those who prize revolutionary action. Corretjer shows a tendency to mutually exclusive, binary, and Manichaean choices, a long tradition among revolutionary writers. As Segundo Ruiz Belvis wrote of abolition, the companion activist cause of the 1800s, "no hay, ni puede haber etapa intermedia entre la esclavitud y la libertad" (Corretjer, *La lucha* 71; there is no, nor can there be an intermediate stage between slavery and liberty). In reality, however, the vast middle of Puerto Ricans—those who favor continuing or beefing up the ELA and who have had the most lasting impact on the politics of Puerto Rico not through armed revolt but through constant electoral choices—live precisely between extremes.

Michael González Cruz gives another reason why Puerto Ricans embrace the other two status options: the "assimilationist" political parties, principally the party that supports the Commonwealth, the PPD, harnessed the emotional force of nationalism by co-opting its *cultural symbols*. Certainly, other political and economic forces can and frequently do co-opt pro-independence rhetoric. For instance, the island's *colonial* condition—a designation that has been repeatedly reaffirmed by the United Nations, especially that entity's decolonization committee—long was an *independentista* trademark. Nowadays, however, statehood supporters use the accusation of colonialism to argue that Puerto Rico must cast off its colonial baggage and move to full citizenship *via statehood*.

Puerto Rico's economic reality is a main factor for the choices Puerto Ricans make, one that is acknowledged by all sides. For instance, José Luis González said in 1987 that despite an artificial and precarious consumerist economy, "the overwhelming majority of Puerto Ricans, accustomed to the idea of enjoying a standard of living far superior to all Caribbean and Latin American countries, are convinced that they would have much to lose as a result of a political break with the United States" (*Nueva Visita* 179).

Economic factors are often used to support independence as well as to attack it. Predictably, data can be used both ways to prove how the island has done in its association with the United States; since Puerto Rico has a lower per-capita income than Mississippi, the poorest of the states, it *should* seek independence. On the other hand, since Puerto Rico has a higher per-capita income than Chile, the richest of the Latin American countries, it *should not* seek independence. On the 2011–12 World Economic Forum's global competitiveness index, the island comes in thirty-fifth, between Kuwait (thirty-fourth) and Spain (thirty-sixth). The United States ranks number five.[21]

There is another important socioeconomic factor for the lackluster electoral performance of independence. The *jíbaros*—the iconic rustic country folk—started migrating to the United States in large numbers at around the time when independence had its highest showing at the polls (19 percent in the 1952 elections) (Marrero García and Rodríguez). Some election scholars think that the *jíbaros* had been strongly supportive of the independence party, which then failed at the polls when they were encouraged by the government to leave the island—in what has been called a social safety valve measure.

Those who remained behind on the island became more and more invested in the Puerto Rico–United States relationship. At the present point in the island's history, an important consideration in Puerto Rican hesitation to embrace sovereignty is the *fear* of losing contributions to and investment in U.S. social programs. Political *independentistas, by the way,* seek to allay this dread by explaining that their plans encompass a republic that would have a special relationship with the United States (Rivera 25).

This fear is expressed memorably by the protagonist's grandmother in Ángel Lozada's novel *La patografía* (from 1996). It is worth quoting at length because the character's support for statehood (which is still rare in Puerto Rican literature) is based on her desire to retain her hard-won benefits. Benefits (such as a welfare subsidies and $7 billion in stimulus money after the 2008 crisis)[22] are what lead her to say:

> Hace seis meses que me cambié de partido. Ahora soy de la palma. Soy PNP y trabajo en colegios. Dejé el partido popular porque no aguanto más a Rafael Hernández Colón. Ese tipo es un vampiro. El partido popular era bueno bajo Muñoz Marín, pero ahora no, ahora se ha dañado [. . .] Lo que quiere Hernández Colón es la independencia pa' Puerto Rico, y déjame decirte, yo no voy a permitir que a mí me quiten los cupones ni el chequecito del Seguro Social, después que me maté como un animal cosiendo y limpiando teatros pa' los gringos de Nueva Yol. (68)

> Six months ago I changed parties. I'm now of the party of the palm. I'm for the PNP and I work in polling stations because I can't stand Rafael Hernández Colón. That guy is a vampire. The Popular party

was good under Muñoz Marín, but now, it's been damaged. [...] What Hernández Colón wants is independence for Puerto Rico, and let me tell you, I'm not gonna let them take away my food stamps or my little Social Security check, after I killed myself working like an animal sewing and cleaning theaters for the gringos in New York.

Lozada's character represents working-class Puerto Ricans who are profoundly vested in the U.S. benefits system. The ties that bind are also important because more often than not their daughters, sons, cousins, *abuelos*, and *tíos* live in the States. Moreover, the ways of staying connected with them have increased with the explosion of social media leading to an increase of the back-and-forth exchange of ideas, values, and social perspectives that Juan Flores calls "cultural remittances" (*Diaspora Strikes Back* 24).

Puerto Ricans in Puerto Rico are bombarded in myriad ways every day by arguably the most powerful global culture. They sit at home and watch American shows on their TV sets or go out and see Hollywood fare in the movie theaters; they are tempted to buy a cornucopia of American products in Wal-marts near their homes; they can stuff themselves with hamburgers and fries at the Burger King around the corner; they carry dollar bills in their pockets and have American passports; their environment is both polluted by U.S. corporations and protected by the EPA; when their local agencies get too corrupt, the Feds intervene, etc., etc., etc. It is nothing short of a tribute to their creative powers that culture producers dreamed a dream nation and offered a counterpoint to the omnipresence of the United States even though, paradoxically, they did so by ignoring the voting inclinations of the largest part of their fellow citizens.

In the Caribbean Sea

Another powerful force in Puerto Rican political choices is their Caribbean context. On the one hand, the dream of independence has been bolstered by the example set by Cuban *independentista* movements since the nineteenth century. Cuba was always a point of reference for Puerto Rico's identity as a nation. Nineteenth-century Puerto Rican *independentistas* were comrades to Cuban counterparts and often lived in Cuba when exiled from Puerto Rico. The feeling among Romantic nineteenth-century authors was that the two were island "sisters." The Romantic/sentimental image of Cuba and Puerto Rico as the two wings of a bird was coined by the famous Puerto Rican nineteenth-century *independentista* poet Lola Rodríguez de Tió, who wrote the oft-quoted lines, "Cuba y Puerto Rico son / De un pájaro las dos alas, Reciben flores y balas / Sobre el mismo corazón" (*Mi libro de Cuba* vii; Cuba and Puerto Rico are / the two wings of a bird, they receive flowers and bullets / Upon the same heart).

Absent from that image, of course, is the third Spanish-speaking Greater Antille, the Dominican Republic; as the critic Juan Flores clarifies, "There is a wing missing, of course, from Lola's emblematic antillano mascot, the Dominican Republic" (*Diaspora Strikes Back* 61). Flores addresses the three islands' similar independence themes and rhetoric; he highlights the beloved musician Davilita, who was a fervent nationalist and whose popular songs were fraught with the theme of independence. In Davilita's song "Son tres" about the three "sister" islands, Flores finds the belief in a common thread of *independentista* heroism at the heart of Caribbean solidarity:

> Fue en Cuba José Martí quien luchó su libertad,
> Y Duarte fue por Quisqueya, y por Borinquen, ¿quién será?
> Son tres, son tres, las islas hermanas
> Que las quiero ver, las quiero ver, las tres soberanas
> Que no me quiero morir sin ver la unión antillana
>
> José Martí fought in Cuba for their freedom,
> And Duarte was for Quisqueya, and in Borinquen, who will?
> There are three, three sister islands
> I want to see, to see them, sovereign three
> I don't want to die without seeing the Antillean union
> (quoted by Flores, *Diaspora Strikes Back* 56)

Flores stresses that while in the nineteenth and early twentieth centuries the islands were a "three-part cultural family," by the middle of the twentieth century their political history became increasingly dissonant due to Puerto Rico's dependent status and failure to achieve sovereignty. Specifically, Flores points to how Cuba and the Dominican Republic "can hail their founding leaders in Martí and Duarte" whereas Puerto Rico failed and its independence icon Albizu Campos "languished in a federal penitentiary" (*Diaspora Strikes Back* 57). Hence the Hispanic Caribbean enclaves in the United States (his subject matter) are no longer like siblings, having become more like "cousins, and distant ones at that" (*Diaspora Strikes Back* 58).

The awareness of the historical route taken by the sister islands is, on the other hand, a reason why Puerto Ricans reject sovereignty. They choose to *not* throw in their lot with independence because they are aware of the harsher life in neighboring sovereign Caribbean islands, which have been subject to dictatorships, economic and social strife, and, in the end, forms of neocolonial dependency on the world's great powers despite their independence. Furthermore, Ramón Grosfoguel argues that Puerto Ricans have benefited from the close association with the United States not only in financial terms but also in other highly significant ways, such as environmental oversight as well as labor laws and the expansion of women's rights. He says that by seeking ties to strengthen the connection to the United States, Puerto Ricans are merely being pragmatic. Grosfoguel is part of a group of highbrow critics, living mostly in the United States, who have questioned the orthodoxy of *independentista* thinking. In *Puerto Rican Jam*, an indispensable and controversial book of essays on the Puerto Rican sociopolitical condition in the 1990s, Grosfoguel and Frances Negrón-Muntaner state that islanders have decided against sovereign status because Puerto Ricans are well aware of the negative repercussions of sovereignty in the island-nations that surround them: "The popular rejection of nationalism as pro-independence [. . .] can be read not as a symptom of a colonized mind but as a reaction against several regional and world processes that Puerto Ricans tend to be critically aware of" (4–5). Grosfoguel, Negrón-Muntaner, and their group of like-minded intellectuals propose a plan for a "radical statehood," that is to say, a redefinition of statehood to include a broad range of progressive social schemes "supporting the struggles of diverse oppressed subjects, such as blacks, women, youth, gays, lesbians, and workers" (71).[23]

Silvio Torres-Saillant, a Caribbeanist, speaks of a complex web of contextual Caribbean reasons for the lack of popular support for independence. He quotes the founder of the ELA, Luis Muñoz Marín, as saying in 1978: "I tell you that independence is impossible because Puerto Ricans don't want it. . . . What is Puerto Rico? An overpopulated Caribbean island. What can we compare it with? With Cuba and Santo Domingo, which are also Caribbean islands. . . . Are those countries really independent?"[24] Torres-Saillant states that everyone was aware of the Soviet subsidies that propped up Cuba during the heady days of the 1960s and 1970s and until the dissolution of the USSR. As he says, people don't forget the neocolonial dependency of the "sovereign" islands, "[n]or has the continued hegemony of the United States and Western Europe in the economic world system into which the region is trapped allowed individual Caribbean nations to attain real autonomy" (147).

Other Caribbean islands struggle with the same dependency issues; in 2010, five Dutch Caribbean dependent islands changed their status: Curaçao and St. Maarten became autonomous countries within the Kingdom of the Netherlands; and Bonaire, St. Eustatius, and Saba became "autonomous special municipalities" of the kingdom. Aruba had reconstituted its political structure in 1986. Tellingly, in the referendums prior to the constitutional change, "None of the islands voted for independence" (*BBC News* 10 Oct. 2010).

What Do Puerto Ricans Really, Really Want?

Independence has been what the cool kids flaunt. There is a frequent life-story arc in which young Puerto Ricans embrace *independentismo* because it offers the feeling of being in-your-face, of *épater les bourgeois*, of thumbing the nose at the middle class. Mayra Santos Febres is eloquent about how she revolted against middle-of-the-road norms at an early age: "A los trece me afeité la cabeza harta ya de lisados, aprendí a fumar en los *parties* de marquesina, me rompí una pierna corriendo *skateboard*, escribí poemas y me declaré independentista" (*Sobre piel y papel* 206; At thirteen, weary of hair straighteners I shaved my head, I learned to smoke at patio parties, I broke my leg skateboarding, I wrote poems, and declared myself an *independentista*).

Independentismo, which was demonized by the government and the middle and upper classes from the 1930s to the 1970s (and perhaps beyond), becomes for many young people a countercultural act of defiance of bourgeois norms. Yet by the time they start voting, the inclination stops. This leaves a huge gap between ordinary folk and the island's cultural producers who, as a community, continue to lean Left later in life. Agustín Lao has pronounced the breach between the voting public and the cultural aspirations for sovereignty an "enormous social and cultural distance between the *independentista* 'left' and the popular sectors" (173). In larger than average numbers, culture critics and producers customarily favor independence and somehow remain true to the dream nation, the idea that at heart all Puerto Ricans want their own free state. Why? In part due to the weight of literary tradition, also perhaps because the cultural community is small and interconnected, or maybe because, as Luis Rafael

Sánchez says, "ser nacionalista en la isla acarrea un secreto prestigio" ("La guagua aérea" 15; being a nationalist on the island entails a secret prestige).

As we shall see, there are performers, filmmakers, writers, as well as everyday bloggers (on the island and in the United States) and sympathizers in general who passionately defend independence to this day. In support of *la lucha*, take, for instance, "La Proclama de Panamá" (The Panama Proclamation), which was a nonbinding document in support of Puerto Rican independence signed by group of prominent island and even more prominent Latin American writers when they attended the Congreso Latinoamericano y Caribeño por la Independencia de Puerto Rico (Latin American and Caribbean Congress for Puerto Rico's Independence) in 2006. Among the literary lights reaffirming their support for the cause were contemporary stars Luis Rafael Sánchez, Ana Lydia Vega, and Mayra Montero, who represent different generations of writers. Championing the (lost) cause were also Nobel Prize–winning Gabriel García Márquez (Colombia), Ernesto Sábato (Argentina), Mario Benedetti (Uruguay), Eduardo Galeano (Uruguay), Frei Betto (Brazil), Jorge Enrique Adoun (Ecuador), and Pablo Armando Fernández (Cuba). To paraphrase Ramón Grosfoguel, why are so many culture producers divorced from the people they write about?

The present book contends that independence, as a symbolic gesture, has creative and emotional pull even though it distances culture from the will of the people. Equally important is that since it has been defeated as a political status option, it consequently remains on the periphery of the political decision-making process and therefore appeals to culturati who, following the perennial logic of die-hard avant-gardism and hipsterism (everywhere, not just in Puerto Rico), want to retain outsider standing. Being on the periphery has been the preferred scene for culture buffs since at least the nineteenth century. There is little desirability in claiming to be the power at the center inasmuch as the center itself is regarded with suspicion, as the place of orthodoxy, of the fat cats, of the enemy.

The emotional pull of the dream nation also reflects a desire to grow up into what many regard as full national adulthood. This is the political stance of the PIP. They explain the aspiration in sociofamilial terms, using *La Gran Familia Puertorriqueña* trope: "independence means to countries, what the command of one's home means for adults" (www.independencia.net). This comparison anthropomorphizes the historical and economic conditions of the island and connects strongly to the notion of the *destiny* of nations. And also the dream of independence hits an open nerve when it conflates personal and national identity since the template suggests that freedom means becoming a consummate nation, a real one.

Another factor in the cultural persistence of independence is that its supporters are newsworthy. For instance, President Obama's visit in June 2011 was preceded by much planning on the part of the nationalist movements. The PIP called for a march to reclaim independence and the liberation from prison of Oscar López Rivera (*Claridad* 10 June 2011). Their spirited claim—which falls back on a nationalist *hero*—was noted in a *New York Times* article about the president's visit, even though the party is a minority movement. The Gray Lady too probably thought calls for sovereignty are logical and inevitable.

Independence makes for better press copy in part because of attention-grabbing demonstrations. On 6 May 2009, six protestors interrupted a session of the U.S. Congress—disrupting Representative Barney Frank (D-Mass.) midsentence—abruptly singing and holding posters in favor of independence. Most of the press coverage flashed back to the violent protest fifty-five years earlier in which Puerto Rican nationalists fired shots inside that very chamber. The lack of violence in the twenty-first century was not, however, the most fundamental change in the protestors' attitude: that would be their effort to focus attention on Puerto Rico's colonial status so that the *United States* will decide for Puerto Rican independence, thus preempting and bypassing the pesky lack of popular support on the island. The United States would then decide the status issue just as it imposed citizenship in 1917; the irony is biting.

Independence retains public visibility in other eye-catching ways: in 2007, the Ateneo Puertorriqueño, one of the premier cultural institutions on the island, set an "eternal" flame burning until "colonialism" has been vanquished, and in 2012, it reaffirmed its *independentista* institutional commitment citing the familiar trope of Nation = House and using two hallmarks of independence: the nineteenth-century independence stalwart Ramon E. Betances and the Grito de Lares. With such fervent *independentista* spirit, the publicly funded Ateneo declared itself a "national house at the service of the Country and its Culture, but not before acknowledging a historical commitment forged in the memory of the Grito de Lares with the father of the homeland Dr. Ramón Emeterio Betances to fight for the decolonization of Puerto Rico" (ateneopr.org Sept. 2012).

Another compelling moment of the work for independence was signaled by the UN's anticolonial resolution #1514 (XV-1960), which

FIGURE 3. Street in Lares, 2012. (Photo by María Acosta Cruz)

affirmed that independence was the "normal goal" of non-self-governing territories (Musgrave 95). The year 2010 saw a celebration in Puerto Rico commemorating fifty years of this international solidarity by honoring the *éminence grise* of independence, Juan Mari Brás.

Evidence of the continuing centrality of nationalism is the esteem and respect for iconic Pedro Albizu Campos; all seventy-eight Puerto Rican municipalities (none of which has a PIP administration) have a road or avenue named in his honor.

Just one of the Facebook pages devoted to the independence martyr has been *liked* by tens of thousands of people. His face remains a long-standing visual meme in Puerto Rican graphic arts as well as in the marketplace of patriotic knickknacks. The publicity for a recent documentary, *Who Is Albizu?*, summarizes his continuing attraction, which is due to his life of uncompromising principles and tragic heroism as a "Puerto Rican Malcolm X," that is to say, "the symbol of Puerto Rican identity, culture, and resistance" (www.whoisalbizu.com). Albizu retains a firm presence not only in the popular imagination but also in literature. For instance, Magali García Ramis says she had originally wanted one of her most famous characters, Uncle Sergio in her hugely popular novel *Felices días, tío Sergio*, to be "una cosa imposible: un tío Sergio que era una mezcla de Pedro Albizu Campos y Pedro Navaja. Era guapo, perfecto, maravilloso, era el héroe ridículamente imposible pero dentro de mi infantilismo era lo que quería" (Pérez Rivera; an impossible thing: a mix of Pedro Albizu Campos and Pedro Navaja. He was handsome, perfect, marvelous, he was a ridiculously impossible hero but in my infantilism, he was what I wanted). Mayra Santos Febres wrote a study of Albizu as literary figure titled, simply, "Albizu." In it she dwells on the martyrological iconography surrounding him, using as her starting point a

Chicago mural depicting him crucified—one of many ways in which she traces religious meanings tied to this nationalist hero. She then examines how the leading poets Juan Antonio Corretjer, Julia de Burgos, Francisco Matos Paoli as well as seven later poets use the varied sacred overtones of Albizu as a vital nationalist icon. Aurea María Sotomayor further looks at the multiple appearances Albizu has made in Puerto Rican prose in an essay titled "La imaginería nacionalista: de la historia al relato" (Nationalist imagery: From history to storytelling). Carlos Pabón discusses this persistence of Albizu at length as well in *Nación postmortem*.

The rise of the Internet has been a boon for *independentista* outlets, with shifting websites showing the enthusiasm of assorted factions of nationalists. The PIP's bilingual web page[25] and YouTube links[26] are a gateway to anyone interested in Internet content for Puerto Rican separatism. In addition, the *independentista* newspaper *Claridad* has substantial online content. There are other nationalist activists on the Internet: Partido Independentista in Rincón;[27] blogs like *Ciencia e independencia* (Science and independence)[28] maintained by Ramón López Alemán, a University of Puerto Rico physics professor and self-proclaimed "whole-hearted *independentista* and militant in the PIP"; *Lugares Imaginarios* (Imaginary places)[29] by writer and historian Mario R. Cancel often scrutinizes *independentista*-related literature (like the novel *Seva*), as does *El vuelo de la garza* (The flight of the heron) by Tomás L. Vargas;[30] Ángel Collado Schwarz's radio program transmissions, most on national history, are available on mp3 format.[31] There are also many pages dedicated to Pedro Albizu Campos.[32] Adál Maldonado has a fascinating web page called *elpuertoricanembassy.org*, which features dream nation artwork such as imaginary Puerto Rican passports, mail stamps, national coins, etc.

Independence also sells. Visit any online store about Puerto Rico and you will find dozens of commodities proudly displaying the Puerto Rican flag, which was originally a nationalist symbol. These web stores prove it is far easier to wear or decorate with symbols of nationalism than to vote for the PIP.

On the serious side, helping prolong the cultural weight of independence was the victory won (by coalitions, peaceful protests, and civil disobedience) in Vieques against the U.S. Navy. Also significant was the 2008 global economic crisis, which gave new breath to nationalists because the financial upheaval upset the U.S. economy, on which Puerto Rico is entirely dependent, sharpening a crisis that nowadays extends to all parts of island life; in 2011, for example, the Pew Hispanic Center said the unemployment rate topped 16 percent, the poverty rate 44 percent, and the median annual income was a lowly $14,400. Furthermore, that year "violent crime has gotten so bad that last year Governor Luis Fortuño had to call out the National Guard" (Padgett). The hoped-for silver lining is that the island's colonial condition has been detrimental on so many levels that the situation can't help but lead to change.

Even though consistently on the losing side of elections, *independentistas* can also act as gadflies on the status topic and have a public voice on social issues. In the bleak socioeconomic climate of the early 2000s, where the solutions proposed by the government were a bitter pill,[33] pro-independence activists saw an opening to restate their calls for radical change. An editorial in *Claridad* spoke to the possibility of rebirth if all this upheaval hastened the end of the colonial model that they claim was instituted in 1898 ("El camino hacia la independencia" [The road to independence 25 Sept. 2009]).

In the rest of the book, we will see how *cultural* fictions of national freedom are sustained by:

- tradition
- patriotism
- nostalgia
- a left-leaning intelligentsia
- a need for heroes
- a marketplace for nationalist iconography
- notions of national authenticity

I also want to note that *political* dreams of sovereignty are, for the minority that supports it as a viable political path, fuelled by:

- the resentment caused by well-documented abuses by the United States;
- the political and economic limitations imposed by the island's colonial condition; and
- the desire to escape the two-party system.

As we will see, Puerto Rico may lack sovereignty, but it has not lacked cultural symbols to direct attention to what became a *dream nation*—one that capitalizes on heroes and history, on national allegories such as the house and the family (a.k.a. *La Gran Familia Puertorriqueña*), and on nostalgia for the lush panorama of La Isla del Encanto.[34] Independence appears in wide-ranging ways in the great works taught in schools, the literary corpus—the living body—of Puerto Rican literature. All these and many more symbolic places in the Puerto Rican national imagination are laden with more emotional resonance the closer they get to the failed dreams of nationalism. Time and again, against all odds, independence continues as a touchstone in Puerto Rican culture perhaps following a contrarian impulse of a "cultural nationalism that works for an objective it finds is persistently being frustrated by the democratic vote" (Lass 4).

The fiction of verdant land that yearns and fights for independence with all its will is fruit of a culture so steeped in one ideal for so long that it denied itself representations of conflicting political action; other hopes for La Isla were locked out of the house.

A great part of the attraction to the dream nation is its long-standing appeal to patriotism, a clarion call to higher, nobler national emotions, leading to what Ramón Grosfoguel labels "the romantic rhetoric of the pro-independence movement" ("The Divorce of Nationalist Discourses" 69). Luis Rafael Sánchez, a defender of sovereignty, makes the distinction between patriotism as love of land and "patriotería" (jingoism). Brilliantly, he comes down on the side of love when he talks about his obsession with "El país cuya canción, dulce o amarga, quiero cantar" (cited by López-Baralt in *Llévame alguna vez* 51; The country whose song, sweet or bitter, I want to sing).

What is the Puerto Rican nation? I study it in this book as a cultural entity immersed in contradictory impulses for and against sovereignty, one in which many cultural stories, themes, and symbols connected to independence have inspired, agitated, and provided an outlet for inchoate sentiments about the beloved dream nation. Even though the ordinary person on the street has long abandoned independence as a viable political solution to the island's ills, and even though more recent culture is becoming increasingly distanced from the mythic nation, that dream nation is a wound that has not been healed, a rage that has not been stilled.

Road Map to *Dream Nation*

Chapter 1, "Literary Tradition and the Canon of Independence," explores how the fight for sovereignty acquired the status of cultural orthodoxy in Puerto Rico; it uses as case study a comprehensive anthology of twentieth-century literature, Mercedes López-Baralt's *Literatura puertorriqueña del siglo XX: Antología*. Her choices in shaping the classics of Puerto Rican literature—that most traditionally nation-building of arts—highlight the symbols and stories, the fictions of independence that portray the fears and anxieties as well the love for the dream nation.

Chapter 2, "Breaking Tradition," analyzes the few writers of consequence who have openly critiqued the nationalist cultural project. First is a detailed study of José Luis González's groundbreaking work questioning the tenets of traditional *independentismo*. Rosario Ferré and Edgardo Rodríguez Juliá (and many other writers) are also examined as representing the spectrum of opposition—from her rejection of independence to his distrust of all political projects. The chapter also explores how newer generations of writers (including fashionable so-called minorities such as the LGBT contingent) have become more critical of strictly nationalist cultural projects.

Chapter 3, "From the Lush Land to the Traffic Jam," looks at the complicated shifts in the meanings of the nation that have taken root in Puerto Rican culture based on two patterns: nostalgia and idealization of the agrarian past, yearning for the natural beauties of land and sea (using as exemplar the painterly tradition of Francisco Oller), and then the chapter transitions to its opposite, particularly recent allegories of the island as Traffic Jam, as a colonial society trapped in modernity that spurs dystopia, stagnation, and overdevelopment.

Chapter 4, "Dream History, Dream Nation," discusses prominent (and lesser-known) examples of Puerto Rican culture's penchant for revisiting and rewriting history using heroic as well as antiheroic fiction to mythologize the precolonial and Spanish times. Starting with the centerpiece of alternative history, Luis López Nieves's *Seva*, it reviews how storytellers manipulate the past in relation to the stories of independence (Olga Nolla, Rosario Ferré, Magali García Ramis, Edgardo Rodríguez Juliá, Gina González de Freytes, and others). The chapter also looks at newer literature that explores diasporic and global historical contexts.

Chapter 5, "Dreaming in Spanglish," considers how the principles explored in earlier chapters play out in Puerto Rican Latino cultural production. At issue is how writers in the States construct/remember/fantasize Puerto Rican and Latino identity for the U.S. cultural marketplace. How do these writers replicate the island's cultural patterns and/or perpetuate the view of the islanders as crusaders for independence? How are Latinos telling other stories? Esmeralda Santiago's pro-independence work, shaped by nostalgia, is contrasted with Judith Ortiz Cofer who eschews romanticized views of the island.

1 / Literary Tradition and the Canon of Independence

In his most famous novel, *La guaracha del Macho Camacho*, Luis Rafael Sánchez presents those who follow the dream of independence in lyrical, transcendent terms:

> Sueño vivo, sueño agazapado en la mirada de los muchachos y las muchachas que altisonan y venden *Claridad* y *La Hora* [. . .] Sueño vivo, sueño trémolo o esa transparencia agresiva que se muda o demuda en los rostros que oyen hablar a Mari Brás: deslumbrados porque la historia los invita a hacer el viaje; habla Mari Brás y ellos lanzan el pecho hacia el mañana porque en las manos les conversa la construcción de la libertad. (*La guaracha del Macho Camacho* 128)

> A living dream, a dream crouching in the gaze of the young men and women who holler and sell *Claridad* and *La Hora*.[1] [. . .] A living dream, a tremulous dream, or that aggressive transparency that changes or ranges across the faces listening to Mari Brás: dazzled because history invites them to take the journey; Mari Brás speaks and they thrust out their chests toward the morrow because the construction of liberty is in their hands.

His fictional young activists listen to and are inspired by the living dreams of the real-life Juan Mari Brás, the militant pro-independence founder of the Puerto Rican Socialist Party. What stands out about this section of the novel is that it crops up as a contrast to Benny, the uncaring, ignorant, and profoundly bourgeois scion of Senator Vicente Reinosa. The earnest *independentista* youngsters are the polar opposite to the main characters, themselves repellent caricatures of the status quo (with the exception of Doña Chon, the salt of the earth, motherly character whose sympathies lie with striking workers).

Furthermore, in the passage cited above, the idealistic youngsters—representing a strictly *independentista* vision of the future—disrupt the traffic jam that is the novel's allegory for twentieth-century, modernized Puerto Rico. They are the only force in the novel that does so, since it depicts a stand-still dysfunctional society in which chaos is as ever-present as the smoggy air the characters breathe, an indictment of a beaten-down dream nation. So broken down are all social systems that a "proper" man in the tumult concludes, "the country doesn't work, the country doesn't work, the country doesn't work" (11). Sánchez's *independentistas* are the only shining spot of optimism in a novel that stridently and penetratingly proclaims all that is amiss with Puerto Rico. At the bitter pit of all the wrongness is the island's colonial situation because Puerto Rico is the "successive colony of two empires" (5). And so the dream nation, which persists only in the shouting *independentista youth*, is the sole calling of hope.

Sánchez is a good author to consider in terms of the influence of the independence ideal because of his deep connections with it. For instance, the protagonist of one of his most famous plays, *La pasión según Antígona Pérez* (The passion according to Antigone Pérez) was reportedly based on Olga Viscal Garriga, a member of the Puerto Rican Nationalist Party. All the same, throughout his career he has stated that his emotional bond to the island is in no way jingoistic *patriotería*. But like any great tragedian, he can see the world in stark binaries, which, as we've seen, have a long tradition in the revolutionary fervor of *independentismo*. In "La guagua áerea," for example, he talks about two mutually exclusive ideologies, "el discurso patriótico y el contrainterrogatorio anexionista" (13; patriotic discourse and its annexionist cross-interrogatory), that is to say independence versus selling out.

Writers and intellectuals do not, for the most part, cling to the ideal of independence blindly or unwisely. They are, more than many other folks, devoted to thinking and reading and consequently are often realistic, even grim, about the island's deficiencies. One need look no further than Sánchez's comments in 2012 upon receiving the Eugenio María de Hostos medal from the Hostos Community College in New York (an institution that itself is proof of the strength of communities of Puerto

Ricans). On that occasion, he spoke of his complicated feelings toward his country's flaws, "me amarga mi país, me desconcierta la vulgaridad, el cretinismo político, me intimida la descomposición cultural, me asusta el que tanta gente talentosa no tiene un lugar allí" (*Primera Hora* 1 May 2012; I am embittered by my country, I am bewildered by the vulgarity, the political idiocy, the cultural decay intimidates me, it scares me that so many talented people have no place there). The dream nation is one way to avoid dwelling on that quagmire. Its fictions offer respite.

At first glance, it seems that most major (and quite a few minor) Puerto Rican writers have, until recently, supported independence. Beginning with the nineteenth-century and early twentieth-century stalwarts like Eugenio María de Hostos, Lola Rodríguez de Tió, José de Diego, and José Gautier Benítez, going on to the Generación del 30,[2] Antonio S. Pedreira, Tomás Blanco, Emilio S. Belaval, Nilita Vientós Gastón, Julia de Burgos, Juan Antonio Corretjer, and others, and the Generación de 1945 or 1950, René Marqués, José Luis González, Abelardo Díaz Alfaro, Pedro Juan Soto, Francisco Matos Paoli, and others, most were writers who openly supported independence. And if they didn't support it, they kept their doubts to themselves. In the 1960s and 1970s, the Puerto Rican literary and cultural scene was a hotbed of admiration for the main beliefs of the Cuban revolution, among them Caribbean sovereignty free of U.S. influence. Paradoxically, this era saw the solidification of the voters' inclination to association with or statehood in the United States.

The culture as a whole leaned left; the journal *Guajana* (founded in 1962), for instance, was actively dedicated to a politicized, militant literature centering on independence. Proof of the journal's continuing significance in the twenty-first century was that in 2005 the island chapter of the PEN Club gave its award Gran Premio Alejandro Tapia y Rivera de Las Letras to the journal which they shared with Josefina Rivera de Álvarez, another pillar of the literary establishment.

In the 1960s and 1970s, cracks began showing in the unanimity of the intellectual community's support for *la lucha*. René Marqués and José Luis González, for example, were critical of the establishment independence party. Ana Lydia Vega declares in a humorous piece in 1989 that "the majority of Puerto Rican writers are *independentistas*" while poking fun at them because, as she put it, three-quarters of their oeuvre went unpublished (*El tramo ancla* 282). Rosario Ferré, who was initially pro-independence, by the end of the 1990s had embraced the cause of statehood. Ferré is at an extreme of the continuum; more common is

Vega's trajectory: while sometimes critical of independence tactics, she reaffirmed her commitment to the cause in the 1990s.

Pedro Juan Soto was a writer of fierce *independentista* credentials, which is easy to understand given that his son was ambushed and killed by anti-*independentista* government forces in the Cerro Maravilla debacle. Soto unhesitatingly characterized his entire generation (that of the 1950s), as well as the preceding generation (of the 1930s) as being pro-independence, "Todos surgimos a la sombra del Estado Libre Asociado y todos nos rebelamos. [. . .] todos continuamos [. . .] las prédicas de la Generación del 30: *independencia política*, exploración en materia de vida puertorriqueña, defensa del vernáculo" (Hernández, A viva voz 22 [my italics]; We all emerged in the shadow of the Commonwealth and all of us rebelled. [. . .] we continued [. . .] all the preaching of the Generation of 1930: *political independence*, exploration of Puerto Rican life, defense of the vernacular). His fellow writer Emilio Díaz Valcárcel put it differently: "Nosotros éramos todos un *pain in the neck* para el gobierno" (Hernández, A viva voz 52; We were all a pain the neck for the government). Díaz Valcárcel claims there was no contradiction in supporting independence while working for the ELA government because "nuestro trabajo era educativo, no ideológico" (Hernández, A viva voz 52; our work was educational, not ideological).

All the writers mentioned gave generations of Puerto Rican schoolchildren a national culture that reaffirms the dream of independence in myriad ways. Díaz Valcárcel, for instance, says they wrote books for the government about topics fully embraced by the independence movement (although he does not label them as such) like the "movimiento obrero, la historia de las mujeres, la historia y el arte de Puerto Rico" (Hernández, A viva voz 52; the labor movement, women's history, the history and art of Puerto Rico).

Juan G. Gelpí puts a different spin on the recurrence of certain themes, motifs, and stories in Puerto Rican literature, saying that the national literature shares a preoccupation with certain problems that surface time and again (López-Baralt, *Antología* 169). For Gelpí, the repetition of these cultural themes (he zeroes in on tropes of the nation related to sickness, infantilization, and the allegory of the house) are *problems* that the rhetoric of cultural nationalism tries to solve; in that case, independence, which occurs in a complex series of tropes and fictions, is one of the leading problems being percolated through cultural production.

Independentista intellectuals work to shape and develop these themes not just through their writing but also through their participation in institutions like the Universidad de Puerto Rico at Río Piedras (UPR-RP), the Ateneo Puertorriqueño (Puerto Rican Atheneum), and the Instituto de Cultura Puertorriqueña (ICP, Puerto Rican Institute of Culture), among other institutions that promote Puerto Rican culture. An endeavor that has until recently been highly centralized in the greater metropolitan area where the UPR-RP is located. This continues in large part to be the case, as a glance at the list of authors involved with the recent *Colectivo Homoerótica* (www.homoerotica-pr.org/autores.html) shows; many of these hip new authors also went to the UPR-RP. The Puerto Rican literary canon therefore was and is still often defined and passed on by a tightly knit, interconnected literary establishment bonded by friendship (although sometimes they are more like frenemies) and shared beliefs, educated in a uniform system of higher education and cultural diffusion shaped by prominent *independentistas*. Like north on a compass, independence is a point of reference that Puerto Rican culture has institutionalized. In this chapter, I look at how it acquired the status of orthodoxy in Puerto Rican culture and examine a canonical anthology as a case study.

Carmen Dolores Hernández's book of interviews with Puerto Rican writers, *A viva voz*, reveals that all but two of the seventeen important Puerto Rican writers she interviews went to the UPR-RP. That campus was by mid-twentieth century a cultural bastion for *independentismo*. A case in point is the UPR-RP's pro-independence student group (Federación Universitaria Pro-Independencia, or FUPI), which was a force in the 1960s and 1970s and is still active in student protests. Arcadio Díaz Quiñones and Pedro Juan Soto say in their interviews with Hernández that the UPR-RP's bureaucracy during the 1950s and 1960s, on the other hand, was part of the government establishment and therefore against independence. The ethos of the institution later shifted toward independence precisely because Soto and Díaz Quiñones, as well as other famous *independentista* writers, started teaching there in the 1960s. (Hernández, *A viva voz* 33, 131).

The UPR-RP and cultural institutions like the Ateneo and the ICP influence and support the culture as a whole. Because the island is small, a majority of writers were until recently involved in the same cultural institutions. In Mercedes López-Baralt's anthology (discussed below), a staggering 59 out of 112 authors taught or were administrators at the UPR-RP; furthermore, an additional 12 did so at other UPR campuses.

The unifying cultural views on the dream nation respond to the outlook and training of a writerly class that until recently has been the enclave of professors, or, as Carmen Dolores Hernández says, "a fundamental characteristic of our literary landscape [. . .] is its reliance on academic circles. In the absence of the possibility of subsisting as writers because of the smallness of the market and the weakness of the publishing establishment—which is unable to project them beyond the island—the Academy is, if not a refuge, a resource that provides some stability" (*A viva voz* xiii).

In areas where the government had a controlling hand, such as public education, *independentistas* influenced the culture by flying under the radar; for instance, the government's División de Educación de la Comunidad (Division of Community Education) employed pro-independence writers such as René Marqués, Emilio Díaz Valcárcel, Abelardo Díaz Alfaro, and Pedro Juan Soto, and artists such as Rafael Tufiño and Lorenzo Homar during their early careers (Hernández, *A viva voz* 29, 51).

Important journals such as *Asomante* (1945–1970)—later *Sin Nombre* (until 1984)—were led by pro-independence sympathizers like Nilita Vientós Gastón, who had a substantial cultural footprint. She was president of the Ateneo Puertorriqueño, hostess of a long-standing salon at her house, and a lawyer who was instrumental in getting the Puerto Rican Supreme Court to designate Spanish as the official language of the island. Other major cultural figures have been independence sympathizers; such is the case of Concha Meléndez, who founded the chair of Hispanic American Literature at the UPR-RP; Ricardo Alegría, director of the ICP for eighteen years (1956–1979); and Francisco Arriví, the playwright, who was also associated with the ICP.

A majority of Puerto Rican writers and critics at some time in their careers (usually when younger) belonged to the PIP and followed its agenda—at least until century's end. Even today an apolitical stance is the closest that most major writers get to rejecting independence; in fact, few writers identify openly with the ELA and fewer still with the pro-statehood cause, with the exception of Rosario Ferré.

There are, however, newer culture venues that bring the possibility of more diverse opinions. Outlets such as virtual portals for new writers like *En la Orilla: Una virtual experiencia de la joven literatura puertorriqueña,* and online journals like *80Grados*—although the latter proves that progressive, pro-nationalist sentiment is still the default mode for Puerto Rican culture. Publishing houses have also become less directly beholden to traditional establishment communities; for instance Editorial Isla Negra, which publishes many of the young, hip crowd, is newly ascendant just as the UPR's publishing venues have suffered budget cuts. Also the UPR-RP has been weakened by massive government budget cuts and the resulting strikes so that its hold on the literary production is therefore diminished because its publishing and journalistic arms have been immobilized. If newer writers like Pedro Cabiya and Elidio La Torre Lagares are any indication, e-books will also have an impact in bringing Puerto Rican literature to light. Some writers, such as award-winning Eduardo Lalo, bypass the island publishing houses. Of course, true diversity would entail important tropes, symbols, and stories that consider whether/how, say, the people's wish for statehood is a part of the national identity.

Clearly, the ideal of independence had tremendous ferocity and longevity with Puerto Rican writers in earlier times. The nineteenth-century writer Eugenio María de Hostos is representative of the early period. His support for the island's sovereignty appealed to raw nationalist emotions via heartfelt pleas for social justice, "Hay que insistir todo [sic] los días en decir y repetir que Puerto Rico ha sido robada de lo suyo, de su libertad nacional; de su dignidad nacional; de su independencia nacional" (López-Baralt, *Antología* 13; We must insist every day in saying and repeating that Puerto Rico has been robbed of its own, of its national freedom, of its national dignity, its national independence). Hostos and many others believed that independence was the birthright of nations, and that only by achieving sovereignty could Puerto Rico recover the *dignity* wounded by its colonial condition. Liberty and dignity became entwined in the Puerto Rican national imagination.

How to achieve independence was not so clear-cut. Hostos thought a conversion into sovereign nationhood was only possible by means of a legal plebiscite or some other form of representative election. He also recognized that no island is an island, at least in terms of realpolitik, and pleaded for international legal mechanisms to undo the territorialization of Puerto Rico. For instance, he urged the U.S. Congress to grant the island the same freedom it was about to give Cuba and the Philippines. It did not.

Like Hostos, most writers of the nineteenth to mid-twentieth century passionately agitated for Puerto Rico's legally binding sovereignty free from all attachments to foreign powers, but especially free from the

United States, a country already regarded by Cuban *independentista* luminary José Martí as a threat to Latin America.

Exploring Pro-Independence in the Twentieth Century: An Anthology as a Case Study

National literatures depend on anthologies to codify what gets taught in schools, to represent the nation, to spread the word. How do anthologies do this? Ordinarily they provide the reader with the collected works of a nation, a period, or a group in one place and at a good price (sparing her/him from having to choose and buy many disparate books). *Vocabulary.com* amusingly defines anthologies as "the heavy textbooks that span the literature of an entire culture and that school children transport in over-sized backpacks with wheels." John Guillory reminds us that the main constituency for anthologies is university students (30) and states that the authority exerted by these tomes springs from the complex power relations churning inside institutions (like universities) where the anthologizing authorities decide for the public what constitutes the canon (or list of great works). For my purposes, the Puerto Rican anthology studied below bolsters the *independentista* nation-building canonicity of great Puerto Rican works in the twentieth century.

As Guillory says, the debate over the canon concerns what gets taught in schools so that there is "an imaginary cultural unity" (38) crucial to "a supposedly national culture" (39). Well, there's nothing "supposed" about the reality of Puerto Rican national culture, and one of the reasons for this is precisely the persistent impact of a literature steeped in independence, which was to a large extent the useful, binding agent of the culture's national enterprise.

In the case of Puerto Rican literature, anthologies, curricula, and syllabi have all reinforced certain ideas of the nation—for instance, a country identified with an idealized agrarian past—and, it has most often been the case, a country linked to the one political option viewed as most patriotic: independence.

My argument is that the selections in an A-list anthology reveal the deep scar of that one ideal on the corpus of Puerto Rican literature. To prove this, I explore Mercedes López-Baralt's *Literatura Puertorriqueña del siglo XX. Antología* (from 2004) in order to sort out how independence works as a guiding principle of the standard literary canon in overt and hidden ways. Mostly I look at the prose genres (essays, short stories, testimonies, and novel fragments) because that is my chief area of practice; however, I will mention some poems from the anthology (which excludes drama) whenever they are relevant.

There are several anthologies of Puerto Rican literature of the twentieth century; I chose López-Baralt's because of her stated preference for independence; because it was published in the twenty-first century, which means it is still very much in print; and because it covers many genres. The stature of the anthologist was also a factor: López-Baralt is a *grande dame* of Puerto Rican letters, and her tome is the largest such endeavor, with 1,045 pages. In comparison, Edgar Martínez Masdeu and Esther M. Melon's twentieth-century anthology, published (somewhat prematurely) in 1972, has 439 pages.

In the introduction to her anthology, López-Baralt focuses on the theme of national identity, which has deep roots in the ideal of a dream nation. She deploys transparently pro-independence rhetoric in speaking of how literature interacts with nationalism (a closely coded sister-word to independence):

> El resurgimiento de la autoestima colectiva de nuestro país, lastimada por cinco siglos de sujeción colonial, es fruto finisecular. Si bien nunca faltó el abono de la lucha centenaria de nuestro pueblo por su soberanía, tanto en el autonomismo como en la independencia, la gesta de la Isla Nena contra la marina norteamericana ha nutrido en los últimos años del siglo y en los albores del veintiuno un nacionalismo para el que afortunadamente ya no hay vuelta atrás. El lugar de las artes, y sobre todo, de las letras en este despertar de la conciencia colectiva, es invaluable. (xx)

> The resurgence of our country's collective self-esteem, wounded by five centuries of colonial subjection, is fruit of the turn of the century. If in fact the nourishment provided by our people's century-long struggle for their sovereignty was never missing, both in the search of autonomy and independence, the saga of the Baby Island [Vieques] against the U.S. Navy has nurtured in the last years of the century and in the dawn of the twenty-first a nationalism from which thankfully there is no turning back. The place of the arts, and especially the *belles-lettres*, in this awakening of the collective consciousness, is invaluable.

In this quasi-manifesto, she uses key terms from *independentista*-speak: "collective self-esteem," "colonialism," "sovereignty," "autonomy," "independence" (of course), and, finally, the "epic" of Vieques. Given this will to be guided by nationalism, the anthology makes a compelling example of how the dream nation works in Puerto Rican literature since it is grounded in notions of Puerto Rican *identity* arising from a long literary tradition that favors revolutionary nationalist fervor. In contrast, Martínez Masdeu and Melon merely say that they aim to provide a panoramic view of Puerto Rican literature (6). A comparison of twentieth-century Puerto Rican literature anthologies would be fascinating but is beyond the scope of this chapter.[3]

López-Baralt's definition of literature is *therapeutic*, following the logic that the dream of independence is the unvarying site of trauma that needs healing through art. In fact her words inspired (in part) the title of the book you are reading because, as she states, "La isla deviene hoy territorio libre hecho de palabras, más allá de la geografía telúrica" (xix; The island becomes today a free territory made of words, beyond the reach of earthbound geography). The dream nation is the written nation.

Her introduction, as we can see, is written in a high-serious style in keeping with the weightiness of the tome as well as the traditional rhetoric of independence, which often tends toward earnest humorlessness.[4] The tone ties in with the anthologist's mission of casting literature as a vehicle for sociopolitical aims, one meant to awaken collective conscience and to bolster national self-esteem (which she hopes will lead to actions similar to Vieques). The introduction also sets up the dream nation of freedom fighting, of a culture that struggles, that refuses to lay down its rhetorical arms or its language, since she holds the use of Spanish is a prime battleground of Puerto Rican nationalism. Because it is taken for granted that the aim of literature is to correct or to save the so-called colony from history (xxi) and to give us a truer nation.

First, of course, comes the affirmation of independence as a cultural landmark in Lopéz-Baralt's introduction (quoted above). The reader cannot help but note that one of the guiding criteria for inclusion in the volume is *independentismo*. Since the word "anthology" comes from, as Bárbara Mujica says, "the Greek word for 'collection of flowers,' a term implying selection" (203), what we have here is Professor López-Baralt's handpicked bouquet, to extend the metaphor. As expected, the choice of some writers, but not others, caused much friction in the island's literary scene because the pool of writers is in some ways like a clan (or a dysfunctional family). Case in point, Pedro López Adorno says, "a recent anthology of Puerto Rican literature by Mercedes López-Baralt, *Literatura puertorriqueña del siglo XX* [. . .], has caused much uproar [. . .]

because of some unlikely inclusions (i.e. writers with no significant publications to their credit) and a number of exclusions" (16). That would be the case with any anthology, not just López-Baralt's.

Of course, she didn't choose the works in the anthology based solely on the writers' or the texts' faithfulness to independence—she wouldn't have to because from the nineteenth to the latish twentieth century the only way to avoid independence in Puerto Rican literature was to *not read it*.

Still, here is a major compilation of great works where the anthologist herself articulates her desire for a specific political option in the introduction to the volume. Her ardent praise of the island's need for sovereignty makes López-Baralt's book an exemplar of how the flow of Puerto Rican literature is channeled through independence, canonizing writers and works that present overt as well as symbolic references to the dream nation.

That is not her *only* criterion; the anthology also includes writers and works that ignore the question, since an apolitical stance was the closest most major writers in the twentieth century ever got to rejecting independence. With the notable exception of Rosario Ferré, no major writer cast her/himself as pro-statehood openly and unambiguously. Defense of the ELA can be figuratively laid at the feet of the centrist Edgardo Rodríguez Juliá, though he has identified with all three status options at one time or another. A writer's preference for political independence, on the other hand, has always been flaunted in Puerto Rican literature. Lately, as we shall see, culture producers are bypassing the dream nation and its issues, transitioning from local island affairs into global and diasporic matters.

An important question, of course, is, Does a pro-independence *political* stance consequently show up in a writer's *creative* work? Not necessarily. Puerto Rican literature is about many things, and independence is only one, albeit an important feature. In addition, most activist writers have other axes to grind, other causes in which they take part in (ecology, social inequalities, women, and LGBT and workers' rights, for example). But chances are that if a writer supports independence, it will be present in overt or symbolic terms in their writing. For example the quote from Luis Rafael Sánchez's *La guaracha del Macho Camacho* that opens this chapter.

While the present book looks at themes, symbols, and stories associated with independence in (mostly) literature, it is interesting to trace the degrees of separation between the authors' real-life opinions and activism and the dream nation. In this regard, López-Baralt's brief biographies at the end of her anthology highlight the overt connections of a large number of writers directly to independence institutions or causes. (Please see the Biographical Appendix to *Dream Nation* for a list of writers who appear in the anthology's biographical section as having ties to independence.)

A writer's support for *la lucha* doesn't necessarily lock their work into any of the key components of independence-oriented literature (heroic templates, nostalgia for the Lush Land, rewriting of history, *La Gran Familia Puertorriqueña*, etc.). López-Baralt, however, views art as having a consciousness-raising purpose. Given the perfect storm of canon-forming academic authority (represented by her stature and the anthology's length) and the near-universal support for independence on the part of so many writers up to the latter part of the twentieth century, the themes, stories, and symbols of the dream of an independent nation formed and enhanced, as well as stifled, the Puerto Rican canon as it appears in this anthology. Stifled, I say, because its centrality comes at the expense of literary explorations of the other two status options, which have more often than not been invisible.

Let's look closely at the works in the anthology. The choice of first genre (essays) and the title of that first section, "Pensando la nación" (Thinking the nation), already tilts the anthology from the beginning toward themes of nationalism. Puerto Rican essays throughout the twentieth century (particularly the early part of the century) frequently appealed directly to the issue of political status as an identity marker. Not every essay in the anthology, however, discusses deep political/identity issues; for instance, there is a topical essay by Mayra Montero on the controversial British royal Camilla Parker Bowles. The anthology, however compiles a majority of essays that delve in the familiar territory of the national.

The first two essays are by iconic nationalist militants, Eugenio María de Hostos and Lola Rodríguez de Tió; they are usually regarded as belonging to the nineteenth century, but López-Baralt shoehorns them into the twentieth. Both essays are epistolary—giving the reader the benefit of a personal, direct voice sometimes absent in the genre—and both exalt independence. If he was the father of independence (although Betances has an equal claim to the honorific), Rodríguez de Tió has the privilege of being regarded as mother of calls for independence—one of her poems later became "La Borinqueña," the song of Puerto Ricanness. Both Rodríguez de Tió and Hostos show their era's positivist bent, trusting in the inevitability of *progress* toward independence.

In her 1900 essay "Carta a mis amigas de la vuelta abajo" (Letter to my woman friends from close on by), Rodríguez de Tió flatly states that the people have only one aim: "la independencia absoluta de la patria" (3; the absolute independence of the motherland). She was writing from Cuba, where she spent part of her life, and her belief that the two islands were called to the same destiny led her, in one of her most quoted poems, to call them the two wings of a bird. The underpinning of Caribbean solidarity, particularly the closeness between Cuba and Puerto Rico, was key to the momentum of the meaning, symbols, and stories of early twentieth-century writers like Rodríguez de Tió. For instance, the eleventh selection in the anthology, José Ferrer Canales's essay "José Martí y José de Diego" is symptomatic of the insistent search for similarities between the two islands (in his case, heroes of patriotism). The shared Cuban/Puerto Rican political struggle would again rear its head in 1959, when the Puerto Rican intelligentsia, like that of most of Latin America, latched onto Castro's revolution as the new model for nationhood because, as the critic Ed Morales puts it, "it was Latin America's great 'fuck you' to Yankee domination, a defiance Puerto Ricans can only dream of" (*Living in Spanglish* 226).

Another rhetorical stance of late-nineteenth- and early-twentieth-century writers like Rodríguez de Tió and José de Diego is their attachment to the religious resonance of the dream nation. In her essay, independence is "el sublime ideal de la santa causa" (4; the sublime ideal of the holy cause). That strident religiosity later fell into disuse, although it still crops up, ossified; Mario A. Rodríguez León speaks in 2013 of the dream nation as a "patria cristiana" in a *Claridad* column titled "El altar de la Patria."

The second work in López-Baralt's anthology is by Eugenio María de Hostos, one of the great heroes of the nineteenth-century struggle for independence from Spain. Hostos addresses the legal situation of Puerto Rico after the United States has taken command of the island by "brute force." For him, the island's sovereignty was a matter of ethics: "No es ya sólo el patriotismo, que nos obliga a defender la patria [. . .] es también la conciencia quien manda hacer lo que es bueno" (10; It is no longer just patriotism that requires us to defend the homeland [. . .] it is also conscience that commands us to do what is right). Hostos's "Carta" (Letter) works the trope of the *madre isla* (the mother island). His moral defense may sound hyperbolic now, but it was a common rhetorical custom in his day. Nowadays no one would say of the danger of assimilation that "para absorber a Puerto Rico es necesario exterminarlo" (10;

in order to absorb Puerto Rico it is necessary to exterminate it) because the term "exterminate" echoes in our post-twentieth-century ears with genocidal overtones. But Hostos was not prefiguring Hitler, Stalin, or Pol Pot; for him, the battle between right (independence) and wrong (the United States and its island defenders) entailed the possession of the island's body and soul. Hostos's warning of cultural extermination is one of the dread-inducing scenarios that some still fear will come to pass.

In this manner, these first two works in the anthology center on the dream nation, an independent cultural entity that fights for freedom, as the foundation of twentieth-century Puerto Rican literature. The third essay, from 1911, is by lesser-known writer Rosendo Matienzo Cintrón, "La guachafita fa" (The hubbub here), a sardonic diatribe about the worthlessness of U.S. citizenship for Puerto Ricans. Just like religiosity, the anti-American bluster he strikes will be a rhetorical note beaten throughout the century in many nationalist writings.

Next, from better-known Nemesio Canales comes "No servimos" (We do not serve), an essay that reinforces the essentialist idea that nations must be sovereign, discusses the likelihood of U.S. citizenship (in 1915), and concludes, in relation to that possibility, "esto no es Puerto Rico" (25; this is not Puerto Rico). He uses the even then well-worn stereotype of Americans as utilitarian and materialist, "metódicos, rutinarios, puritanos, fríos e ingenuos" (26; methodical, routine-oriented, Puritans, cold and naïve) and contrasts it to a self-serving description of the essential characteristics of Puerto Ricans that is romanticized and equally stereotypical, "vehementes, imaginativos, soñadores, algo holgazanes, irónicos, rebeldes a toda disciplina, un poco filósofos y un poco poetas" (26; vehement, imaginative, dreamers, somewhat lazy, ironic, rebellious to all discipline, a little bit philosophers and a little bit poets). That Manichaean view of the two national personalities—itself a dubious concept, as if nations could be so univocal—will continue to bring highly charged emotionalism in defense of the dream nation throughout the twentieth century.

Antonio S. Pedreira, a major essayist of the twentieth century, appears next, arguing against the threat of dissolution of national identity, which, as we have seen, is a common theme of the essays chosen by López-Baralt. The anthology includes excerpts from his most famous essay, *Insularismo*, which laid down the template for future culture discussions. It also became, as Alfredo Villanueva Collado says, "the *bête noire* of Puerto Rican cultural production" (182) for its racist, homophobic, and sexist underpinnings. In any case, the essay hits dream nation themes of nostalgia for an Edenic past, for a more authentic Puerto Rico, and it is opposed to modernization (i.e., the twentieth century U.S.-dominated island). Pedreira's fear that the war between *norteamericanos* and *puertorriqueños* would blur Puerto Rican national identity leads to his conclusion that the real nation hinges on a careful and systematic rejection of so-called modernity and its "democratizing" educational goals. Pedreira considers that none of the "civilizing" effects coming from the United States outweighs the deficits of the moral vacuum of dependency. He sees a struggle in which the loser is anyone who mixes the basic principles of Americanness (machinism) and Puerto Ricanness (soul). Pedreira also raises the specter of racial confusion and borrows a term from Luis Palés Matos, the famous Afro-Caribbean poet, *burundanga* (comparable to the civil rights era's notion of mongrelization of the races, or miscegenation). This *burundanga* he assails as the product of a "pseudodemocratic" culture spread via the public schools.

Tomás Blanco's "Elogio de la plena" (In praise of the *plena*), which is the next essay, equally rejects modernity and stresses the same fear of a cultural, "burundanga [. . .] una mal cocida mezcla de componentes dispares—con frecuencia antagónicos—que coexisten, como matrimonio mal avenido, sin mutuo provecho ni armonía: mescolanza sin sentido, como algazara de loros; disparatada, como olla de grillos; pretenciosa y absurda" (54; burundanga [. . .] an undercooked mix of disparate components—often antagonistic—that coexist, like an ill-assorted marriage without mutual benefits and harmony: as a meaningless jumble, as a racket of parrots; crazy as a madhouse, pretentious and absurd). Blanco seems to have liked the negative use of the word; he uses it in another of his essays (not in the anthology): "Reflexiones finales del prontuario histórico de Puerto Rico" (Final thoughts on the historical handbook of Puerto Rico), as a term of opprobrium about the "bridge between two cultures" metaphor being used for Puerto Rico during his time (Mari Brás 205).

Blanco and Pedreira's elitist, white-only ethos would later be hung like an albatross on orthodox *independentismo*, not least by José Luis González in his formidable essay "El país de cuatro pisos" (The four-storyed country). It is clear that the early to mid- twentieth century produced much angst about national identity centering on status questions: "¿Adónde vamos? ¿Cuál ha de ser el *status* definitivo de la isla? ¿Estado federal? ¿República independiente? ¿Autonomía con protectorado?" (29; Where are we going? What should be the definitive status of the island? Federal state? Independent republic? Autonomy with protectorate?).

In the 1930s, independence was still conceivably a viable political option, but Pedreira's defense of sovereignty for the island, based as it was on patriarchal, elitist values built on the cultural legacy of Spain, would doom the impact of his thinking for future readers. José Rodríguez Vázquez says Pedreira aspired to be a "literate voice directed at elites who are owners of high culture" (42). In sum, Pedreira's Hispanophilic nostalgia (and its attendant anti-American reflex) led him to disdain the "sordid" times he lived in because material progress would lead to dreaded egalitarianism. Echoing José Enrique Rodó, who in *Ariel* spoke of an "aristarchy" of culture, Pedreira's classist, misogynist viewpoint of a severely critical "meritocracy" (that is to say, an aristarchy) sees cultured Puerto Ricans, for him "superior men," increasingly disrespected by the mediocre masses.

It is almost too easy nowadays to dismiss Pedreira for his elitism, misogyny, and racism; however, to do so would ignore Pedreira's foundational definition of Puerto Rico as a country divided between cultures and races and that the dualism, the dichotomies, in part set the template for future nationalists who cannot abide the mix of cultures or languages. Later, Pedreira's model was used to portray how patriotic people (on one side) defend the nation and its independence on moral grounds against (on the other) the alienated Spanglish-speaking masses that support ties to the United States.

One presumes that the selection of works for an anthology is subject to many forces, such as consensus among the anthologist and her cohorts. Accepted presence in the field is one way to define which great works get included because they promote a certain story of the nation; works and writers also receive recognition and attention through awards and prizes and through their works' use in school and university curricula. One supposes a desire to redefine the canon is also at work when an anthology appears. These opposing needs of the anthologist—using popularly accepted works versus discovering hidden gems—*might* explain the altogether curious choice of José Ferrer Canales's (*not* Nemesio R. Canales) obscure essay "José Martí y José de Diego" as a canonical work of literature. But if the anthologist wanted to rescue an arcane essay(ist), why not Antonio J. Colorado? Or if she deemed José Ferrer Canales ripe for canonization, why not his far less bombastic "Acentos Cívicos y Gandhi" (Civic accents and Gandhi)? The choice of this particular essay proves that *independentismo* and its literary tradition are at the heart of this anthology.

Neither Ferrer Canales nor the essay feature prominently, or at all, in the usual lists of great Puerto Rican works—primarily because his sentimental, pompous language has long since fallen into disfavor. He is certainly not present in Martínez Maseu's anthology. But the *dream of independence* is clearly singled out by Ferrer Canales: "La Independencia, la soberanía es la libertad matriz y primaria de los pueblos" (97; Independence, sovereignty is the matrix and primary freedom of the people). The crux of his essay is the exaltation of the nineteenth-century apostle of Puerto Rican patriotism, the poet José de Diego, for whom the fight for independence was a sacred undertaking. De Diego's prose and poetic stylings are grandiloquent relics steeped in essentialist pontifications about independence, such as "Las Islas son y deben ser independientes por la voluntad de Dios y la obediencia a la Naturaleza" (91; The Islands are and should be independent by the will of God and obedience to Nature). Even though his birthday commemoration is a Puerto Rican national holiday to this day, among the intelligentsia nowadays de Diego's stock has plummeted and not just because of his bombastic style but also because of his values. Mario R. Cancel says de Diego's nationalism served to defend "Catholicism, language, Hispanism, and Antilleanism" (*Anti-figuraciones* 108). While de Diego's poetry is legitimately representative of a moment in Puerto Rican culture and should be in an anthology (and is included in the poetry section), the essay by Ferrer Canales has the sole merit of linking de Diego to the far more famous and prestigious Cuban *independentista* José Martí.

Since literary canons reflect the main ideas of their times, assuming this anthology was compiled in the latter days of the twentieth century and the first few of the twenty-first, then we have to wonder what was the attraction of this particular essay by Ferrer Canales for an anthologist who must have been impacted by late-twentieth-century shared cultural notions that privileged irony over sentimentality, postfeminist multiculturalism over Hispanophilic religious/patriarchal machismo. The choice of Ferrer Canales, which runs counter to all of these cultural markers, signals a selection dictated by a tradition in support of independence.

Nationalists born in the nineteenth century such as Hostos, Rodríguez de Tió, and de Diego subscribed to the thinking about the right of nations to sovereignty and against tyrannical oppression from *empire* as well as to the emotional and pseudo-religious feelings deployed to defend that right. The selections in the anthology underscore the corollary concept of national *dignity*, a cornerstone to *independentismo*. For instance, the anthology has two central works of *independentismo*: José de Diego's poem "En la brecha" (Into the breach) (1916) and Abelardo Díaz Alfaro's short story "El josco" (The fiery one) (1947). Both were nation-building works taught in schools, and both use Nature, specifically bulls, as symbols of the island to inspire the combative spirit necessary to rescue wounded national dignity. De Diego uses animalistic strength as a call for rebellion:

> ¡Levántate! ¡Revuélvete! ¡Resiste!
> Haz como el toro acorralado: ¡Muge!
> O como el toro que no muge: ¡Embiste! (714)
>
> Arise! Seethe! Resist!
> Do as the bull at bay: Bellow!
> Or like the bull that doesn't bellow: Lunge!

This poem's *cries de coeur*, prodigious use of exclamation points, and melodramatic intensity are as far from late-twentieth-century tastes as they are far from, say, José Martí's writing. Compare any passage in the Cuban's defense of Latin America in his splendid "Nuestra América" (Our America) to de Diego's sentimentaloid Catholic religiosity: "¡Donde no se olvida, y donde no hay muerte, llevamos a nuestra América, como luz y como hostia!" (102; Where it is not forgotten, and where there is no death, we carry our America, as beacon and as communion wafer!).

If we know one thing about Puerto Rican literature, it is that, like many other national cultures, it quite often used to correlate the physical land with the nation. As is to be expected from a work written in the earlier part of the twentieth century, Díaz Alfaro's "El josco" manages to be shockingly chauvinist as well as nationalistic when the symbolic male bull strides the virgin land. In that one phrase, which encapsulates the ethos of the story, the (redundantly) male bull stands atop (on top of) the feminized land (a feminine noun in Spanish). So of course the heroic enterprise of freedom seeking, with its strength and defiant stance (like the *macho* bull) dominates the landscape, always personified as virginal and in need of protection. Note the longevity of both the poem and the story, which have proven amazingly resilient to the ravages of time, as allegories of Puerto Rico and its struggle for freedom.

Lest it seem too easy for such a metonymical scaffolding to nail down the bullishness of the dream of independence, the anthologist notes that de Diego and Díaz Alfaro coincide in their message of nationalist affirmation. Díaz Alfaro's "El josco" is for López-Baralt, "el epitafio de la dignidad isleña" (xxxv; the epitaph of the island's dignity). Dignity, always dignity. So significant does she find the story that despite a copyright problem that prevented her from including it in the anthology, she left a blank page in its honor.

Support for independence isn't, of course, the only factor for the anthologist's choices because Puerto Rican literature in the latter part of the century began angling toward criticism of *independentista* orthodoxy. José Luis González was probably the first writer of consequence to speak at length against conventional *independentismo*. López Baralt's anthology employs the second section of his essay "El país de cuatro pisos" (The four-storyed country) (1978), one of the best known and most widely read essays in Puerto Rican literature. She anthologizes the section titled "Literatura e identidad nacional en Puerto Rico" (Literature and national identity in Puerto Rico) bypassing the eponymous first section of the book in which González lashes out against old-guard *independentismo*, the national literary canon, and, especially, the sacred cow that is Albizu. González was militant in the Communist Party when he was seventeen (Díaz Quiñones 15), so that a writer with such solid nationalist credentials could afford to lash out against standard ideas of a unified dream nation. At the time González was writing, he had long been in exile in Mexico, which had an effect on his willingness to speak against what was at the time hard-core devotion to heroes of independence like Albizu. The portion of the essay in the anthology highlights groundbreaking aspects of González's redefinition of Puerto Rican culture, such as his belief that culturally, Puerto Rico is firstly grounded in African and mulatto legacies.

Nevertheless, the next essay in López-Baralt's anthology, lesser-known Rafael Castro Pereda's "Morir en español" (To die in Spanish) (1984) runs completely counter to José Luis González's message. The foundational dream nation principles of idealizing the landscape and of patriotism are triumphant in Castro Cepeda, who regards telluric definitions of the nation as the proper sphere of "Hispanic-American writers who faithfully express national sentiments" (146) such as the Mexican author Juan Rulfo.

Nevertheless, González was not just a prophet in the desert; he was a harbinger of questionings to come. Following his lead, by the late twentieth century some culture buffs critiqued blind devotion to the dream nation. For instance, in her commentary to the next essay,

Juan G. Gelpí's "Literatura y paternalismo en Puerto Rico" (Literature and paternalism in Puerto Rico) (1993), López-Baralt describes the essay as being in a debate with González. Gelpí doesn't, however, so much debate as build on González. In fact, he critiques the role of a literary canon as a substitute for national sovereignty (169).

For Gelpí, as for González, the Generation of 1930 institutionalized a paternalistic culture that idealized the nation, which is evident in the traces it left on the literary canon (157). He states that Antonio S. Pedreira was the "consolidation" of paternalism and René Marqués its last pure exemplar, one who was dealing with the crisis of nationalism. For Gelpí, their works show symptoms of a culture linked (as González had stated) to the worldview of the landowners. Gelpí also demolishes the conflation of nation and family, pointing out how this fundamentally paternalistic symbolic system excluded women from the literary canon (except a few, such as Julia de Burgos) (159). López-Baralt includes a second essay by Gelpí called "Reescrituras del clásico" (Rewritings of the classic) (1993), which argues for new ways of interpreting Puerto Rican cultural orthodoxy along the same lines as the essay just discussed.

No anthology of twentieth-century Puerto Rican literature and its obsession with the nation could fail to include Luis Rafael Sánchez's "La guagua aérea" (The airbus) (1983), which changed the popular notion of the imagined community of Puerto Rico from the island *as an island* to an allegory of a floating nation going to and from San Juan and New York. He replaces the iconic topography of La Isla with a crowd in a transnational setting: Puerto Rico is an airbus full of loud, irreverent, tragicomic characters telling tales in the middle of nowhere. The dreamed-of nation may not be an island anymore but is made of fiction; the nation is in the telling.

While the territory, La Isla, is no longer the sole defining factor of Puerto Ricanness, some qualities of the nation are the same. For instance, the people still believe in their own exceptionalism as they tell stories in which Puerto Ricans are placed at the "centro absoluto de la picardía, de la listeza, del atrevimiento, de la malicia, de la maña, del ingenio" (199; absolute center of playfulness, shrewdness, daring, malice, cleverness, wit). Sánchez mocks telluric nationalism (with a clear swipe at René Marqués): "Anécdotas telurizadas por el estilo arroz y habichuelas. Anécdotas protagonizadas por un jíbaro que no habla dócil" (199; Anecdotes rooted in a rice-and-beans style. Anecdotes featuring a *jíbaro* who does not speak in a docile manner). He had already changed the allegory of the nation from the Lush Land into that of a gargantuan traffic jam in

La guaracha del Macho Camacho; in "La guagua aérea," he uproots the nation from the idyllic land, which he now labels an uninhabitable Eden. The punch line of "The Airbus" is that it turns out that for the travelers the territorial extension of the island encompasses the other side: New York City is just another *pueblo*.

Nevertheless, proving that López-Baralt's canon keeps pulling back to nationalist fundamentals, the next essay, Carmen Dolores Hernández's "Escribiendo en la frontera" (Writing on the border) (1997), restricts the definition of the nation to linguistic (Spanish-only) terms. For her, the fusion of bilingual and binational art and identity leads to confusion (another kind of *burundanga*, like Pedreira and Blanco). The purity of the Spanish language, a linchpin in *independentista* definitions of the nation, is once again paramount.

Hernández turns around Sánchez's uproarious air-bound crowd and casts the situation of Puerto Ricans in the United States as a dire, calamitous state of nonbeing, neither-here-nor-there, "nadando entre dos aguas, atrapados entre dos fuegos, enmarcados dentro de dos horizontes de referencias culturales" (209; swimming between two waters, trapped between two fires, framed within two horizons of cultural references). Given her stature as one of the island's main literary critics, it is surprising that Hernández's essay runs counter not only to Sánchez's notion but to so many theoretical assumptions of the last decades of the twentieth century such as the inherent value of fusion, of so-called *hybridity*, and goes against the wider cultural climate that was at the time guided by theories such as Gloria Anzaldúa's *Borderlands*, which prizes border cultures. Hernández will have none of that; she diagnoses a bicultural trap that puts Puerto Rican writers in the United States in a cultural bind so that they end up rejected on both sides. Such may have been the case for the Nuyorican poets in the 1970s, but the concept lacked force in 1997 (the date of publication of the essay) when a rapprochement between island and stateside intellectuals was resurgent, so why bring it up? Hernández's essay shows the persistence of the identity question, "Who is a Puerto Rican?" anchored to the Spanish language.

In this, Hernández and López-Baralt see eye to eye. For them and many other culture critics, Spanish is the sine qua non of Puerto Ricanness, a cornerstone, because as Hernández says, "Como patrimonio y también como símbolo y afirmación de una identidad cultural, el español de Puerto Rico es pues, una de las características más fundamentales—*si no la más fundamental*—de nuestra identidad colectiva" (210 [my italics]; As heritage and also as a symbol and affirmation of cultural identity,

Spanish in Puerto Rico is thus one of the most fundamental features—*if not the most fundamental*—of our collective identity).

And she's not alone. The centrality of the Spanish language is reaffirmed by many other critics. The anthology called *Los nuevos caníbales* (2004) explicitly makes the connection between the island's dependent status and Spanish: "After over a hundred years into our special relationship with the United States of America, we believe it is pertinent to emphasize the younger narrative, which, through the use of Spanish [. . .] continues intertwining Puerto Rico with the Caribbean and the rest of Latin America" (191). To be fair, López-Baralt anthologizes a few poems written in English by Puerto Rican writers in the United States.

According to Hernández, the purpose of literature written by Puerto Ricans in the States is to document lives lived in the belly of the beast. These Latino Scheherazades write, she says, in order to survive by envisioning "un Puerto Rico soñado, a veces idílico, por lo general mítico" (214; a dreamed-of Puerto Rico, sometimes idyllic, usually mythic). Again, the dream nation.

Next up in the anthology is an odd essay/testimonial written by the anthologist's sister, Luce López-Baralt. Called "Escribirlo es llorar: La crónica del 98 de Esteban López Giménez" (To write it is to weep: Esteban López Giménez's Chronicle of 1898), the essay, from 1998, is a centenary tribute to the scars of national history—specifically the trauma of 1898, one of the most symbolic cornerstones of the dream nation. The essay centers on the memoirs of the sisters' Spain-loving great-grandfather and taps into the yearning for national founding father/heroes common to the independence-prone imagination: "seguimos estando nostálgicos de heroicidad, de un mito fundacional honroso sobre el cual descansar nuestra mirada histórica retrospectiva. Prueba de ello es que nos hemos visto precisados a inventar este mito de origen, como demuestra dramáticamente el relato *Seva*" (224; we continue to be nostalgic of heroism, of an honorable foundational myth with which to look back with our historical gaze. Proof of this is that we have been compelled to invent this origins myth, as demonstrated dramatically by the story *Seva*). Therefore, the stain that needs cleansing is the dishonorable conduct of Puerto Ricans in 1898 who were indifferent to the Americans or, even worse, received them with open arms.

She offers as counterbalance the real-life tale of resistance of her great-grandfather Esteban López Giménez, who was an ardent sympathizer of Spanish rule and in the quoted excerpts, sheds tears of shame that all it took was thirteen marines to take over his hometown (222). López

Giménez's anguish is strikingly conflicted about identity and nationhood: "si bien odiaba los gobiernos de España aquí, amaba a mi madre Patria; a mi raza hispano latina; a mi religión católica apostólica romana; a mi idioma" (223; while I hated the governments of Spain here, I loved my mother Country, my Latin-Hispanic race, my Roman Catholic religion, my language). Race, religion and language are here the hallmarks of national identity. Even though Luce López-Baralt points out that her ancestor didn't take into account the African and indigenous influences on the nation (223), she validates the primacy of Spanish-language heritage for Puerto Rico—as does her anthologist sister. She also scorns postmodern thinkers (i.e., those who question the dream nation) as assimilationist traitors who ridicule "la defensa de la lengua y de la cultura nacional—como los asimilistas a ultranza" (225; the defense of language and national culture—like extreme assimilationists). She sees writing in Spanish as the last defense against the dissolution of Puerto Rican identity yet paradoxically notes the ferocious nationalism that can strike Puerto Ricans abroad (which in traditionalist mode she labels exile, not migration): "nuestros compatriotas del exilio, convertidos ya en minorías norteamericanas, muestran a menudo una puertorriqueñidad más combativa que los criollos anexionistas que hablan la lengua de Cervantes" (225; "our compatriots in exile, already having become American minorities, often show a more militant Puerto Ricanness than annexationist Creoles who speak the language of Cervantes).

Mayra Santos Febres's essay "La promesa" (The promise) strides a middle ground in this language/identity divide. On the one hand, it resonates with nineteenth-century overtones of religious views of patriotism as a sacred feeling, "el camino del santo" (217; the way of the saint). On the other hand, she follows Luis Rafael Sánchez beyond the telluric definition of the nation, writing that it is not a place or land but a choice to stay—a very real decision given the hundreds of thousands of Puerto Ricans who have come to the States, particularly in the late twentieth and twenty-first centuries. So for Santos Febres, nationhood represents a poetic desire, a belief, a projection to the future: "un país no es un canto de tierra y cemento que se posee, ni una vergüenza que se esconde, ni un 'patrimonio' que se hereda por casualidad [. . .] un país es una proyección hacia el futuro" (217; a country is not a piece of land and cement that one owns, nor a hidden shame, nor a 'heritage' that is inherited by chance [. . .] a country is a projection into the future).

Post-nationalist literature moves beyond the strict independentista definition of a fixed territorial national identity (La Isla). Playing both sides of the aisle, Santos Febres lays claim to an emotional connection to el país with a promise of the heart, even after she dismantles the ideology of nationalism by acknowledging the paradoxical forces of Puerto Rico. For her, the "one nation" myth has yielded to multiple, sometimes competing identities, concerns and constituencies, especially those that became important in key social issues in the late twentieth and early twenty-first centuries: "mujeres, gays, americanos, pentecostales, internacionalistas" (218; women, gays, Americans, Pentecostals, internationalists). Her postmodern view of many identities leapfrogs the "country above all" loyalties demanded by traditional nationalism to affirm the promise (utopian though it may seem) of a politics of higher meaning and functionality: dialogue, shared life, interaction between all parties and parts of the nation.

In the following essay, "De cómo y cuándo bregar" (Of how and when to deal), Arcadio Díaz Quiñones leans away from strict *independentismo* and gives a centrist definition of Puerto Ricanness based on the pragmatic choices in daily life. For him, national identity isn't about *what* you are but about *how* you live. It's about attitude. He believes living as a Puerto Rican revolves around a way of looking at life, which he summarizes with a street-language term, *la brega* (roughly, "coping"). Interestingly, Juan Mari Brás, the late secretary general of the Partido Socialista Puertorriqueño, a rabid *independentista* if there ever was one, singled out that very word, saying: "'Bregar.' Ese es el verbo predilecto de los populares, 'bregar'" ("*Bregar.*" That is the preferred verb for the *populares*) (Marrero-García and Rodríguez, chapter 4); *populares* is the moniker for members of the Partido Popular Democrático, defenders of the middle-of-road status quo.

Popular or not, Díaz Quiñones still holds to traditional Puerto Rican thinking by embracing exceptionalist views of nationhood. *La brega* comes down to "una especial sensibilidad cultural y política para la negociación" (26; a special cultural and political sensibility for negotiation). The difference is that, as opposed to old-guard nationalism, *la brega* signals a dedication to pragmatism. In a wonderful display of *bregar*, Díaz Quiñones himself navigates the tumultuous waters of Puerto Rican intellectual history in a nonjudgmental way that fully embraces the pride in national culture yet does not ally his thinking to any stated political choices. He, like many late-twentieth- and early-twenty-first-century writers, sees the status issue as a dead end, locked into specific political agendas in so many ideological fiefdoms. Nevertheless, no Puerto Rican essayist worth his/her salt can stay away entirely from the gravitational pull of the status issue; Díaz Quiñones says the existential no-man's-land is due to a fed-upedness with the trials of daily life on the island. Díaz Quiñones rejects the Left *and* the Right as having led to the present status quagmire: "*la brega* se ha ido formando como maniobra defensiva frente a las 'retóricas de la intransigencia,' tanto las 'progresistas' como las 'reaccionarias'" (250; *la brega* has been formed as a defensive maneuver against the "rhetoric of intransigence," both "progressive" as well as "reactionary"). In his open criticism of the Left, he follows José Luis González when he speaks, for instance, of the failures (plural) of leftists (272) and is critical of their tendency toward belligerent authoritarianism that alienates those it would convince (257).

Díaz Quiñones also boldly assails the heroic template of revolutionary and nation-building thinking in Latin America. He highlights, for example, that the customary admiration of revolutionary Cuba as heroic—and therefore Puerto Rico as antiheroic—rests on the rhetoric of war and militarization, which he sees as pervasive in Cuba.

Still, like José Luis González, Díaz Quiñones leans toward progressive causes; for instance, he lauds the *independentistas* for the fight against arms storage on the island (267). He bemoans the militarization of Puerto Rican culture because of U.S.-imposed Cold War exigencies. But like José Luis González (and as opposed to traditional leftist thinking), he is also positive about some aspects of the ties to the United States, specifically public education, housing, and health programs as well as veterans' benefits (259).

Despite some balance, every section of the anthology shows the weight of ideas that pro-independence tradition carries.. The short-story section of the anthology features a prime example of *jíbarismo literario* (literary exaltation of the *jíbaro*), a linchpin of the dream nation in mid-twentieth century. Miguel Meléndez Muñoz's "Navidad y Reyes" (Christmas and kings) (1941) nostalgically recalls the olden days of holiday festivities when country folk would renew their bonds of friendship and kinship in *parrandas* (300). The underlying metaphor is nation as family. He offers a national vision of a benevolent landowning lifestyle when the landowners built their manses with such social gatherings (for the entire community) in mind.

As noted earlier, Abelardo Díaz Alfaro's "El josco" (1947) is not reprinted in the anthology due to a difficulty with Alfaro's estate; instead, an editor's note speaks about its significance, and a blank page stands in homage to the story's status as a Puerto Rican classic.

José Luis González, also a masterful writer of realist short fiction, is represented by his famous and widely anthologized short stories "La carta" (The letter) (1948) and "En el fondo del caño hay un negrito" (At the bottom of the channel there's a little black boy) (1954). Both feature heartbreaking social-realist depictions of poverty, racial strife, and hard migrations.

Spiks (from 1956) was a landmark collection of stories by Pedro Juan Soto. Among its strengths was its portrayal of the hard life for Puerto Ricans in the States, which demythologized the "American Dream." From it López-Baralt picks a story, "La cautiva" (The captive), that centers on the airport as the symbolic site for migrating Puerto Ricans who suffer from "desamparo, soledad, osadía, amargura" (320; helplessness, loneliness, courage, bitterness).

René Marqués towered over the Puerto Rican literary landscape in the 1950s and 1960s and is generally regarded as siding with the independence ideal—though not necessarily with the official party. In works like *La carreta* and *Los soles truncos,* Marqués reaffirms many of the formulas of the dream nation: yearning for a return to the land, distrust of urbanized, Americanized modernity, and anti-American nostalgia for the values of Spanish times on the island. The anthology includes Marqués's 1958 story "Purificación en la Calle del Cristo" (Purification on Cristo Street), in which three reclusive sisters mourn the passing of their upper-class world after "la armada de un pueblo nuevo y bárbaro bombardeó a San Juan" (333; the armada of a new and barbaric people bombarded San Juan). As a result, their circumscribed lives are steeped in nostalgia: "la vida toda era un recuerdo, o quizá una serie de recuerdos" (330; the whole of life was a memory or perhaps a series of memories).

The anthology includes, among many other prose works, representative works from the feminist wave of the 1970s and 1980s. Included from this period are Rosario Ferré's "Cuando las mujeres quieren a los hombres" (When women love men) from 1976 and Ana Lydia Vega's "Letra para salsa y tres soneos por encargo" (Lyrics for salsa and three custom-made songs) from 1981. These stories signal the new direction for intellectuals at the end of the century, when the issue of the island's status started taking a backseat to questions of gender/minority inequalities. Both writers were in favor of independence at the time. Many of the pieces from the anthology from the latter part of the century have feminist, minority, or queer theory themes as part of current trends at the time of publication. Independence as an overt theme quite visibly makes way for other concerns in many of the selections.

Luis López Nieves, on the other hand, is a true-blue adherent to the dream. He wrote the most famous and unambiguous tribute to the ideals of independence in the late twentieth century, the novella *Seva*. This tale of a fictional town that fights off the American invaders yet is forgotten by history was not anthologized by López-Baralt at the writer's request (xxxii); the anthologist states that he had asked her instead to include a more recent short story from 1987 called "El lado oscuro de la luna" (The dark side of the moon), which is more conventional and less controversial. It deals with a dysfunctional married couple who are passionate at night and abusive during the daylight hours. Their situation sounds symbolic of a dysfunctional Puerto Rico that accepts its colonial fate during the day but returns to its passionate dream of independence at night.

The rest of the prose segments occupy a middle ground in the ideological spectrum. Edgardo Sanabria Santaliz's "Cierta inevitable muerte" (Certain inevitable death) (1988) is about a protagonist who rejects his grandfather (i.e., his heritage). The grandson seeks to reconcile the older generations' multiple and conflicting feelings of despair, denial, sadness, resentment, and tenderness. The bastard son is torn between two mothers, his own and his father's widow, much as Puerto Ricans are torn between two national claims. In the end, after all, the son chooses to return to the Land, fleeing from a corrupted civilization into the primal landscape.

Kalman Barsy's confounding story "El jardín" (The garden) has overtones of nationalism in its denunciation of modernity and nostalgia for the lost land, although a gender-studies reading is equally called for since his fantastical tale centers on male/female sexuality. In the tale, the protagonist (a professor) discovers his wife's genitalia transformed into a mysterious land and, later, a sea. With a botanist's interest, he tries to catalogue the flora searching for the meaning of this feminized garden of La Isla. Frustrated, he finds the garden—like Puerto Rico—unclassifiable: "no sólo escapaba a toda clasificación botánica, conocida, sino que ni siquiera podría afirmarse en forma unívoca que fuera de naturaleza vegetal" (426; it not only escaped any known botanical classification, but could not even be said unequivocally to be plant-like in nature). Fantastically, he enters his wife's body whole (like the protagonist in Pedro Almodóvar's *Talk to Her*) to find a river that leads to the ultimate mystery of life (427). Apart from the staggeringly patriarchal and essentialist projection of Woman as Land, Nature, and Mystery, could the nationalist symbolism here be the land's (and by extension, its people's) unknowability, uncategorizability? Because a people who do not want independence are, what . . . exactly?

The story was published in 1989, well after the feminist explosion of writing by Puerto Rican women starting in the 1970s, so there is room to interpret it as a sly parody of male desire—as well as a reverse Heart of Darkness-esque representation of the imperialist drive—where the male stands in for the clueless imperialist lackey; this enhances the symbolic ties to the allegory of a dream nation that is overdetermined by the landscape.

Another recent story in the anthology, Edwin Figueroa's story "El amolador" (The grinder) (2000), centers on an old favorite theme: the critique of Puerto Rico's modernity (i.e., overdevelopment) due to the mallification and uglification of the country—and the attendant nostalgia for a pure landscape. Figueroa's story is in many ways a throwback to the old binary pattern: country/authenticity versus urban/alienation. The deserving working classes face the loss of their agrarian, prelapsarian paradise, violently felled by the faceless forces of governmental modernity. Anastacio, the grinder from the title, speaks in a contraction-laden Spanish reminiscent of a stereotypical *jíbaro*: "Yo me siento sembrao en este barrio como el árbol a la tierra" (467; I feel rooted in this barrio like a tree in the earth). His pop-culture, *telenovela*-loving wife urges him to accept the trappings of modernity (a color TV, new food, etc.): "Tú vives en la Luna. Hay que bregar con los tiempos" (467; You live on the moon. We have to deal with the times). With more than a touch of old-fashioned misogyny, *she* buys into the government's promises of a better, government-sponsored life with social safety nets, good schools, health care for all (467) and so urges him to leave the past and all its accoutrements behind. The grinder, however, insists on pushing his cart and playing his flute, which produces a magical sound. In an almost exact replica of tellurism coupled with rejection of modernity that we have traced before, the story continues to a bourgeois McMansion (in the subdivision that replaced the grinder's neighborhood), where miraculously a symbolic tree persists, and where a child hears the grinder's flute and thinks it is a magical bird from a mythical, long-lost Land. In a turn reminiscent of the end of *La guaracha del Macho Camacho*, the grinder is run over by the limousine transporting the upper-class child and his American-loving, Spanglish-speaking parents.

The story ends in an airplane with a sustained vision of a floating nation last seen in "La guagua aérea," as passengers in a U.S.-bound airplane represent Puerto Rico. Here they become united, one people, through the nostalgia for the lost land inspired by the child's playing of the grinder's flute: "Una emoción unánime [. . .] los sume en melancólica añoranza de hondas vivencias que surten de los veneros de la tradición isleña y aflora en ellos el sentimiento de identidad nacional" (473; A unanimous emotion [. . .] plunges them into a melancholy longing for deep life experiences supplied by the springs of the island tradition and a sense of national identity surfaces in them).

Elidio La Torre Lagares's "Unicornio" (Unicorn) (2000) also mourns the lost landscape. Taken together with the previous story, it can give the impression that newer generations of writers are still in thrall to the dream nation, the verdant land, the soul of Puerto Ricanness. In this story, Cristino, a lonely seven-year-old boy, hears nature speaking to him (478). We first see him eating guavas—a fruit symbolic of an authentic Puerto Ricanness, as we shall see in chapter 5. Interestingly, like in Figueroa's story, the woman pushes for modernity. The story takes place in Adjuntas, a mountainous town deep in the island's center, at a time when being a leftist was still dangerous: "ser de izquierda era casi un pecado" (478; being a leftist was almost a sin). Only the children, the usual stand-ins for purity, can feel the language of the earth (478). The child and his friend try to catch an elusive unicorn that also represents innocence just like theirs, which has been beaten out of them by their abusive fathers—like paternalistic governments that engineered the overdevelopment of the Land.

The anthology's section of testimonies has as its title an allusion to "La guagua aérea": "La nación flotante, aquí y allá" (The floating nation, here and there), which indicates the bridge the anthology tries to make between island and stateside writers. The first selection, Bernardo Vega's "Nueva York: Foco de la revolución antillana. Papel de las comunidades cubana y puertorriqueña" (New York: Focus of the Antillean Revolution. Role of the Cuban and Puerto Rican communities), sets a pro-independence agenda for Nuyorican literature, which López-Baralt considers part of the continuum of Puerto Rican literature only as long as it is written in Spanish. Vega describes and praises Hispanic Caribbean participants in the fight for the independence of Puerto Rico and Cuba from Spain.[5] He vividly depicts the life in exile of independence patriots Eugenio María de Hostos, Ramón Emeterio Betances, and Segundo Ruiz Belvis, and how they formed a revolutionary committee that united the (doomed) fight for the islands' independence from Spain. Memorably, Vega describes Hostos as burning for independence: "venía de Europa echando chispas y con el alma incendiada de santo fanatismo por la independencia de su patria" (491; he came from Europe blazing and with his soul afire with holy fanaticism for the independence of his homeland). Vega's testimony of the independence fight of his day is notable not just by its remembrance of major *independentista* public intellectuals in New York but also because he includes women and working-class activists.

Edgardo Rodríguez Juliá's *El entierro de Cortijo* (Cortijo's wake) (1983), an exercise in pop culture and new journalism, moves to a different beat. As he has done many times, he shatters the myth of the *La Gran Familia Puertorriqueña*. The opening section portrays a nation divided and separated by racial and class borders as Rodríguez Juliá peppers the description of the funeral of the popular musician Cortijo with bittersweet observations about a "país chiquito y redundante" (513; small and redundant country). His redefined nation is a mix of tradition (the *baquiné*) and mass culture (Ruth Fernández). Giving balance to the anthology's focus on traditional themes of nationalism, Rodríguez Juliá's gonzo journalism deals with many topics (including death and its attendant rites as well as a meditation on racial politics) but particularly the differences present within a nation, the tribe-like splinters of a country that still thinks of itself as Family.

Next is Esmeralda Santiago's "Como se come una guayaba" (How to eat a guava) (1994), the prologue to her best-selling memoir, *When I Was Puerto Rican*. The guava symbolizes Puerto Ricanness, authenticity, and connection to the Land. The passage highlights Santiago's neonationalist, pro-independence attitude, which is apparent in her books (see chapter 5). The rest of the testimonies in the anthology reflect late-twentieth-century topical concerns (celebrity culture, cinema, etc.) that signal a move away from strictly local, nationalist matters.

The selections from novels present many classics of the Puerto Rican canon. While each one has its own flavor and together they touch a great many themes, many of these fragments reinforce the themes, stories, and symbols common to the dream nation.

Manuel Zeno Gandía's "El negocio" (The business) comes from *Crónicas de un mundo enfermo* (Chronicles of a sick world) (1922) and uses the trope, common in his time, of an island sickened by colonialism. Enrique Laguerre's *La llamarada* (The flare-up, 1935) features the action sequence where the protagonist, Juan Antonio, fights to the death with his foe, Segundo. More importantly, it also includes Juan Antonio's bitter appraisal of the *cañaveral* (sugarcane fields) and the life around the fields as "lakes" of misery. Laguerre sets us in familiar dream nation symbolic territory: island pride, Taíno bravery, Nature as refuge, anti-Americanism, and Catholic Hispanophilia.

The next classic is Manuel Méndez Ballester's *Isla cerrera*, about which has been said, "More than fifty years after its appearance, the novel is required reading in public schools" (Irizarry, "Historiografía"). The very small sample taken from this novel features the early Spanish colony (Juan Ponce de León features prominently) when the protagonist, Ricardo Boadilla, arrives on the island for the first time. It is, partly, a paean to the unspoiled beauty of the island setting the stage for admiration of the Land that is so common in classic Puerto Rican literature. It also presents the heritage of conquest and the different kinds of people who came from Spain.

José de Diego Padró's *En babia* appears in a much longer selection and offers a binary juxtaposition to the preceding selection's unspoiled island paradise because the protagonist, Jerónimo Ruiz, describes a microcosm of Nuyorican life, where he tells of a life of crushing anonymity in the American urban setting. The next selection (the briefest of the fragments) is from an obscure novel by Luis Palés Matos, *Litoral*, and *also* features a description of a country landscape that appears to be a dreamscape, "Todo ha sido un sueño" (604; It has all been a dream).

Emilio Díaz Valcárcel's *Figuraciones en el mes de marzo* (Schemes in the month of March) is next. The novel, which in its full edition is dedicated to "los revolucionarios boricuas" (the Puerto Rican revolutionaries), uses linguistic and formal experimental techniques (a collage of epistolary, dialogues, monologues, news items, among others) and features an *independentista* protagonist living in Madrid. In the selection, the sick protagonist listens to the complaints of his inebriated Spanish doorman reiterating themes of language and power, among them the contrast of language in Spain versus the Americas (to the detriment of the latter).

The anthology has fragments of *La guaracha del Macho Camacho*, particularly the introduction in which La China dances to the *guaracha*. The anthologized segment has *the* key quotation that ties the novel to the themes of independence: "el sol cumple aquí una vendetta impía, mancha el pellejo, emputece la sangre, borrasca el sentido: aquí en Puerto Rico, colonia sucesiva de dos imperios e isla del Archipiélago de las Antillas"(612; the sun wields here a wicked vendetta, it stains the skin, whores up the blood, storms the senses: here in Puerto Rico, successive colony of two empires and island of the Archipelago of the Antilles).

If *La guaracha* looks outwardly toward Puerto Rican society and media, Magali García Ramis's immensely successful novel *Felices días*, tío Sergio[6] looks inward and sees the same panorama of the dysfunction of colonialism. The novel is a tender and bittersweet coming-of-age story about a girl, Lidia, and her bourgeois, independence-hating family. The selection in the anthology opens with a description of the times she lives in, the 1950s, when rapid urbanization was altering the landscape. It shows the family's Manichaean worldview, dividing the world into the side of Good (Catholicism and the United States) versus the side of Evil: communists, atheists, Masons, Protestants, Nazis, and, of course, those demonized "Puerto Rican nationalists and *independentistas*" (617–18). The passage also offers a poignant description of the vexations of growing up in a conservative family: "nos iban educando con una mezcla de conceptos científicos y religiosos, verdaderos y falsos, liberales y conservadores, producto de sus miedos y prejuicios o de sus conocimientos y convicciones, que nos tomó una vida reorganizar y clasificar" (617; they were educating us with a mixture of scientific and religious concepts, both true and false, liberal and conservative, product of their fears and prejudices or their knowledge and beliefs, that it took us a lifetime to reorganize and classify).

The inclusion of Carlos Varo follows the anthologist's stated goal of flexibility in classifying as Puerto Rican also authors not born on the island. Varo is a Spaniard who moved to the island when he was in his thirties—he writes in Spanish, however, so he meets one of the top criteria for inclusion into the canon. His credentials also include pro-independence writing; he has two books that are sympathetic to nationalist culture.[7] A selection from Varo's *Rosa Mystica*, a novel thick with both linguistic and sexual experimentation, probes queer sensibilities. It features two protagonists, a hermaphrodite in drag who is founder of a convent for wayward women in Spain, and Divina, Juniol/Divina, a street youth who turns into an international transsexual celebrity. The selection has Juniol's narration, in heavily Puerto Rican youth-speak and his heartbreak at a tragic misadventure suffered by a friend during an escapade from school.

Arturo Echavarría Ferrari's *Como el aire de abril* (Like April air) is represented by a lyrical description of a beautiful landscape that leads to a seascape as one of the young characters (and his beloved) travel by car, a journey colored by the memory-scape of desire and erotic love. Marta Aponte Alsina's *El cuarto rey mago* (The fourth king) is here a short fragment that finds the protagonist and a dog confronting man's damage to Nature; they are in a forest that at first seems virginal but soon reveals all-too-human trash. It is another comment on the spoiled Lush Land.

The selection from Jorge Luis Castillo's *La estación florida* (The flowering season) offers a taste of the characters' dissipated lives in contemporary Puerto Rico; it's a description of a failed erotic escapade in the midst of modernity. Also dwelling on modernity's ills is Edgardo Rodríguez Juliá's *Sol de media noche* (Midnight sun); the famous author's incursion into the detective novel genre is here a fragment of the narrator's self-loathing, cheerless reflections on his regrets, failings, and failures, both personal and professional.

As we can see, the closer we get to the end of the twentieth century, the more variety of topics that appear in addition to the familiar independence themes and tropes. Kalman Barsy's *Naufragio* (Shipwreck) features a globalized couple (friends/lovers) who are building a boat. In Manuel Martinez Maldonado's *Isla verde (El Chevy azul)* (Isla Verde [The blue Chevy]) the narrator reminisces about his beloved Old San Juan and his first love, erotic awakenings and movie-fuelled dreams. In Alfredo Matilla's postmodern *El españolito y el espía* (The little Spaniard and the spy), the protagonist recollects the option in his youth between Spanish or American citizenship and choosing the latter in order to become an *independentista*. Mayra Montero's *Púrpura profundo* (Deep purple) is here a snippet of a description of a violinist lover of the narrator. Mayra Santos Febres's *Sirena Selena vestida de pena* (Sirena Selena) is here represented with a fragment that describes Martha dressing and applying makeup to her protégé Sirena before the transvestite diva's performance.

The longest fragment comes from Rosario Ferré's *La casa de la laguna* (*The House on the Lagoon*) and has two sections from that novel, which was originally published in English and moves back and forth between competing narratives and histories. The anthology has the episode in the Kerenski ballet school in Ponce for which the contending narrators, Isabel and Quintín, give different versions of the same event therefore questioning the truth-value of stories that purport to document an event.

In aggregate, the intellectual community of Puerto Rican literature as López-Baralt's anthology presents it ranges far and wide and yet remains a testament to the deep roots and persistence of themes, stories, allegories, and heroes of the dream nation up to the very end of the twentieth century. The significance of this case study is not that it is a singular literary document but that it serves also as a magnifying glass that exposes the persistence of the dream nation in that most traditionally nation-building of the arts, literature.

In the next chapter, we will explore the few literary figures who have written explicitly of Puerto Rico's culture as one that remains paradoxically tied to fictions of independence but where the political practice, the everyday choice of the vast majority of people, is dependency. These few voices have come out against the failed dream of independence and the rote literary conventions that it engendered while continuing to use and transform some of the fictions of the dream nation.

2 / Breaking Tradition

Puerto Rican national culture has been built up by the great works of its literary canon, itself shaped by institutions like universities and cultural centers, by documents like classroom syllabi and anthologies, by the media that promote culture, by activities like literary festivals, by communities of culture that award prizes, etc. The communities that produced the early canon believed that culture would directly and unequivocally boost the island's struggle for independence. Until recently, the loftiness of that ideal (as well as peer pressure) meant that few writers dared to break with the dream nation. The traditional literary world in Puerto Rico is a small, clannish enclave that awards its members (who are acquaintances, friends, or mentors) the literary prizes, book contracts, and speaking gigs that merit literary recognition. There are exceptions, such as Eduardo Lalo, whose Rómulo Gallegos award was an external deus ex machina that brought him international attention. Moreover, a majority of the best-known writers have been alums of and professors at the University of Puerto Rico Río Piedras campus (UPR-RP), the state-run institution with a long history of intellectual sympathy for independence.

So most major writers in the nineteenth and twentieth centuries were fervent *independentistas*. However, in the latter part of last century, some important intellectuals broke with convention. Many others, of course, chose to ignore the matter of status altogether and in doing so they paralleled what a large portion of the voters did in the 1993 status referendum, choosing "none of the above" as the preferred status option or, as the voters did in the 2012 elections, casting blank ballots. Few critics or writers own up to being on the right or to the center of the political spectrum, although the information on writers' political preferences other than independence is mostly anecdotal and hard to come by. For instance, Pedro Juan Soto asserts that two luminaries in the generation prior to his, Enrique A. Laguerre and De Diego Padró, were secretly right-wingers, "derechista encubierto, tapado" (Hernández, *A viva voz* 30; undercover right-winger, hidden), and he claims that is why De Diego Padró was not more widely read—which, one notes, was not the case for Laguerre.[1]

Puerto Rican literature, like most of Latin American literature, has leaned left—and the Puerto Rican leftist cause par excellence has been independence. The fact that some major writers questioned the doctrinal stance on the matter should not be attributed to a fondness for the United States, which remains persona non grata to the Left. This dislike persists despite the centrality of U.S. culture to at least one activist cause dear to progressives in the twenty-first century: minority and gender rights. No, the authors who broke with convention beginning in the 1980s did not have newfound devotion for the United States; their reasons were more complex. They were propelled by disenchantment with the feasibility of political independence and by their queasiness with an old-guard *independentismo* whose ossified postures on many issues (racial and gender biases, for instance) had become passé. John Perivolaris sumps up the fatigue of militant *independentismo*; talking about "El cruce de la Bahía de Guánica" (The crossing of Guánica Bay), an essay by Edgardo Rodríguez Juliá (who is, to put it mildly, not a fan of traditional independence), Perivolaris notes that the essay underscores "the anachronism and obsolescence of traditional militancy [. . .] suggested by the few people who turn up for the Socialist rally in Guánica, the tired rhetoric of its activists, and the old-fashioned revolutionary chic à la Guevara and Castro of their dress" ("Heroes, Survivors, and History" 693). Also burned out is the cultural establishment's steadfast insistence that culture is only, or primarily, supposed to be in a perpetual and homogeneous mode of protest.

These writers' break with tradition was counterintuitive to the political atmosphere of the 1960s and 1970s, which saw a formative stage for many prominent writers. Solidarity with the Latin American Left demanded common cause with revolutionary Cuba—which blazed a trail in hemispheric split from the United States. As Daniel Balderston and Mike González write: "In Latin America itself, the overthrow of Batista privileged the Cuban experience in all subsequent political debate. Its methods became the model, and its project for national independence the road to follow" (introduction, *Encyclopedia of Latin American and Caribbean Literature, 1900–2003*).

Habitually Puerto Rican writers and so-called culture producers had supported the pro-independence *political* establishment at every turn. Yet in 1971, René Marqués (a luminary of his time) broke this habit by casting doubt on the party itself when he spoke of "el P.I.P. en naufragio" (the sinking P.I.P.) (*El puertorriqueño dócil* 203). His critique of the political party did not, however, mean that Marqués denounced the ideal of independence itself or that his work differed significantly from earlier work in its use of symbols, themes, and stories of the dream nation. Plays like *Los soles truncos* are steeped in Hispanophilia—looking back yearningly to pre-Americanized Puerto Rico. His best-known play, *La carreta*, rejects the ethos of modernity and casts migration to the United States as an abomination. And his most famous essay, "El puertorriqueño docil" (The docile Puerto Rican), wholeheartedly rejects the cultural influence of the United States. In all, he may have found fault with the PIP as an ineffectual political machine, but throughout his life, he was a hard-core *independentista*.

The Literary Lion Roars

The greatest and most sustained critique of independence orthodoxy came from José Luis González—a giant of his time. González's bona fides as a Marxist defender of sovereignty for the island were never in question. In his *magnum opus* on Puerto Ricanness, *El país de cuatro pisos*, González declares that Puerto Rico's culture had arisen from nationalism (and nationalism was in Puerto Rico always synonymous with pro-independence). But González had a problem with an ideology of nationalism that was beholden—from its inception in the first Puerto Rican book (*El aguinaldo puertorriqueño* from 1843)—to *criollismo* (creolism), which was for him the culture of the white landowning class which he said embraced independence because it dovetailed with their interests (whereas the United States interfered with their privileges).

González, who was arguably the greatest short-story writer of his generation, was the most distinguished writer to come out against the dream nation as it was conceived in the mid-twentieth century. His stance earned him much ill will among those he termed "los independentistas conservadores e hispanófilos que tanto me detestan" (*Nueva visita al cuarto piso* 11; the conservative and Hispanophile *independentistas* who hate me so much).

His rupture with tradition was groundbreaking because of his centrality to the literary canon. His work is featured in every major anthology of Puerto Rican literature of the past fifty years, and his essays and stories are still taught in schools and universities. Despite his critique of how independence was being interpreted in his day, he was not soft on "imperialism," going so far as to renounce his U.S. citizenship, becoming a Mexican citizen and spending most of his life in exile. In a book-length interview with Arcadio Díaz Quiñones, González proclaims himself an advocate for sovereignty for the island, but *not* an *independentista*. Calling himself a "Marxist without a church" (96), he states that independence, while indispensable, cannot be an end in itself. For him, the true end of all social struggles was socialism.

González's objections to the independence project are foundational to all subsequent critiques because his seminal essay, "El país de cuatro pisos," reconfigured the Puerto Rican cultural landscape. His view is that Puerto Rico's culture which he metaphorically casts as a house, was built on the contributions of its historically layered cultures (of the oppressor and the oppressed, mainly) but also of racial cultures, with black heritage as the *base* of the structure; a notion that at least one of his critics, Juan Manuel Carrión, disputes, saying that Caribbean cultures are too transcultured to be cast so uniformly (7). González's contention that different cultures vie for supremacy—as opposed to the view of one land, one national culture—fundamentally altered the very notion of Puerto Ricanness.

González writes of multiple *patrias* that coincide with the historic, racial, migratory, and class divisions among Puerto Ricans (what Edgardo Rodríguez Juliá will later call tribes): "la patria del negro, la patria del mulato y la patria del criollo, cuya integración en una verdadera patria nacional es un proceso que no culmina todavía" (*El país de cuatro pisos* 49; the homeland of the black, the homeland of the mulatto, and the homeland of the Creole, whose integration into a truly national homeland is a process that has not yet culmitated). His critics said this view of a multilayered culture amounted to *divisiveness*.

Furthermore, he specifically opposed the primacy of a culture of traditional *independentismo*, which he labeled as conservative, noting its tendencies toward Catholicism, racial, class, and gender stereotypes, and upper-class prerogatives. This ideological toxic stew resulted, he thought, in literary classics that are in tacit agreement with the entrenched principles of the ruling class. His is a response to the nationalist/*independentista* Catholic, Western tradition represented by Albizu, who, in 1936, said, "Esta nación cristiana surgió bajo la égida de la Cruz [...] culturalmente esta nación se considera una de las depositarias de la civilización grecolatina en este hemisferio" ("Nuestro estatus politico," in *La conciencia nacional puertorriqueña* 88, quoted by Rodríguez Vázquez 233; This Christian nation emerged under the aegis of the Cross [...] this nation culturally is considered one of the repositories of Greco-Roman civilization in this hemisphere).

González also attacks another national cultural feature, the adulation of *jibarismo*, because he says that the stereotypical *jíbaro* portrayed was always white. Consequently, the idealization of the "simple and authentic" country folk in their verdant land—which promotes a sense of national unity and patriotism—was channeling nostalgia for a mythical agrarian past, its unspoiled land and cherished virtues, behind which rode all kinds of reactionary thinking.

By being critical of *independentismo,* González is clearly not rejecting the ideal of liberation itself. For instance, he writes admiringly of late-nineteenth- and early-twentieth-century liberal or progressive *independentismo*, which he opposes to the conservatism of writers like José de Diego. He notes, for instance, that for progressives like Hostos, national identity was not a problem; it was a "project": "El caso de Hostos, por ser Hostos quien era, constituye el major ejemplo de esa conciencia de la fragilidad de la formación national puertorriqueña que hallamos en los escritores más representativos de la época" (*El país de cuatro pisos* 70; The case of Hostos, Hostos being who he was, is the best example of this awareness of the fragility of the Puerto Rican national formation found in the most representative writers of the time). González remembers that Hostos called Puerto Rico "la nacioncita" (the little nation) and considered that when the United States took over it was just not ready for independence. González casts Hostos's "Liga de Patriotas" (League of Patriots) as a failed attempt to unify all three branches of political thinking on the island: autonomists, *independentistas*, and annexionists (a feat only successfully accomplished, for a while, at the end of the twentieth century by the cause for Vieques).

González comes down particularly hard on José de Diego—to this day a popular poet who is taught in schools. González says he represented conservative *independentista* culture and whose reaction to the regime change was to cling to Hispanic values and an identity defined as "esencialmente hispánica, blanca y católica [...] con marcada prescindencia del elemento africano como factor determinante" (*El país de cuatro pisos* 76; essentially Hispanic, white, and Catholic [...] with a marked disregard for the African determining factor). González also blasts de Diego for his professional work as a corporate lawyer on behalf of U.S. sugar interests and for being a foe of the labor movement.

Another cultural linchpin of the dream nation that González assails is "telurismo" (tellurism, or excessive adulation of the land), which he says overwhelms Puerto Rican literature in classic authors like Luis Llorens Torres, Miguel Meléndez Muñoz, Enrique A. Laguerre, Emilio S. Belaval, Manuel Méndez Ballester, and Abelardo Díaz Alfaro.

In reexamining Puerto Rico's literary greats, González sees in Antonio S. Pedreira the coexistence of twin contradictory impulses that split up politics on the island: liberalism and conservativism. Pedreira becomes the figure incarnate of *the* unsolvable clashing impulses of "hegemonía local y participación en la deslumbrante riqueza de la sociedad capitalista norteamericana" (*El país de cuatro pisos* 80; local hegemony and participation in the dazzling riches of American capitalist society). In this part of his critique, González has no problem affirming the admirable strengths of the late capitalism in the United States and its effects on Puerto Rico. His positive appraisal of the United States is reserved nonetheless, for its social legislation benefiting women's rights and labor movements (81).

Despite the intellectual dangers of giving credit to the United States in his day, he acknowledges that country's cultural clout and analyzes how other nations cope with Americanizing influences without fear of diluting their national identities, noting the uses of jazz and blue jeans in France, Germany, and Japan, and baseball in Cuba. He also avoids knee-jerk anti-Americanism by stressing important technological contributions made by the "civilización norteamericana" and goes so far as to praise the United States for being "los creadores de una de las diez o doce grandes civilizaciones originales en la historia de la humanidad" (Díaz Quiñones 129–30; the creators of one of the ten or twelve great original civilizations in the history of humanity).

In relation to the impact of the United States on Puerto Rico, González thought it the height of hypocrisy that voters' rejection of sovereignty should be blamed on the alienation caused by colonialism: "si el independentismo tradicional puertorriqueño en el siglo XX ha sido—en lo político, en lo social y en lo cultural—una ideología conservadora empeñada en la defensa de los valores de la vieja clase propietaria, ¿a santo de qué atribuir a una 'enajenación' la falta de adhesión de las masas al independentismo?" (*El país de cuatro pisos* 36; if the traditional twentieth-century Puerto Rican independence movement has been—politically, socially, and culturally—a conservative ideology bent on upholding the values of the old capitalist class, where do they get off attributing to "alienation" the lack of adherence by the masses to the independence movement?).

In his critique of *independentismo*, González names names; for instance, he says that the lauded Generation of 1930 suffered from "sentimental Hispanophilia" (*El país de cuatro pisos* 82), and René Marqués's work shows, he says, a "militant" nostalgia (84). Most shocking, because of its audacity, is his critique of Pedro Albizu Campos (or his legacy, *Albizuismo*), which takes up seventeen pages of the interview with Díaz Quiñones. To this day, the figure of Albizu holds great emblematic power for *independentismo* since he is regarded as the patron saint and patriot/martyr of militant Puerto Ricanness. His face is instantly recognizable in Puerto Rican graphic arts, being as ubiquitous as the *coquí* (the indigenous frog) or the Puerto Rican flag in both high highbrow works of art as well as in the market for nationalist knickknacks (T-shirts, posters, key chains, etc.). His iconic image also appears in Latino graphic art; for instance, Ernesto Quiñones describes murals in Spanish Harlem featuring the secular heroes of the barrio: "the greats: Zapata, Albizu Campos, Sandino, Martí, and Malcolm" (213; see also the introduction to this volume).

González makes a concerted effort to demythify Albizu first in "El país de cuatro pisos" and later, at length, in the interview with Díaz Quiñones, restating that Albizu was an agent of bourgeois and conservative nationalism. He talks about Albizu's "paternalism" (Díaz Quiñones 107) and brings up his lack of support for the sugarcane workers during the strike of 1934. As proof of Albizu's allegiance to the landowning class, he quotes Albizu's speech from 1930 lamenting exploitation in telling terms: "Cada minuto que pasa cae un nuevo terrateniente puertorriqueño y se levanta un explotador yanqui. Y los pocos boricuas que quedan están fatalmente condenados a desaparecer" (Díaz Quiñones 110; Every minute that passes a new Puerto Rican landowner falls and a Yankee exploiter rises. And the few remaining Puerto Ricans are fatally doomed to disappear). González points out how *boricua* is here synonymous with landowner and knocks down the contention that Albizu's thinking—regarded as progressive by many—was the only option possible, reminding the interviewer of the alternative represented by the Puerto Rican communist party (of which González had been a member) (Díaz

Quiñones 108). Following this line of critique, Mario R. Cancel talks in 2007 of "el nacionalismo oloroso a derechas de Pedro Albizu Campos" (*Literatura y narrativa* 16; the right-wing-smelling nationalism of Pedro Albizu Campos).

González denies that Albizu leaned toward fascism (Díaz Quiñones 117), though he points out that the nationalist leader did not distance himself from European fascism explicitly, but this González thinks was due to his embrace of an "enemy of my enemy" way of thinking. He agrees with Albizu's assessment of the United States because he says Albizu was the first to realize that "la anexión de Puerto Rico a los Estados Unidos entrañaría la renuncia a su propia identidad nacional" (Díaz Quiñones 120; the annexation of Puerto Rico to the United States would involve renouncing its own national identity). Also on the plus side of the ledger was Albizu's work for "internationalizing" Puerto Rico's situation so the matter of its colonial status could be aired out in a broader arena (120). His final assessment is that Albizu was a *prócer* (great man, along the lines of the nineteenth-century patriotic "great man" view of history), but González cautions against "mitificaciones ahistóricas" (ahistorical mythifications) about the nationalist leader (121). González's legacy can be found in recent studies of Albizu like, for example, that of historian Luis Ángel Ferrao, who examines Albizu's authoritarian control over his party and followers. But the pop-culture idealization of Albizu—which for my purposes connects to hero worship and the stories and iconography that it generates—continues to this day.

Time and again, González attacks nationalist nostalgia for Puerto Rico's rural world—a linchpin for the dream nation, the yearning for a pre-1898 paradisiacal unified Land. He affirms that contrary to what "ignorant" and "hypocritical" conservative *independentistas* say, in 1898 Puerto Rico was not undergoing any "spiritual flourishment" (Díaz Quiñones 125–26). Far from being a unified people who were splintered by the U.S. invasion, "la identidad puertorriqueña anterior a 1898 era una identidad bastante deficiente (¡y cómo no iba a serlo en una sociedad donde se había abolido la esclavitud de buena parte de sus miembros hacía apenas veinte años!)" (126; Puerto Rican identity prior to 1898 was a rather deficient identity [and how could it not be in a society where the slavery of many of its members had been abolished barely twenty years earlier!]).

González subscribes to the definition of a cultural nation, although he finds much to critique in it, but never questions the nation defined as a human community tied by bonds of history, geography, language, and, he adds, "psychology" (Díaz Quiñones 127–28). Within that definition he privileged the Afro-Antillean cultural base, which had been ignored by then-established *independentistas,* whom he accused of defending "nuestra hispanoamericanidad" (our Hispanic Americanness) while withholding equal value to Afro-Antilleanness (128). He was following the lines of the Caribbean *négritude* movement of the 1930s, and in his assessment, he was successful; the *majority* of culture producers by the end of the century had backed away from Hispanophilia—and definitely from whiteness—as an underpinning of the cultural nation.

As exemplar of that omission of the island's Afro-Antillean heritage, he quotes Luis Lloréns Torres's "Canción de las Antillas" (Song of the Antilles), a canonical poem that stresses the Hispanophilic whiteness of the islands with its allusion to "Hispanic legions" and racial unity under a "strong Iberoamerican race" (Díaz Quiñones 128). However, as if González had not been heard, López-Baralt in her 2004 anthology praises Lloréns Torres, saying his celebration of "an Antilleanness bound to Hispanic roots" was a response to the American invasion (xxxiv).

González's patriotism was unquestionable, and he defended Puerto Rican culture to the point of exceptionalism. For instance, he extolled the island's cultural production in hyperbolic terms: "no existe en el mundo ningún país del tamaño, la población y la situación política de Puerto Rico con una producción cultural comparable" (Díaz Quiñones 130; there is no country in the world the size, population and political situation of Puerto Rico with a comparable cultural production).

Being unafraid of criticizing the living as well as the dead, González railed in 1987 against the younger generation of poets for their hidebound *independentismo,* going so far as to say that they were "encajonados en la estrecha y esencialmente reaccionaria concepción de lo revolucionario en la poesía, heredada, sin que ellos mismos tuvieran conciencia de ello [...] de José de Diego y José Stalin [quienes concebían] la poesía como un 'arma' al servicio de causas políticas inmediatas" (*Nueva visita* 124; boxed in the narrow and essentially reactionary revolutionary concept of poetry, inherited, not that they were aware of it [...] from José de Diego and Joseph Stalin [who conceived] of poetry as a "weapon" in the service of immediate political causes). This extreme rhetoric is explained on the next page, when he refers to the acrimony that his views had caused among young literati, who had accused him of being a supporter of Nixon, Muñoz Marín, and Hitler (*Antología personal* 235).

González is the first consequential establishment writer to break with tradition and the quality of his writing, his stature as a public figure and his long-standing Marxist credentials ensured that he was not shunned by most literary figures or banned from the canon. It is in his essays that his break with orthodox independence becomes a major force, but José Luis González's short stories are far better known and continue to be read and anthologized, and most were written before his concerted attacks on traditional *independentismo*. So, how do the stories feature independence or its symbols? Well, there are many connections. The world portrayed in the stories centers to a large extent on the *jíbaro* population that is a key element to *independentismo* (but whose mythification González rejects). The majority of his short stories, however, assail nostalgia for an idealized *ruralismo*. González's stories from the 1940s and 1950s explore class and racial divisions in ways that standard portrayals of his time do not. He looks at the perils of a difficult modernization with great nuance.

Many of his neorealist stories from the 1940s and 1950s feature the poor, rural classes as well as urban dwellers. The *central*, or sugarcane-processing plant, dominates the landscape and is the symbol of the evils of Puerto Rico's underdevelopment and colonial status. U.S. sugar corporations, aided by the local bourgeoisie and regional government, wield absolute control over the lives of the *jíbaros* as well as the nation's economy, which is shown under the grip of predatory capitalism. The island, the land itself, is fast disappearing as American corporate interests buy it up, as stated in the aptly titled "La desgracia" (The disgrace) (1943). Sugarcane, the plant itself, symbolizes an alien blight upon the land; as one old *jíbaro* says, in the olden days "God's country" was not afflicted with sugarcane: "en aquellos tiempos, déjenme decirles, todavía quedaba mucho monte con palos de buena madera por estas partes, no como ahora que la caña está acabando con lo que Dios puso entre el cielo y la tierra" (*Cuentos completos* 106; in those days, let me tell you, there was still a lot of country with good wood in these parts, not like now when the sugarcane is doing away with what God put between the sky and the land). In story after story, the small landowners lose their way of life along with their land, and then their only option against starvation is backbreaking, dehumanizing labor in the sugarcane fields.

González, all the same, presents some *jíbaros* as entrepreneurs who try to break from the fatalism of the hard rural life. Such is case of Pichirilo Sánchez in "Santa Claus visita a Pichirilo Sánchez" (Santa Claus visits Pichirilo Sánchez) (1953), who dreams of getting a bicycle from Santa Claus so he can earn an income as a bike messenger to help his mother. Salomé Benítez, the doomed character in "El enemigo" (The enemy) (1953), sees his life as a fight to the death against the sugarcane field, which is "un enemigo sobrecogedoramente poderoso" (an overpoweringly powerful enemy) (*Cuentos completos* 218). Nevertheless, with ingenious entrepreneurship, he finds an alternative way of making a living as a "public car" driver. Despite his ingenuity, he is nevertheless killed by the poisons that the sugarcane company sprays on the fields.

What is Puerto Rico in the stories? The phrase "tiempo muerto" (dead time) highlights the nation's condition. One of the worst curses brought about by the transformation of the economic life of the *jíbaro* was the aptly named "tiempo muerto" when the sugarcane was not being processed and when a punishing workday was replaced by want. The only certain escape from these circumstances is unionization, which is difficult because union busters are an omnipresent and oppressive threat. Many stories feature attempts at unionizing and strikes, with workers clashing violently with strike-busters employed by a powerful mix of corporations and government. Thus, a story about failed attempts at unionizing against overwhelming forces is called simply "Miedo" (Fear) (1945). Another story, "Me voy a morir" (I am going to die") (1946), is told by a dying unionizer who has been shot and knows no one will be brought to justice for the crime. Government representatives are rarely shown at all; they are mostly distant forces and, when seen, look different from the *jíbaros*. For instance, the government official who shows up in "El enemigo" (The enemy) (1953) is a nameless "rubio de bigotito recortado y nalgas grandes" (*Cuentos completos* 219; blond with a trimmed mustache and a fat ass).

González's focus on the humanity, the struggles, and suffering of the *jíbaros* differs fundamentally from the familiar use of the docile *jíbaro* as a quaint folkloric depiction of the heart and soul of the nation. His descriptions of the countryside are in stark contrast to bucolic *paisajismo*; his is a harsh countryside where the beautiful landscape is replaced with decaying housing and filthy, hungry people, for example in "En la sombra" (In the shadow) (1943).

Yet, the pull of Hispanophilic nostalgia and overt references to independence are not entirely absent from his stories. For example in "Paisa" (1950), the grandfather refuses to leave the countryside and proudly reminisces about his days as a soldier for Spain. "El abuelo" (The grandfather) (1956) is different because the grandfather, who is a "pure" Puerto Rican *independentista*, proudly refuses to be allied with *either* Spain or the United States, "los hijos del país no queríamos cuentas ni con los cachacos [the Spaniards] ni con los yanquis. Los únicos puertorriqueños con vergüenza" (*Cuentos completos* 287; we children of the country wanted nothing to do with either the Spaniards nor with the Yankees. The only Puerto Ricans with any shame). He explains to his grandson that the only reason they submitted to the new colonizer was lack of weapons.

No working-class character that I can find in José Luis González's complete stories embraces either modernity or the United States' presence on the island. In stark contrast, he portrays the Puerto Rican bourgeoisie as craven sell-outs who wholeheartedly buy into the political and economic system; such is the case for the racist lawyer in the story "La galería" (The gallery) (1951). The story is an exemplar of González's take on race and class divisions in the colony. It takes the oppression of the landowning class to its most extreme point when the lawyer's father forces a black mother to give her breast milk to his white son, dooming her own infant to die. Nonetheless, sometimes González too falls back on the Land as the route to salvation; the upper-middle-class narrator (who is the son of the family that the lawyer is visiting), repulsed by what he has heard, escapes to the Land: "me levanté, lenta, penosamente, yo sin decir palabra me eché al campo luminoso y abierto. Corriendo sin saber hacia dónde" (*Cuentos completos* 193; I got up, slowly, painfully, saying nothing I went out to the luminous and open country. Running without knowing where to). Like René Marqués's canonical *La carreta*, the family in *Paisa* suffers (each in his/her own way) the negative effects of moving from the country to the city shantytown: "Más que ninguno, el padre sufrió el impacto físico, directo, del cambio. [. . .] Con la madre fue diferente. Ella era la raíz del árbol familiar, el eslabón que los unía a todos al pasado que ahora empezaba a quebrantarse irremediablemente (*Cuentos completos* 19–20; More than anyone, the father suffered the physical, direct impact of the change. [. . .] For the mother it was different. She was the root of the family tree, the link that united everyone to the past that now began to break down irretrievably).

In the patriarchal world González depicts, mother figures are wise, proud, and admirable but hew closely to prevailing gender roles. Nevertheless, González restates his view that colonialism and modernity are complicit foreign-imposed forces destroying Puerto Rican lives, and, significantly, the *jíbara* is the one who senses that their world is dying:

> La jíbara no hubiera podido explicar, por ejemplo, que el antiguo orden, con todas sus injusticias y sus valores falsos, era un momento natural en la historia de un pueblo, sujeto a los cambios y a las rectificaciones del progreso, mientras esto que ella presenciaba

ahora era la desintegración impuesta por designio extranjero. (*Cuentos completos* 20)

The *jíbara* could not explain, for example, that the old order, with all its injustices and its false values, was a natural moment in the history of a people, subject to changes and corrections of progress, while what she now witnessed was the disintegration imposed by foreign design.

The countryside, therefore, contains no happy-go-lucky *jíbaros* playing *cuatro* and watching the sun setting over the verdant landscape. There is no an escape for José Luis González's characters from pain and heartache. Indeed, many stories relate sordid and violent lives (prostitution, beatings, rapes, etc.). Families are destroyed, women abused and prostituted, men ground down beneath the wheels of colonial forces. The bleak picture is almost relentless, with respites few and far between such as, for instance, the happy conclusion to "Regalo de reyes" (Three kings' gift) (1944) in which the child receives a calf for Christmas.

González's stories show a nation caught in the continuing tension between fatalism and the everyday struggle against circumstances. On the other hand, sometimes the stories feature *jíbaros* who have agency over their lives; rather than being just passive victims of fate, they are aware of their oppressions and seek to escape them. Of particular note are the stories that feature unionizers getting crushed but still battling away.

Some characters openly rebel against the status quo, like "el mellao José Orellana" (José Orellana, the gap-toothed) in "En la sombra" (In the shadow) (1943). Orellana refuses to work the sugarcane; "Tú sabeh que yo no le pico caña ni a María santísima. Esa clase 'e trabajo se hizo para los burroh. ¡Y yo soy hombre, no burro, manque no se note!" (*Cuentos completos* 72; You know that I won't cut sugarcane even for the Virgin Mary. That kind of work was made for animals. I am a man, not an animal, even if you can't see it!). His definition of "hombre" is proudly rebellious, in stark contrast to the machismo displayed by many other male characters, who are controlling fathers, brothers, and husbands. Nevertheless, José Orellana escapes being ground down by the system because he lives on the margins of society, the rest of which is fated to oppression by colonial socioeconomic conditions. One of the few examples of an empowered and victorious community is the story "Cangrejeros" (Crab catchers) (1944), in which a tiny community of seven families, when one of their men runs afoul of the law, relocates in its entirety—everyone up and leaves overnight—and manages to escape the system. But their town is premodern, and they can fade into the landscape, an option not open to characters that live in modernity.

Nevertheless, one strong voice, even that of José Luis González, is not enough to break ingrained cultural habits; the principle of the simple *jíbaro* as the nation's *soul* endures to this day, at least in popular culture. A search for *música jíbara* in YouTube, for example, will yield hundreds of videos featuring the mythified, happy, *cuatro*-playing countryfolk.

The Feminist Apostate: Rosario Ferré

Rosario Ferré's works have sometimes ended with houses blowing up and burning to the ground (*The House on the Lagoon*, "Marina y el león"). This explosive end to the familiar allegory for the nation (the house) runs entirely parallel with Ferré's knack for blowing up the metaphorical house of Puerto Rican literature. Ferré is arguably the most famous Puerto Rican woman writer, if not of all time, then certainly of the 1970s and 1980s, a period crucial for Puerto Rican women's writing. She is also the only major writer to have publicly abandoned her early support of independence and embraced statehood. This was, to say the least, controversial.

A feminist of consequence with pro-independence street cred, Ferré changed the landscape of Puerto Rican literature in the 1970s, writing empowering stories about rebellious women such as "The Youngest Doll" that have become standard fare in anthologies of Puerto Rican and Latin American literature. In that decade, Ferré founded along with her cousin, the writer Olga Nolla, a politically tinged left-wing literary journal called *Zona de Carga y Descarga*, about which Suzanne S. Hintz says, "*Zona* became a public organ for preaching social reform and independence politics." Ferré later said the journal had not just been pro-independence but in fact had been more of an "anarchic" literary journal (*Las puertas del placer* 155). Furthermore, she also clarified that the journal's avant-garde vibe was a response to the "anquilosamiento" (paralysis) in Puerto Rican literature due to "criollismo y folclorismo" (creolism and folklorism), a slap at the literary establishment (Hernández, *A viva voz* 103). Beyond independence, she lists a broad spectrum of progressive topics tackled by the magazine: "la liberación sexual de la mujer y el reclamo de su propio cuerpo, la legitimación de la homosexualidad, la visión espiritualista de los flower people [. . .] la lucha contra el racismo y la defensa de los derechos civiles; el uso del lenguage soez como elemento artístico y, ante todo y sobre todo, la defensa de la libertad del escritor ante las presiones políticas, tanto de izquierda como de derecha" (Hernández, *A viva voz* 104; the sexual liberation of women and their claim to their own bodies, the legitimization of homosexuality, the spiritual vision of the flower people [...] the fight against racism and the defense of civil rights, the use of street language as an artistic element and, before and above all, the defense of the writer's freedom from political pressure on the left as well as the right). This last is a broadside at the Puerto Rican establishment's definition of art as an instrument for a nationalist agenda.

She insists that the journal was above politics, never proselytized, and was free of the ideological straitjacket imposed by strict adherence to the PIP. However, her backtracking must be weighed against the journal's pro-independence inclusion of an opinion piece by Rafael Cancel Miranda, one of the militant *independentistas* imprisoned for opening fire on the U.S. Congress (Hernández, *A viva voz* 104). In any case, Ferré insists that the cultural direction of her journal went beyond "los postulados del nacionalismo" (the principles of nationalism) and as proof notes its internationalism in publishing some of the brightest lights of Latin American writing of the 1970s (for example, Severo Sarduy, José Lezama Lima, Julio Cortázar, Ernesto Cardenal, and Mario Vargas Llosa).

Her break from the ranks of the literary establishment became public in the 1990s, when Ferré started writing in English. She says she did so because she felt comfortable enough in a bilingual identity and also because she wanted validation on her own terms, not just as the governor's daughter (Pino-Ojeda 90–91). Likewise, she wanted a wider audience, and in that she succeeded, since her first novel in English had an astonishingly large (by Puerto Rican standards) first edition of sixty thousand copies.[2] With *The House on the Lagoon,* she achieved a new level of transnational success since the novel was a finalist for the 1995 National Book Award. Nevertheless, she must have known that her decision to write in English would cause a stir, given the perpetually contentious role of language in Puerto Rico and the ferocious attachment of the intelligentsia to the bond between Puerto Ricanness and Spanish. Nevertheless, her apostasy of writing in English happened only after she had established a reputation built on *independentista* countercultural views of the 1970s; so that it was in her later works—*The House on the Lagoon* (1997) and *Eccentric Neighborhoods* (1999)—that she challenged the prevailing Spanish-only definition of Puerto Rican writers.

Defiance of the powers that be is an abiding allure of pro-independence thinking, but as this incident shows, there is transgression and then there is transgression. Some kinds of nonconformity are just unacceptable to the cultural establishment. Ferré's turnaround on language ignited a cultural firestorm because—as Carmen Dolores Hernández succinctly states in a preface to an interview with Ferré—in Puerto Rico, language is a "sign of identity" (Hernández, *A viva voz* 94). Hernández adheres to the old-time *independentista* belief that Spanish is more than an identity marker; it constitutes a sign of resistance. The controversy caused by Ferré's use of English spread and multiplied; Juan López Bauzá, one of many who chided Ferré, said that she effectively had cast her lot with Latino writers and ceased being Puerto Rican. Juan Duchesne Winter's spirited reply to López Bauzá points out that such a defense of Spanish heightens a divisive climate of outdated intolerance toward Nuyorican writers. This kind of exchange is the mark of an old culture war around notions of purity and hybridity that has raged since at least Pedreira and Blanco's attacks on cultural fusion, which they labeled *burundanga*.

But Ferré's true heresy (as far as traditionalists are concerned) happened when her *political* views on the island's status changed. An 1998 op-ed article called "Puerto Rico, U.S.A." in the *New York Times* asserted her willingness to support the island's ties with the United States for two reasons: first, because changing times had brought about a permanent rapprochement between the United States and Puerto Rico; and second, because the American cultural landscape itself, with its expanding Latino demographics, had become a more welcoming environment. Many people assailed her op-ed piece immediately. Ferré became, for many pro-independence supporters, persona non grata. The blogger Robert Guzmán is blunt: "As long as she was an *independentista* well then she was the 'darling' of the local intellectuals. When she turned pro-statehood she caught literary leprosy in the eyes of many" ("Critical Mass").

Reflecting on the shock that Ferré caused, Bridget Kevane comments (in her interview with Ferré in *Latina Self-Portraits*): "Ferré has always provoked controversy on the island. While her father, Luis A. Ferré, was governor from 1968 to 1972 and promoted statehood, she remained a radical pro-independence activist. However, she recently declared her support of statehood for the island, which, *needless to say*, created a furor" (Kevane 60; my italics). Kevane's "needless to say" stems from the *assumption* made by pretty much everyone in the Puerto Rican literary establishment that any prominent Puerto Rican writer will, as a matter of course, be pro-independence and never, ever, favor statehood. Since then Ferré has been pegged as a polemicist: "Ferré's work is ultimately polemical, whether she is criticizing patriarchy or nationalist politics, commenting on identity, or fighting for a version of the truth" (Stark, Lecheler, and Anunson).

Ferré says ties to the United States make sense because she's using a different definition of Puerto Ricanness than the traditional "one island, one language" characterization. In an interview in the *New York Times* in 1998, she asserted that "to be Puerto Rican is to be a hybrid. [. . .] Our two halves are inseparable; we cannot give up either without feeling maimed" (quoted by Liz Ruark). With this attitude, Ferré goes against the long tradition of a unified Puerto Rican identity based on linguistic and territorial integrity. That old-guard point of view is typified, for instance, by Nilita Vientós Gastón's essay "Los 'puertorriqueñistas' y los 'occidentalistas'" (Puerto Ricanists and Westernists) (1962): "¿Cómo puede sentirse integrado un hombre que tiene dos patrias, dos banderas, dos constituciones y dos himnos?" (López-Baralt, *Antología* 81; How can a man who has two homelands, two flags, two constitutions, and two hymns feel integrated?). Ferré countered this push for national purity by embracing hybridity, a postmodern term much in favor of the bi- and multicultural criticism of the late twentieth century.

Is her oeuvre symptomatic of some kind of oedipal conflict? Such an interpretation oversimplifies the complexity of her opinions and writing. Yet Ferré's writing has always been seen through the prism of her biography. For José Luis González, her family's wealth and influence were at the center of her social critique; he said that her work offers the most devastating condemnation of ruling class from within (Díaz Quiñones, *Conversación* 137). But despite her early success as a pro-independence writer, when the scandal of her support for statehood arose, much importance was again attached to her father's influence. Blaming her father's sway does not explain the arc of her political opinions—independence as a young woman and statehood as an older writer—a common enough arc for regular Puerto Ricans but not so much for public intellectuals.

Her decision to support statehood resulted in an explosive literary spat in Puerto Rican culture when she was attacked by Ana Lydia Vega—an *éminence grise* who had been a fellow feminist Young Turk back in the day. The Ferré versus Vega controversy pitted sister against sister, caused a cultural hullabaloo, and signaled the end of the united front of pro-independence writers and culture producers. Claudia Macías de Yoon says Vega's letter "reproves her *betrayal:* 'Who were you, when in

'76 you gave birth to the unforgettable pages of a luminous book that opened paths of freedom for a generation of women writers? Would you be the same who a few days ago, under the hackneyed slogan 'Puerto Rico USA,' handed over to the *New York Times* a sad apology for assimilation?'" (my italics; "Historia de arroz con habichuelas de Ana Lydia Vega" [Story of Rice and Beans by Ana Lydia Vega]).

In the full letter, Vega goes on to say witheringly, "¿Serías la misma que, el pasado 19 de marzo, proclamándose 'más americana que John Wayne,' le anunciara alegremente a nuestros conquistadores que por fin habíamos llegado a ser como ellos?" ("Carta abierta a Pandora" [Open letter to Pandora]; Would you be the same who, on March 19, proclaiming herself "more American than John Wayne," announced gleefully to our conquerors that we had finally become like them?). Vega reproaches Ferré on *personal* terms for the latter's reliance on the cultural shield of hybridity, in other words, the belief that Puerto Ricans can remain Puerto Ricans while striding two cultures and two languages. For Vega, personalism lies at the heart of Ferré's about-face: "Aunque todo esto de la hibridez podría resultar muy fascinante como exploración autobiográfica, la pretensión de proyectar tu condición personal sobre la totalidad del país me parece un tanto arriesgada" ("Carta abierta a Pandora" [Open letter to Pandora]; While all this hybridity could be very fascinating as autobiographical exploration, the aim of projecting your personal condition on the whole country seems to me a little risky).

Lisabeth Paravisini-Gebert discusses the broad sweep and massive import of Ferré's change of heart and its impact on Puerto Rican culture by analyzing Ferré's book of conversations with her father. In that volume the political and the personal merge, a situation never far from island discussions of Ferré and her work (as evidenced by the popular and widespread use of the diminutive name "Rosarito" to refer to the august writer).

Ferré's works indeed span from the committed feminism of her initial *Papeles de Pandora* (Pandora's papers) to her later novels that work against heroic visions of the dream nation. In truth, *Papeles* was more about women's independence than any crusade for political sovereignty. By advocating for the right of women to break gender patterns, Ferré, who at the time defended independence as a political option, brought an *independentista* sensibility and fiery feminist spirit to her fiction. She later deployed the same ideological alloy ironically in *The House on the Lagoon* when Quintín, the male historian, accuses Isabel, the female novelist, of writing not art but "a feminist treatise, an *Independentista manifesto*" (386; my italics).

The writing of history is the battleground in works like *The House on the Lagoon* and *Maldito amor*. The truth value of history is put into question—in a *Rashomon*-like manner—by showing different versions of the family stories. In *The House on the Lagoon,* the female writer contradicts the parochial male so often that, as Susan Devine says the novel essentially denies the nostalgic view of an all-encompassing, uplifting history of the dream nation, "the notion of Puerto Rico as a paradise lost because of a U.S. conquest" (73). With *The House on the Lagoon*, Ferré—much as José Luis González had done in his short stories—blames the local bourgeoisie, and not just the United States, for many of the nation's problems; Ferré focuses on class conflicts and lays the responsibility for the misery of the poor and the working classes on the greed of local landowners more than on the pressure of the United States (see a full analysis in chapter 5).

Man in the Middle: Edgardo Rodríguez Juliá

Rodríguez Juliá's arc is similar to Ferré's. Like some writers of their generation (1970s), youthful enthusiasm led to pro-independence sentiments, which were then cast off in later life. For instance, Rodríguez Juliá speaks of his early affinity to the dream of independence while reminiscing about a visit paid as a teenager to the famous nationalist poet Juan Antonio Corretjer (see *San Juan ciudad soñada* 10–12). Nowadays Rodríguez Juliá has written much about his doubts concerning the feasibility of the political success of independence. In 2010, for example, he spoke openly of the defeat of independence and (somewhat ambivalently) espoused statehood and, trying have it both ways, bemoaned the dysfunction of the ELA while *still* declaring himself one of "aquéllos que proponemos la independencia" (those of us who propose independence) in an article pointedly titled "¿De qué país estamos hablando?" (What country are we talking about?). Nevertheless, in it he defends statehood and questions the existence of the Puerto Rican nation itself. In baroque fits of despair, he declares the game over because of the grim socioeconomic conditions on the island as well as the larger number of Puerto Ricans in the States than on the island. Rodríguez Juliá then endorses statehood as the only workable solution to the island's *identity* problems and ends by stating that nationhood goes beyond territoriality. The entire passage reads:

> De hecho, la estadidad sería, con todas sus dificultades, la solución más evidente y con el menor embrollo humano y jurídico a

esta encerrona. Aliviaría, sin duda, nuestra cada vez mayor emigración al Norte. Sería el reconocimiento jurídico del estado actual de cosas, porque de ocurrir lo "concebible," es decir, que el llamado "americano" nos atragante la soberanía o independencia, quedaría lo "impensable," o sea, una revuelta boricua en la isla para que no nos quiten los cupones, los cheques de estímulo Obama ni las becas Pell, con la previsible fuga, abandono del barco zozobrante, a nuestros lares norteños. Allí donde viva un solo puertorriqueño, estará la patria. ("¿De qué país estamos hablando?")

In fact, statehood would be, with all its difficulties, the most obvious and least messy humane and legal solution to this trap. It would ease, no doubt, our increasing emigration to the North. It would be legal recognition of the current state of things, because if the "conceivable" happened, that is, that so-called "America" pushes sovereignty or independence on us, all that would be left would be the "unthinkable," that is to say, a Puerto Rican revolt on the island so that they not take away our food stamps, or Obama's stimulus checks, or the Pell Grants, with the expected flight, abandoning of the sinking ship, to our northern places. Where a single Puerto Rican lives, there will be the homeland.

At least one blogger saw this as an admission of defeat, "the inevitable capitulation of an '*independentista* writer' before the imminent end of the Commonwealth" (Álvarez).

Rodríguez Juliá's general stance on authority—all authorities—helps explains his defiance of the dream nation in literary orthodoxy. Consider how many characters in *El entierro de Cortijo* defy and mock authority, especially in the last pages, when several young women mock Rubén Blades, who is regarded as the epitome of leftist progressive *cool*. One of the main themes of that book is how *el pueblo-pueblo* mocks and repudiates Authority, something the embedded writer clearly admires.

As a commentator on all things Puerto Rican, Rodríguez Juliá has gotten progressively fed up with the state of things on the island and therefore with the pointlessness of discussions about the national status. Nowadays, he is equally disgusted by the anti-Americanism associated with hardened *independentismo* and the Latin American Left. This comes out clearly in his critique of Calle 13's René Pérez, who as I've noted is the most internationally famous *independentista*. The rapper was also sympathetic to Venezuela's Hugo Chávez, whom Rodríguez Juliá called "an autocrat" ("La calle al revés" [The street upside down]). The writer proves almost as emphatically opposed to contemporary popular music (in the form of the reggaeton) as he was to Chávez's brand of leftism.

Rodríguez Juliá is a man in the middle also because his historical fiction and essays circumnavigate issues of independence and the island status; they touch many points of view about the island and its history but commit to none. For instance, his seminal *El entierro de Cortijo* shows the seeds of his discontent, portraying Puerto Rico as an urban nation (as opposed to agrarian models of the country) devoted to popular (not folkloric) music. His work attacks the concept of *one* nation, instead representing the country as a gathering of social tribes, and it does not attempt to rhapsodize about the love of Land. Both of his famous historical novels, *La noche oscura del Niño Avilés* (The dark night of the Niño Avilés) and *La renuncia del héroe Baltasar* (The renunciation of the hero Baltasar), offer the very opposite of nostalgia: dystopian cityscapes. His works show no longing for the rural landscape of yore, and in its place are tortured gardens (in *La renuncia*), fiery apocalipsis (in *La noche oscura*), *and* the housing projects and the popular music of Cortijo, Cheo Feliciano, and Ruth Hernández instead of the folkloric music of the *jíbaro* (in *El entierro*).

Another way he avoids the standard nationalist-inspired cultural agenda is that the *héroe Baltasar* is the opposite of a national hero. Baltasar is in every respect an antihero just as much of Rodríguez Juliá's writing is devoted to undermining the very concept of heroism, of epic deeds. The only national heroism in sight—which is not inconsiderable—is being able to live within the colonial condition. John Perivolaris refers to this reverse-heroic strain in Rodríguez Juliá's chronicles, saying that everyday exigencies are what the chronicler (and the novelist, one would add) focuses on: "Rodríguez Juliá's 'crónica' is taken up with the day-to-day survival of most Puerto Ricans, rather than self-sacrifice, and with all the ambiguities that colonial survival entails" (694). And indeed it is in his chronicles that the writer focuses on *la plebe*, the irritating, always loud, and often vulgar mass that nevertheless consistently inspires tenderness in the author. The common people parade around in events like Cortijo's funeral and the crossing of the Guánica Bay and overwhelm the landscape, leaving no room for the solemnity of the heroic nation. The very tackiness of the *hoi polloi* is the primary device by which Rodríguez Juliá makes one of his main points, that the age of independence heroes is over and that like it or not, the people who support either statehood or the ELA are here to stay. As if that were not enough, he seriously and systematically undermines all notions of individual and collective heroics in his historical novels (see chapter 4).

In terms of politics, Edgardo Rodríguez Juliá has chosen (like roughly half of the electorate) to not choose, proclaiming himself sympathetic to *independentismo* as well as being an acute observer of the ELA and later supporting statehood. In his nuanced (or waffling, depending on your viewpoint) way, he includes himself as part of "aquéllos que proponemos la independencia, o una mayor soberanía dentro del Estado Libre Asociado" ("¿De qué país estamos hablando?"; those of us who propose independence or greater sovereignty within the Commonwealth). In light of that, his oeuvre is that of a writer struggling to make up his mind about which "nation" to write about. In his fiction as well as his New Journalistic essays there is always a lost nation, or rather a nation in search of itself, from the clashing of tribes in *El entierro de Cortijo*, through the nightmarish vision of the nation's history as a conflagration caused by the war of hierarchies, a petulant and insane Afro-Antillean hero in *La renuncia del héroe Baltasar*, through the lost foundational city of *La noche oscura del Niño Avilés*, or the search for the island's place in the Caribbean in *Caribeños*.

The literary generation of 1970 to which Rodríguez Juliá and Rosario Ferré belong signaled a concerted break with the ranks of the literary establishment. Another nonconformist was poet José Luis Vega, who in 1972 founded a poetry journal called *Ventana*, regarded as a split from the diehard pro-independence journal *Guajana*. Vega says that the founders of *Ventana* wanted poetry to be open to "other concerns that were not exclusively those of political testimony" (Hernández, *A viva voz* 290).

The 1990s saw renewed discussions pro and con independence; in particular about the viability of the whole independence political project. The group of so-called *posmodernos* (postmodern critics)—so labeled by independence stalwarts as a term of derision—reject both the cultural and the political aims of independence. The *posmodernos* lean left for other causes, though. Many of them are residents of the United States and affiliated with American universities and cultural institutions and have declared openly that it is time to move on from the standard ways of the cultural establishment on the island.

Puerto Rican Jam, edited by Frances Negrón-Muntaner and Ramón Grosfoguel, was a manifesto of the movement. Intellectual descendants of José Luis González, they declare that the cause of independence "is only powerful among elite minorities" (4–5) and that support for different forms of alliance with the United States does not constitute proof of a colonized mind. Like González, the writers in *Puerto Rican Jam* assail the mythification of pre-1898 Puerto Rico, particularly the idealized agrarian past along with the attendant lament for its destruction by the Americans. Negrón-Muntaner et al. explain that Puerto Ricans readily accepted U.S. rule in 1898 and beyond, stating that ordinary Puerto Ricans saw the change as a far better alternative to the Spanish regime, "an authoritarian, repressive, and backward form of cultural domination with no positive political legacy to be remembered by" (45). Furthermore the United States had two "key factors" to recommend it: one was the positive perception of its rule as bringing "political rights, democratization, prospects of prosperity, and so on," and the second the antagonism felt by emerging social groups from "those promoting the virtues of *la puertorriqueñidad*" (45).

In an equally strong line of argument, Negrón-Muntaner and Grosfoguel openly speak about how the majority of Puerto Ricans have rebuffed independence. This rejection they attribute primarily to Puerto Ricans' awareness of the grim history and poor living conditions of neighboring sovereign island nations seen as "regimes of state-orchestrated terror, International Monetary Fund intervention, pauperization of the population, illegal emigration, foreign debt, and a lack of strength to forcefully negotiate with the economic centers" (8). This cautionary tale they claim is made stronger by Puerto Rico's knowledge that liberation by arms in Caribbean and Central American nations can be defeated through superior arms or "strangulated economically" by the United States (9).

Mariano Negrón-Portillo (also in *Puerto Rican Jam*) agrees with José Luis González in seeing Pedro Albizu Campos as problematical. Negrón-Portillo catalogues many of the ideological flaws in Albizuism: "His discourse was based on the defense of *La Raza*, animosity toward North Americans (who were viewed as foreigners), assimilation of many elements of the Catholic conception of the world, reverence toward national heroes, Hispanism, and an authoritarian view of political and social struggles" (50). Like González's, this assessment has yet to affect many *independentistas* on and off the island, and if contemporary iconography is to be believed, Albizu's face still remains as popular as Che Guevara's in the marketplace of *independentismo*.

Los posmodernos do not sugarcoat the negative elements of the island's colonial situation, among them economic dependency and subordination as well as lack of political representation in the U.S. system. However, they point to real, lasting improvements to the Puerto Rican quality of life brought about by the association with the United States, chief among them the cultural empowerment of minorities. They clarify over and over that this was not the product of United States' altruism but grew out of the exigencies of the Cold War and of Puerto Rico's role as a model affiliated Caribbean territory—as the anti-Cuba.

Negrón-Muntaner et al. are not defenders of the United States' handling of Puerto Rico; they note, among other negative factors, that Puerto Rico has a lower per-capita income than the poorest state in the United States. But in their view, realpolitik precludes the attachment to old-fashioned notions of independence. They point to the dependent experiences encountered by the Palau Islands after their dissociation from the United States, and Grosfoguel goes on at length about the disastrous turn of events when Guyana was liberated from, or, rather, was cut loose by Holland.

These and other critics and writers also argue against any *one* definition of the Puerto Rican nation along the lines of the usually homogeneous portrait inspired by patriotism. Like Rodríguez Juliá, Negrón-Muntaner et al. point out that the island is splintered into diverse socioeconomic groups. Like José Luis González, they accuse establishment thinking of elitist ways that are antagonistic to social groups such as the working class (particularly union members), blacks, women and gays, groups not afforded space in the nation as it was romanticized by *independentismo*. In fact, this is no longer an accurate assessment of many contemporary *independentistas* since *Claridad*, for one, has embraced women's and LBGT rights.

What Now?

How does current culture use the dream nation? While some young and older writers and other culture producers continue to embrace the establishment-sanctioned love of independence and nostalgia for the verdant Lush Land that fights for its freedom, there's a new openness to critiquing the dream nation. In part because the issue of national identity is no longer as pressing a matter. Critic Lilliana Ramos Collado says that the topic of "el problema identitario" is fading: "the identity problem hardly appears as a topic, increasingly less urgent in our literature. And we should add that it appears dressed in literary forms and metaphorical systems that are increasingly stagnant" ("Escritores, fin de siglo: un documento" [Writers, end of century: A document]). True or not, the fact that Ramos Collado assigns the start of modernity to 1898 means independence (for her) still has a symbolic place in Puerto Rican culture.

A writer hailed as a leader of postfeminism, Mayra Santos Febres, represents a generational attitude of wanting greater freedom from the strictures of conventional *independentismo* yet having a soft spot for its *je ne sais quoi*. In the introduction to *Mal(ha)b(l)ar*—an anthology of her generation—and in an effort to give a cohesive quality to the group, she defines their shared characteristics as: use of popular language, support of multicultural interests (women, homosexuals, blacks, workers, etc.), intertextuality (a popular feature of 1980s literary theory), and a non-nationalist orientation, "an almost complete absence of evidently Puerto Rican geographic and linguistic referents" (19–20). Besides that, she says that her contemporaries take an opposing attitude toward the nationalist dictum of "the traditional role assigned to Puerto Rican literature as the maker of a national-social conscience" (19–20). Another generational quirk (one she doesn't mention) is apparent in the title of the collection, *Mal(ha)b(l)ar*, with its play on words through clever use of parentheses.

Newer generations of culture producers like Santos Febres stake the claim that they are free from the monomaniacal search for national identity (i.e., dependent/independent) and the deep identification with and love of tellurism. Perhaps the starkest difference in her cohort is the lightening up in the tone and purpose of culture, with their increased use of irony and humor that allows them to play with tradition. There is also more freedom to be different, to not march in lockstep with one belief or even with one another, which is why Santos Febres points to "substantial differences" among those she chose for her anthology.

It is vividly apparent that new writers have different paths to take, but Santos Febres herself proves that there are still connections to a shared ideal (or at least its heroines). For instance, her short story "Dilcia M." features as protagonist an imprisoned patriot reminiscent of the real-life independence crusader Dilcia N. Pagán, who served twenty years in federal prison for her connections with the Machetero movement. Its companion story, "Act of Faith," references Blanca Canales, an *independentista* champion who proclaimed Puerto Rico free during the Jayuya uprising of 1950; Santos Febres compares her to Joan of Arc. The microstory "Act of Faith" is therefore an affirmation of the heroic power of nationalist women's activism.

Most of twenty-first-century Puerto Rican culture eschews purely local concerns and follows the Western trend of gritty hyperrealism or, better yet, brutal realism featuring multicultural migratory characters, especially those with nonbourgeois sex lives. The most famous Latin American writer in the early part of the twenty-first century, Chilean Roberto Bolaño, exemplifies that sensibility. Following the trend represented by his fiction, younger Puerto Rican writers are no longer bound to the venerable questions about Puerto Ricanness, "¿Qué somos? ¿Cómo somos?" (What are we? How are we?). To use just one example, Elidio La Torre Lagares's novel *Correr tras el viento* (Running after the wind) is a noir thriller that takes place in (among other places) Argentina, Cuba, and Switzerland. Its peripatetic characters, who are similar to those of Bolaño, have globalized, non-Hispanic names such as Brad Molloy (the protagonist), Dolo, Anna Lee, Hammer, and Sergei.

There are, as Santos Febres says, many cultural notions her contemporaries share with Latin American and Western literature in general; for instance, support for queer theory and LGBT characters is the norm in newer writers/filmmakers like Frances Negrón-Muntaner, Eduardo Lalo, Ángel Lozada, and Daniel Torres. Also conforming to their times are writers who stride two Caribbean nationalities, like Cuban-born Mayra Montero and Dominican native Eugenio García Cuevas. These kinds of culture producers are less interested in or beholden to the old ideologies and literary communities.

Two writers who focus on queer themes and characters, Ángel Lozada and Luis Negrón, openly question the Puerto Rican literary establishment. In Lozada's novel *No quiero quedarme sola y vacía* (I don't want to be left lonely and empty), the protagonist rails (in Spanglish) against the centrality of that most recognizable of Puerto Rican literary establishments, the UPR-RP. Santos Febres, by contrast, embraces the centrality of the UPR-RP inced the introduction to the anthology quoted earlier. But Lozada's protagonist denounces that institution's stranglehold on the production of culture:

> Oh, Bitches of the UPR, haven't you notice [*sic*], that I can write veintisiete. Haven't you notice, Bitches of the Puerto Rican Academia, what's going on here? Lo que pre / prosigue sólo puede catalogarse como irresponsabilidades descuidos y cosas raras, como horrores otrográficos y gramaticales: oh, Bitches with PhDs y con el pelo mal-pintado con Wella hair products: la novela tiene errores y muchos dos puntos, pero les advierto, que le responderé a todas con un 'a-mí-plín.' (20)

Oh, Bitches of the UPR, haven't you notice [sic], that I can write twenty-seven. Haven't you notice, Bitches of the Puerto Rican Academia, what's going on here? What pre / proceeds can only be classified as irresponsible carelessness and weird things like othergraphic and grammatical horrors: oh, Bitches with PhDs and hair badly dyed with Wella hair products: the novel has many errors and many colons, but I warn you, I will answer you all with an "a-mí-plín."

Since the last phrase is an allusion to la China Hereje from Luis Rafael Sánchez's *La guaracha del Macho Camacho*, Lozada isn't rejecting Puerto Rican *literature*. He is rejecting what are, to him, the island's academic grammar and ideological police, the literary establishment.

The narrator in Eduardo Lalo's *Simone* also portrays a caricaturesque academic establishment. The intelligentsia's gatherings are vacuous, unnecessary, and incomprehensible, for example the Derridian or Lacanian litcrit analysis at a literary congress where the presenters are all foolish, pompous, boring. Puerto Rican sociological writing is also caricatured, for instance the high seriousness of a book ridiculously devoted to the "cultural ethnicity" of the small town of San Sebastián. The last part of *Simone* is as much a representation of the failures of academia as of a love story. The narrator's rival for the affections of Li Chao embodies the worst traits of academia; Carmen Lindo is an academic player eager to participate in intrigues and spread rumors and proud to be well-connected to the Puerto Rican and Spanish literary establishments. She also receives all the rewards of the cultural establishment: she gets to be center of attention at well-attended parties, she's offered a well-placed job in California, and in the end she (seemingly) gets the girl.

Newer fiction also mocks nationalist tradition. Luis Negrón has a character in *Mundo Cruel* who jokes that, like all protagonists in Puerto Rican literature, he should always follow at least one element of *independentismo*. His self-reflexive riff on literature signals a break because Negrón, moreover, places statehood centrally, visibly in his story (an idea *verboten* in earlier Puerto Rican literature): "Tengo una casita en Santurce, por la parte de atrás del Antiguo Comité General del PNP. (Valga aclarar que es por pura casualidad que vivo allí pues yo, como casi todo protagonista de la literatura puertorriqueña, cuestiono la presencia yanqui)" (22; I have a little house in Santurce at the rear of the Old General Committee of the PNP. [Let me clarify that it is by chance that I live there because I, like almost every protagonist in Puerto Rican literature, question the *yanqui* presence]). Unpacking this passage means first highlighting the novelty of the very *mention* of the pro-statehood party (PNP), an almost unheard-of incidence in the dominant literature up to the end of last century. In the passage, the pro-statehood political party is symbolically *a fixture* of the urban landscape in which the narrator lives—it is the new *palma* in the landscape of La Isla.

Far more common, as we've seen all along, is the belief, the credo, that to be Puerto Rican you have to be *authentic* and to be authentic is to favor independence. In keeping with literary tradition for example, Marcos Rodríguez-Frese mocks statehood in "Décimas de la estadidad" (*Décimas* of statehood) (20 June 2012). In this albeit minor work of popular culture, we see the usual dismissive attitude toward statehood. As is usual in satirical *décimas*, the author ridicules and challenges an idea: statehood for Puerto Rico will come to pass "cuando paran las gallinas / y ponga huevos la puerca") (i.e., when pigs fly). Rodríguez-Frese identifies (as tradition dictates) with rural Puerto Rico.

On the other hand, a highbrow cultural product like Negrón's book goes against tradition and taunts the PIP establishment. For instance, in the story "La Edwin" the eponymous character falls for a guy described as "un fupista de esos que ponen bombas y que quieren al ROTC fuera de la universidad . . . como no pueden liberar la patria ahora se van a liberar sexualmente" (40; a *fupista* of those who plant bombs and want the ROTC off campus . . . because they cannot liberate the country they are now going to liberate themselves sexually). Negrón exploits the stereotypical depiction of the FUPI (the pro-independence university students federation) as "bomb-setting *fupistas*," which harks back to the 1970s and turns to Luis Rafael Sánchez's heroic picture of the students as the hope for the future in *La guaracha del Macho Camacho*. Sánchez, in turn, had reversed an earlier stereotype by having the *fupistas* be the target of a right-wing bomb. Negrón goes even further, mocking heroes and heroic events sacred to the Left: Che Guevara, Fidel Castro, the Cuban Revolution, and Vieques (40–41). The punch line to the humiliating anecdote is that after being led on by the bogus leftist, in the end the *fupista* ditches La Edwin for a statehood supporter from the ritzy part of town.

It is beyond the scope of this book to offer a panoramic survey of Puerto Rican culture of the past thirty years. While independence remains an important character and characteristic of Puerto Rican literature, recent writing shows ample signs of having overcome the monomaniacal focus on a dream nation of earlier generations. Often they do so teasingly, given the spirit of irony in recent generations. A case in point is Juan Pablo Rivera's short story "Vida y obra de Marta la Diabla" (Life and times of Marta la Diabla), which says of its protagonist that her only concession to patriotism is the printed logo "Puerto Rico" on her leather flip-flops (Caleb Acevedo, Rosario, and Negrón 164). That Rivera's story can be read as an *homage* to Rosario Ferré's "Cuando las mujeres quieren a los hombres"—because of its doubling and intertwining identities featuring a proper lady and a transgressive, black, lower-class prostitute—complicates and enhances the connections between the generations of Puerto Rican writers.

Nonetheless, it would only be possible for contemporary Puerto Rican literature to forget nationalism if it also forgets all literature that came before, which is near-impossible since, as Santos Febres points out in the summary quoted before, current literature is often intertextual, that is to say, literature is often about literature. For instance, the online culture magazine *8ogrados* features many of the newer left-leaning culture producers (such as Ana María Fuster and Alfredo Villanueva Collado) and their politics often veer left: toward the causes and principles dear to *independentismo*. What has changed is that nowadays irony is allowed to ride shotgun with the dream nation.

A remarkable example of this tongue-in-cheek tone occurs in a poem by Federico Irizarry Natal titled "Camp," where *the* independence icon, Pedro Albizu Campos, is the focus of sad ribbing. Describing a poster in a bar, the poet muses on the celebrity status that Albizu has achieved in Puerto Rican iconography and popular culture. What is new is the acknowledgment of the trendiness, faddishness, and consumerism that nowadays get dragged in the wake of Puerto Rican nationalism:

> yuppies y barbies nacionalistas
> que te reclaman,
> divo de la nación.
> como indiscutible salvapatrias,
> cual peluche patriótico,
> como su mascota revolucionaria
> . . . .
> Albizu Camp,
> Albizu Pop
> Albizu Kitsch   (Kitsch 27)

> yuppies and nationalist Barbies
> reclaim you,

divo of the nation.
as indisputable savior of the motherland,
as patriotic teddy bear
as revolutionary mascot
....
Albizu Camp
Albizu Pop
Albizu Kitsch

Even Albizu, the icon of independence, has devolved through the inexorable passage of time, through the rough sieve of consumerist culture, into a kitschy cultural artifact.

As we have seen, starting in the 1970s cracks began to show in the intellectual support for the dream nation. Times have changed, and public intellectuals of consequence have pushed back against canonical literary orthodoxy, bringing a thaw to the *exclusionary* emotional hold of the independence ideal on the Puerto Rican national imagination. In the next chapter, we will explore the tradition and the contemporary challenges to one of the most common ways of channeling the dream nation, through the rose-colored lenses of nostalgia for a verdant, Lush Land.

3 / From the Lush Land to the Traffic Jam

Puerto Rican culture from every era shows a deep and abiding love for the island itself, for the geographic territory (in its olden incarnation), which is more often than not referred to as La Isla; the capitalization is the mark of an exceptionalist conception of the nation. This affection for the scenic beauties of the land is in many ways tied to nationalist emotions, to patriotism, to the hoped-for independence, and it contributes greatly to the dream nation.

The patriotic love of land took hold of the national imagination during the Romantic movement, when it was tied to nineteenth-century Latin American independence movements and their nation-building literature. For instance, Andrés Bello, the quintessential Venezuelan poet of independence, connects Nature, rusticity, patriotism, and independence in his *Silvas* (written between 1823 and 1826), an unfinished ode to all of the newly independent Latin American nations:

> Oh, jóvenes naciones, que ceñida
> alzáis sobre el atónito Occidente
> de tempranos laureles la cabeza:
> honrad al campo, honrad la simple vida
> del labrador y su frugal llaneza   (Rodríguez Alcalá 39)

> Oh, young nations, who lift your heads
> with tightly fitted new laurels
> toward the astonished West:

honor the simple life
of the farmer and his frugal simplicity

Love of land and its simple country folk later finds its evil twin: the denigration of Western modernity. In Puerto Rican culture in the twentieth and twenty-first centuries, the ravages of modernity became more ubiquitous as the result of ecologically and aesthetically disastrous overdevelopment by greedy developers aided by lack of government planning. In this chapter, we look at how the Puerto Rican national imagination transitioned from an admiring mode into a lamenting mode, that is to say how during much of the nineteenth century, *paisajismo,* or the pictorial beauty of the island's lush landscape, became synonymous with the dream nation and was entrenched in the national highbrow as well as popular culture. When the landscape itself changed, Nature's beauty morphed into imagery and allegories of its despoiling, what Ana Lydia Vega terms "ecocide" in a column called "Marejada de los muertos" (Tide surge of the dead) in which she laments the pollution of air, sea, and land and the "extermination of the flora and fauna." What was in the nineteenth century pure extolled landscape turns into an urban scene choking in roads, traffic jams, Burger Kings, and smog.

Both modes of gazing at the land/nation coexist because, despite that sad reality of overdevelopment, who wouldn't dwell on the splendorous greens and sparkling blues of the Painted Nation in, say, the paintings of Francisco Oller? That beautiful countryside remains at the heart of the belief in the uniqueness of Puerto Rico so that the pull of patriotism, nationalism, and nostalgia still leads many works to revere the *patria* as a Lush Land.

Writers from every era have written of the Land with deep and abiding love. From María Babiana Benítez, Puerto Rico's first woman poet (1783[?]–1873), to Esmeralda Santiago (the best-selling Latina/Puerto Rican writer), there is an earnest certitude in regarding the island in Edenic terms. Benítez's 1832 poem "La ninfa de Puerto Rico a la Justicia" (The nymph of Puerto Rico to Justice) antecedes the book from 1844 that is regarded as the first Puerto Rican work of literature, the *Aguinaldo puertorriqueño* (Puerto Rican carol). Benítez's poem has three of the traits that tie together Puerto Rican literature and, I would add, much of die-hard *independentista* culture: "the Edenic vision of Puerto Rico, cultural Hispanophilia and political commitment" (Torres Caballero). One can find all three elements in just one stanza: "Yo, desde Luquillo en la alta cima, / contemplo mis riberas, / que Ceres misma anima, / cubiertas de frondosas sementeras, / yo bendigo al monarca que me estima" (Rivera de Álvarez 67; I, from Luquillo's high summit / contemplate my riverbanks, / which Ceres herself animates, covered with lush fields, / I bless the monarch who esteems me).

Almost the entire output of nineteenth-century Puerto Rican literature uses the land as a reference point. For instance, Alejandro Tapia y Rivera reveals the sentimental, intimate connection between self and land that many writers have felt:

> Existe un motivo poderoso para que asocie mis
> *Memorias* con la tierra en que nací; aquéllas son mi vida
> y ésta me la dio. Desde entonces, el vínculo de amor
> que a ella me liga, tal vez contra todas mis conveniencias,
> y acaso como fuente de todas mis pesadumbres, parece
> obra de una imperiosa fatalidad.
>   (Alejandro Tapia y Rivera, *Mis memorias*)

> There is a powerful reason to associate my
> *Memoirs* with the land of my birth, the former are my life
> and the latter gave it to me. Since then, the bond of love
> which binds me to it, perhaps against all advisability,
> and perhaps as a source of all my sorrows, seems
> the work of an peremptory fatality.

Tapia lyrically then lists telluric components of the nation that speak directly to his heart: the gentle breeze, the mornings and afternoons, the verdant fields, the beautiful sky, the splendidly moonlit nights, the cloudy days, the shadowy nights. An important factor in this heartfelt sentimentality about the land was that Tapia, along with many other nineteenth-century writers, looked at the beauties of the landscape through the veil of remembrance, their nostalgia made keener by exile.

Nineteenth-century Puerto Rican lyric poetry in particular has many writers like Romantic poet José Gautier Benítez, who perpetually swoon over the beautiful landscape because the sentimental gaze of a remembered landscape fortified their political attachment to Puerto Rico. Many of his standard school-fare poems are paeans to the landscape with titles like "A Puerto Rico," "Puerto Rico," and, yes, "A Puerto Rico (regreso)" (To Puerto Rico [return]). In one of many examples (from a poem called "Puerto Rico"), Gautier Benítez brings together yet another three traits of the dream nation: the paradisiacal beauties of the land, the feminine incarnation of the *patria*, and the rustic (i.e., authentic) life of the Taínos, who represent an idealized connection to the past:

¡Risueño Edén! Soñado paraíso
de aborígene raza, que en su orilla,
con el hueco bambú y el cedro liso
labrábase la choza y la barquilla,
único ajuar a la ambición preciso
de una existencia rústica y sencilla   (Acevedo Marrero 274)

Smiling Eden! Dreamed-of paradise
of an aboriginal race, which on its banks,
carved the hollow bamboo and cedar
smooth into the hut and the skiff,
only attire necessary for the ambition
of a rustic and simple existence

So deeply has this vision seeped into the Puerto Rican national imagination that Justice Sonia Sotomayor borrows a line from "A Puerto Rico (regreso)" for the title of her memoirs. She also includes the entire poem as a coda to the story of her formation in the Bronx where the island was a far-off small-town paradise seen on summer vacations and through her mother's stories of the 1930s and 1940s. Then, during an adult trip, Sotomayor also saw, along with the natural beauties of, for example Isla de los Ratones off the coast in Cabo Rojo, massive traffic jams in Mayagüez during an election cycle. She recognizes the usefulness of Latino nostalgia as a "rose-colored" (36) enhancement of the land left behind, one crucial for connecting the migrant community to a universe "parallel" to the grim life in New York (65).

The telluric nationalism of romanticized island imagery is linked in the wider culture to pictorial depictions of the landscape's beauty which always hark back to a time perceived as having been better (*O tempora! O mores!*). The leap made by the poets, painters, and patriots from *nature* to *nation* fuels people's love of land and the conviction of their nation's exceptionalism. In other words, the belief that there is something unique in the landscape and the people born to it is deeply intertwined with depictions of the dream nation as it *once* was (supposedly), a reversion to an ancestral time when we were somehow purer, truer to ourselves. A time when we were free.

Silvia Álvarez Curbelo sees direct ties between love of land and twentieth-century nationalism. She traces how this important connection between politics and culture appears in Pedro Albizu Campos saying that his alliance with "Fuerzas Vivas," a political movement of the mid-1920s, had strong links to "a venerable defense of land linked to the likes of Matienzo Cintrón, Manuel Zeno Gandía [an important naturalist novelist], and Miguel Meléndez Muñoz [chronicler of the life of the *jíbaro*], the latter two leaders of farmers and editorialists" (89).

A downside to love of land often was solidarity with the interests of landowners and, subsequently, ignorance of the realities of the working classes, as José Luis González never tired of pointing out. He specifically denounced the sentimental love of land he called *telurismo* as a cultural prop for the ideology of the landowning class:

> El telurismo característico de la literatura producida por la élite puertorriqueña en el siglo XX no responde [. . .] a una desinteresada y lírica sensibilidad conmovida por las bellezas de nuestro país tropical, sino a una añoranza muy concreta y muy histórica de la tierra perdida, y no de la tierra entendida como símbolo ni como metáfora sino como medio de producción material cuya propiedad pasó a manos extrañas. En otras palabras: quienes ya no pudieron seguir 'volteando la finca' a lomos del tradicional caballo, se dedicaron a hacerlo a lomos de una décima, un cuento o una novela. (*El país de cuatro pisos* 33)

> The tellurism characteristic of the literature produced by the Puerto Rican elite in the twentieth century does not respond [. . .] to a disinterested and lyrical sensibility moved by the beauty of our tropical country, but to a longing for a very specific and very historic lost land, not the land understood as symbol or metaphor but as a means of material production whose ownership was taken over by strangers. In other words, he who could no longer "patrol the farm" on the back of the traditional horse, set out to do so on the back of a *décima*, a story or a novel.

Furthermore, he was vehemently disgusted by the ongoing use of images of an unsullied and *gendered* island: "Lo que es verdaderamente morboso y reaccionario en este país es seguir cantándole a una 'isla doncella' que perdió su virginidad desde el momento mismo en que el energúmeno Juan Ponce de León se le echó encima hace casi cinco siglos" (*Nueva visita* 150; What is really morbid and reactionary in this country is to continue singing to a "maiden island" who lost her virginity since the moment that the lunatic Juan Ponce de León leaped on her almost five centuries ago). González probably referred to Antonio Cabán Vale's famous *independentista* hymn "Verde Luz," which uses precisely that phrase, "maiden island."

Lilliana Ramos-Collado states that this kind of myth—inherited from eighteenth-century cultural Puerto Rican production—still permeates modern-day culture: "Todavía estamos combatiendo ese mito que nos ata al imaginario terruño 'primitivo' (conquistable, civilizable) de nuestra América" ("¿Arte queer?"; We are still battling that myth that binds us to the imaginary "primitive homeland" [conquerable, civilizable] of our America).

That primeval virginal land often entails a gendered view of the nation. Olga Nolla exploits this in her novel *El castillo de la memoria* (The castle of memory) when a crew member in Columbus's first trip remembers the Admiral's sexualized description of the islands as a naked, fragmented woman: "no son pocas las veces en que lo he escuchado comparar estas tierras con una mujer: la lozanía de su piel fresca y húmeda, la generosidad de sus pezones duros y sus muslos redondos" (16; not a few times I've heard him compare these lands with a woman: the luxuriance of her fresh moist skin, the generosity of her hard nipples and rounded thighs). The fragmentation in that image mirrors the conquistador's will to conquer the land.

So the idealization of the landscape is a constant refrain in the dream nation. One corollary to the unquestioned adulation of the bucolic land is, as I've mentioned, fear and loathing of modernity, particularly city life. One of the best-known examples is René Marqués's canonical play *La carreta,* with its dread of the soul-killing city, a trope that permeates Puerto Rican literature in the mid- to late twentieth century, including Nuyorican writers. An example of the latter is Miguel Algarín's poem "A Mongo Affair," where the "mongo" (bloodless, spineless) is a Puerto Rican who has moved to the city ("mongo es el boricua / who's been moved / to the inner-city jungles / of north american cities") (Stavans 1347).

Poetry is particularly susceptible to the phenomenon we are exploring because of the strength of the nineteenth-century Romantic movement, which produced masterworks in praise of the land/nation. The inclination, however, was still going strong in the twentieth century when the profoundly pro-independence poet Juan Antonio Corretjer reaffirmed his love of land. The critic Benjamín Torres Caballero regards Corretjer as the national poet of Puerto Rico because of works like "Regresemos a la montaña" (Let us return to the mountain) from 1929. Torres Caballero states that the passionately nationalist poet created "a mythical image of Puerto Rico." Corretjer too uses the gendered metaphor for the nation; the island is "virgen bella." The back-to-the-land agrarian impulse is present because, as Corretjer says, the land fuels the soul of the nation: "Regresemos a la montaña / urna de nobles promesas / factoría de espíritus fuertes / donde se hace la patria / con viandas y leche de vaca" (Colón López 196; Let us go back to the mountain / urn of lofty promises / factory of strong spirits / where the homeland is made / with victuals and cow's milk).

To this day these kinds of depictions, gendered or not, are cornerstones in works that allude to independence. In a paroxysm of irony, the same Land-oriented imagery is frequently co-opted by the government/chamber-of-commerce marketing machine that promotes the island's tourism and industry.

Nevertheless, representations of the land can be explicitly political. When she contemplates the "tierra rota" (broken land) in her poem "Desde el puente Martín Peña" (From the Martín Peña Bridge), Julia de Burgos shows Marxist ferocity: "¡Alzad, alzad vuestros brazos / como se alzaron en Rusia!" (88; Raise, raise your arms / as they were raised in Russia). In her "Campo 1" (Countryside 1), she gives an explicitly revolutionary meaning to the landscape in which "la esperanza está ardiendo" (307; hope burns), a patriotic trope that harks back to such poems by José de Diego as "¡Pitirre!" or "Aguadilla," in which the palm fronds are like flags. But de Burgos's gaze envelops the flora and fauna, and she sees the human revolutionary impulse embedded into the landscape itself since the horizon is "armado de llanto de campesino" (armed with peasant tears) and the earth opens up "quemada de injusticias" (307; burned by injustices). The countryside is still primary for this nationalist poet; the critics Sherezada Vicioso and Lizabeth Paravisini say the landscape in de Burgos's poems is politically charged with the rural/urban dichotomy where the negative view of the city "symbolizes, in its growth and development at the expense of the countryside, the metropolis in relation to the colony" (676).

From the *Hacienda* to the *Hacinamiento*

Puerto Rican culture has often indulged in exceptionalist views of the nation and habitually contrasted the landscape as heaven and the city as

FIGURE 4. Francisco Oller, *Camino a la Hacienda Aurora* (1898–99)

hell or the traffic jam/modernity. Both can be found in the real-life island landscape, which to this day retains (in spots) the beauties admired in painterly imagery but which in most places has suffered overdevelopment that turned it into a cityscape of overcrowded urban areas rife with damaged ecosystems.

Pride in the beautiful land is not exclusive to the dream of independence, but it is an effective catalyst for patriotic nostalgia, for pre-U.S. times, and for renewed accusations about the damage wrought by colonialism. And from the Lush Land frequently springs the dream nation.

To illustrate what I mean, look at the *paisajismo* in a gorgeous landscape by the impressionist painter Francisco Oller titled *Camino a la Hacienda Aurora* (1898–99). In the painting, the light from the sky depicts the broadest, most beautiful Nature. The beautiful land and, upon closer inspection, the buildings and the people in it together represent the nation. In this instance, below the sky and to the left of the buildings are Afro-Caribbean figures (including a woman caring a burden) walking low along a country road. The composition and perspective of the painting have the buildings on a higher plane as reminder of the hierarchical power relations of the island: the *central*, or sugarcane-processing plant, with its red-brick smokestack occupies pride of place along with the mayoral mansion set on the low horizon. We cannot see where the path that the figures are following begins or ends, yet it curves up from the *hacienda*, which is vital to their lives. Those structures of power in turn are dwarfed by the far-off mountains and the stunning sky, which brings the landscape into a sharper meaning. Like Julia de Burgos's poem, Oller's painting tells a complicated story that goes beyond just extolling the beauties of landscape. Rosario Ferré critiques the placid implications of romanticized depictions of the nation in *The House on the Lagoon* when she describes early photographs of the island commissioned by an American governor. She reminds the reader of the Lush Land and of its hidden human toll, since the photographs show "the island in all its splendor: there were angel-hair waterfalls, cotton-candy clouds, sugar-white beaches, cows pasturing up and down velvet-green hills and not a single starving peasant to mar the beauty of the landscape" (125). In sum, it is the kind of traditional depiction of the land disconnected from humanity.

Such is not the case with a great painter like Oller, who, as we see, does not fall into the trap of the colonial mind-set; *Camino a la Hacienda Aurora* is not a contemplation of a landscape devoid of humans; it carefully crafts a commentary on the *scale* of human beings in relation to the socioeconomic life *within* the landscape.

The *New York Times* review of a 2007 exhibition titled *Mi Puerto Rico: Master Painters of the Island, 1780–1952* points out these salient features of Oller's landscapes (he also painted other genres): "Oller also painted *lovely Puerto Rican landscapes*, though he focused on scenes of the island's agriculture, development and modernization. Sugar cane fields and processing factories are prominent subjects in several paintings (which is not surprising given that during the nineteenth century, sugar cane was the island's main export), along with plantations and harvest scenes. *Most of the images have a low horizon, showing off the wide Caribbean sky*" (Genocchio; my italics).

The sky, the land, the sea, and the socioeconomic underpinnings of life on the island all are contained in images that have become so beloved, so treasured that they have become embedded in the popular imagination. So much so that Jack Agüeros, for ten years director of the Museo del Barrio in New York, grumbled about the expectations created by this kind of art and his struggles whenever he curated avant garde and younger painters because the public "wanted to see nostalgic recreations of the Puerto Rican landscape. They wanted to see pictures of cows and *flamboyanes*" (the iconic orange-red blossom tree) (Hernández, *Voices* 30).

Literature also often defaults to the Lush Land, which is conventionally identified with the Nation, one that later became despoiled by modernity, itself regarded as synonymous with the island's colonial entanglement. Modernity is almost always viewed as poisonous to the paradisiacal dream nation. This process appears in traditional Puerto Rican literature and influential works such as René Marqués's *La carreta*, which portrays urban Puerto Rico and New York as dystopias.

Margot Arce de Vázquez's essay "El paisaje de Puerto Rico" (The landscape of Puerto Rico) typifies the feeling that "la isla es paisaje puro" (López-Baralt, *Antología* 72; the island is pure landscape). Published in 1939, it reflects the ethos of its time, with quaint sexism and Hispanophilic tones united to contemplation of the flawless landscape, but primarily it reaffirms the belief that the island's geography is its identity. The land, though beautiful, is infantilized: "la gracia infantil de Puerto Rico" (74; the childlike grace of Puerto Rico), and its green forms and hills look like "toys." Beautifully, Arce extends the sea into the island using a metaphor of gentle waves morphing into the island's hilly landscape: "tierra adentro con un ritmo de ondas suaves que ascienden poco a poco y sin violencia hasta la cordillera central" (74; inland has a gentle rhythm of waves that rise slowly and without violence to the central mountain range).

Why does this kind of depiction never mention the ubiquitous hurricanes that habitually lash the island and that have been recorded since 1515? Arce's sugarcane fields are equally placid and liquid, "su oleaje de lenguas verdiazules y sus guajanas de un violeta delicado, que repiten la imagen de la espuma marina" (72; its waves of blue-green tongues and its plumes of a delicate violet, repeating the image of the sea foam). The tranquility of the landscape is its most notable feature, and from it flows the personality of "el hombre de esta tierra" (the man of this land), whose simplicity and "admirable disdain" for material things would later have its requiem on an island that has the largest mall in the Caribbean.

The sea, always the sea, surrounds and mirrors this magnificent island of Arce's, like it has in countless writers and artists. True to her times, she compares it, however, to European (Mediterranean) scenery: "mar amplio, fuerte y tranquilo que recuerda al Mediterráneo en su luz y su hermosura viril" (70; a broad sea, strong and calm which reminds us of the Mediterranean with its light and its virile beauty). But American colonialism, with its "bitter, inhuman tumult," encroaches the sweet "eclogue" that is Puerto Rico. True to her time, she identifies authentic Puerto Ricanness as being opposed to Americanness, and she uses the common invective for any denatured Puerto Rican who imitates American ways: *pitiyanqui*.[1]

Mind you, if one goes back to the earliest Puerto Rican literature, one finds that Manuel Alonso's *El gíbaro* already bemoaned a beautiful rural world that was *passing* (he was writing from a distance of seven years of exile), so that even in that golden age things were already going to pot:

> no podria [sic] pintar [. . .] sino en el período de su civilizada decadencia [. . .] el sol cubierto con un lienzo de nubes que debilitaba su ardor tropical, templado además por la brisa diaria en aquel clima durante las abrasadas horas del dia [sic], alumbraba el recinto de una ciudad, que ya no ecsiste [sic], tal es la␣trasformacion [sic] verificada en ella en tan corto espacio de tiempo. (1849 edition, 21–22)

> I could not paint [. . .] but in the period of its civilized decline [. . .] It was ten o'clock in the morning, the sun, covered by a canvas of clouds that weakened its tropical heat, tempered further by the daily breeze in that climate during the scorching hours of the day, illuminated the walls of a city that no longer exists, such is the transformation established in such a short space of time.

Benjamín Torres Caballero notes that the colonial "rural world he had captured in *El gíbaro* was disappearing" so that already the feelings toward *la patria* were nestled in a yearning sense of loss and nostalgia, always a powerful cultural cocktail. Even so, cultural nationalism à la the nineteenth century endures. It reappears in Puerto Rican culture in the United States; J. Jorge Klor de Alva sees a connection to another important Latino nationalist political movement, Chicano politics: "Like the mythical Aztlán, Borinquen was transformed in the ethnic mythology of the times into a lost tropical paradise, 'all pregnant with sweetness.' It was the repository of all cherished values, the wellspring of resistance, and the object of nostalgic remembrances. In poems, novels, paintings, and pronouncements, Borinquen, like Aztlán, was held up as the promised land of hope" (75).

Precisely because the Lush Land has never been entirely forgotten, newer stories and symbols for the nation respond to the land's overdevelopment and morph into the evil twin to the Lush Land: the Blighted Land and its allegories of dystopia. In fact, soon after the failure of Albizu-led nationalism and following the ELA's program of massive urban development, the vivid depictions of the Lush Land become images of a ruined landscape. Ana Lydia Vega paints a vivid picture of the alteration in 2008: "los tapones crucifican la paciencia. Las bocinas taladran la cabeza. Las curvas invitan al desbarranque. Las maromas de los conductores cortan la respiración. [. . .] *El paisaje, precisamente el paisaje*, es lo que está ausente" (*Mirada* 36 [my italics]; the traffic jams crucify one's patience. The car horns drill into one's head. The curves invite one to go over into a sheer drop. The antics of the drivers stop one's breath. [. . .] *The landscape, precisely the landscape*, is what is missing). An added complication is the toll of criminality, which Vega says changes the panorama into a charnel house: "En patios, carreteras, bosques, montes, llanos, ríos y playas, una descomunal mortaja de huesos arropa este arrecife a la deriva entre dos continentes" ("La pelona"; In playgrounds, roads, forests, mountains, plains, rivers, and beaches, a huge shroud of bones envelops this reef adrift between two continents).

Also emblematic of the Blighted Land is Hugo Ríos Cordero's 2010 story "Coloso" (Colossus), which presents a view covered by the miasma of violent death and singles out our old friend, the sugarcane *central*, as "una silueta perdida en el paisaje verde del valle" (11; a silhouette lost in the green landscape of the valley). This story hinges on a discarded corpse in the abandoned *central*; a metonymy for the island, a dead body in a dead colonial economy. The nameless narrator watches the genderless body rot and become absorbed *into* the soil, becoming a stain on the landscape, "una silueta marrón en el suelo verde" (12; a brown silhouette in the green ground). A bitter return to the land, indeed.

For a Latino writer, the disillusionment that comes from the contrast between the idyll and the real island can result in feelings of betrayal and even hatred. Abraham Rodríguez Jr. stated that he "hated" the island on his last visit because "it was all concrete" (Hernández, *Voices* 145).

A comparison to the French Départements d'Outre-Mer (Martinique and Guadeloupe) is useful. Both areas (Puerto Rico and the DOMs) suffered similar processes of modernity. Alain Anselin says that the changes on the French islands are similar to Puerto Rico's in that they were a "profound mutation" that resulted from "declining sugar exports, emigration, and *the increasing number of cars*. A rural, colonial world quickly vanished" (113; my italics). The commonly accepted verdict on the death of the landscape, in the French islands as in Puerto Rico, is that neocolonial forces—overcrowding along with developers' greed and government lack of oversight—paved paradise with roads.

This does not mean that the landscape ceases to exist in the National Imagination; on the contrary, popular patriotism can cling to those images and their sentimental values even more. Given the push-pull cultural forces outlined in earlier chapters, it's no surprise that the Lush

Land is usually *implicitly* bemoaned when the island is represented as the Blighted Land.

But the real-life map of the island itself offers the blueprint of environmental disaster, if one wants to contemplate the rise of the concrete wasteland. The real topographic map of Puerto Rico (not the commonly pristine cultural icon) shows an astonishing density of roads. Gone is the nineteenth-century sublime landscape, along with the painterly images of green land and blue sea lauded in dream nation depictions, which now remain mostly in nationalist nostalgia or, to the chagrin of highbrow culture buffs, in marketing campaigns for commodities and for the tourism industry. How did we get from the verdant land to the stifling asphalt?

The change from green to gray in a car-bound life is confirmed, surely, by the general transport data for workers in Puerto Rico.[2] The daily commute, like the nation's path in general, is difficult. *Tendeciaspr.com* says that, "One in eight people takes more than an hour to get to their jobs" (23 Aug. 2009). The statistics cover the time of departure of workers from 12:00 a.m.(!) to 7:00 a.m. Why so many cars? According to the data, 98 percent of the population works outside the home but only 5 percent have access to and use public transportation. In one of these statistical comparisons that attempt to put visual value to data, it turns out that "Puerto Rico now has 25,647 kilometers of road [. . .] if all the roads in Puerto Rico were placed in a straight line one could get to Australia, China or India, and still have left over more than 14,000 kilometers."

Given the prevalence of roads on the island's map, it is easy to see why, since the late twentieth century, so many allegories and stories single out the road, the car, and the traffic jam as representations of Puerto Rico, with its people shown stuck in the middle of a journey, on a road trip to nowhere.

Luis Rafael Sánchez led the pack with his novel *La guaracha del Macho Camacho*. This now classic book was a landmark that responded to Sánchez's vision of the destruction brought on by the irredeemably colonial condition of the country as "esta desamparada isla de cemento" (34; this desolate island of cement) whose problems include but are not limited to three new national traits: a calcified class system, a corrupt government, and a stomach-turning culture of trashy mass media. The stifling island traffic jam (which the book blames on neocolonial socioeconomic conditions) leads Sánchez to neobaroque linguistic flights of fancy in his "búsqueda de una redención por *el paisaje*" (*Macho Camacho* 99 [my italics]; search for redemption by *the landscape*).

Sánchez presents a Traffic Jam Nation that cannot move forward despite—in fact, ironically, because of—the many roads laid out over the landscape. The streets of the novel are either mired in traffic jams or thronged by strikers. This depiction of modern misery is not new to this particular work since, as Efraín Barradas says, "with *En cuerpo de camisa* Sánchez begins to describe a new path that represents a break with a long Puerto Rican literary tradition: the idealization of the peasant" (*Para leer* 69). It also represents a break with the idealization of the landscape.

Sánchez's oeuvre progressively hammers at the degradation of the landscape and the people who inhabit it. A writer who has remained committed to the ideal of independence, he highlights the island's dilapidation, making sure to blame the colonial condition and atrocious lack of planning for the Traffic Jam Nation.

The characters in *Macho Camacho* are of a piece with the nightmarish urban landscape. What ties them together is the traffic jam choking their lives on a Wednesday at 5:00 p.m.; both time and movement are at a standstill. The characters are caricatures or stereotypes, distortions of another common patriotic allegory, *La Gran Familia Puertorriqueña*. The gap between the wealthy (Vincente, Graciela, and Benny) and the poor (La Madre, who is Vicente's lover, her son, and her neighbor Doña Chon) is signaled by their mode of transport: the rich travel in Mercedes Benz and Ferraris; the poor take the bus.

Macho Camacho's language also echoes the trauma of daily living. Vicente's speech, for instance, is a parody of the Constipated Nation; his redundancy, tautology, and snakelike meandering speech lead nowhere, just like the traffic jam. Later Sánchez found an ingenious solution to the problem of the traffic jam and the cacophony of roads in his equally famous "La guagua aérea," which leapfrogs the clogged streets and takes the allegory of nation into midair.

The long reach of *Macho Camacho*'s influence appears still in 1995 in Daniel Torres's novel/graphic novel *Cabronerías o historias de tres cuerpos* (Cabronerías or stories of three bodies), which features the main verse from *Macho Camacho*'s guaracha as its first epigraph. Torres's work can be read as an homage to Sánchez since most of its lead characters are variations of Vicente and La Madre, but with a queer spin. *Historias de tres cuerpos* also parodies the symbolic Family Home (and its extended meaning of the Nation) by calling a homosexual whorehouse *La Casa*.

Ana Lydia Vega also reconfigures the allegories of the journey, the car, and the road in her story "Cuento en camino" (A tale on the road), which begins with an epigraph from Chaucer's *Canterbury Tales*, signaling that the Puerto Rican nation is again in transit, telling tales (and writing the nation) on the road. Vega represents the Puerto Rican nation through different community types crammed into a public car, a Puerto Rican mode of transport for the poor and working classes with many inconveniences in common with buses. The characters, who are from different walks of life, tell stories about a variety of social situations. Vega's portrayals of the national idiosyncrasies are, like a road trip, full of interruptions, repetitions, pauses, and unexpected stops. Gender and race issues remain the subtext of the travelers' conversations. One of the things the story notes over and over is how machismo continues to be rampant on the island.

Anarchic machismo is the obvious subject of the tale-within-a-tale of a father with thirty-seven children and thirty-seven women. This exaggerated fertility rate shows how neocolonial dependency makes a man abandon his responsibilities, becoming reliant on government handouts and leading to his families' dependency on the informal economy. The father character is also Vega's spin on the old *jíbaro*. According to the dude telling the tale, the peasant supported his thirty-seven households by planting a little, but was mostly dependent on the informal economy and food stamps provided by Uncle Sam (*Falsas crónicas* 178).

Vega, like José Luis González before her, makes the folkloric figure a cunning villager who tries to defeat the big-city folk, the capital bureaucracy, and, in sum, colonialism; he is like a contemporary Juan Bobo—the hero in Puerto Rican folk tales who always comes out ahead. When Vega's *jíbaro* has a tax problem and needs to explain his finances to the Treasury Department, he takes his children and instructs them to make a commotion in the government offices so that in the end he doesn't have to answer to the government.

This "happy" ending brings up strong objections from another of the characters in the public car, a religious lady from one of the charismatic faiths who indignantly protests that the father in the story (who was admired by all for his hyperfertility) didn't really contribute much to his families since the most hidden, alternative economy is still women's labor, "¡Qué bonito, ah! Como a él no le tocaba cambiar culeros sucios ni guayar plátanos pal sancocho" (178; That's rich, ha! Because he didn't have to change dirty diapers or grind plantains for the stew). The story has a self-reflexive ending in which the writer (with a capital *W*) who had been in the public car but had refused to tell stories, uses these stories for her own written tales.

The main character in Mayra Santos Febres's story "Dulce pesadilla, Abnel" (Sweet nightmare, Abnel) also lives the daily torture of having to take public transportation in a crowded, congested bus (like Sánchez's La Madre in *Macho Camacho*). Santos Febres depicts the experience vividly, the inside of a bus is like intestinal walls. This visceral metaphor reappears in the story called "Oráculos urbanos" (Urban oracles) in which the street is labeled an intestine. The public bus in "Dulce pesadilla" is like a world apart with its own graffiti, which is in turn like the flow of the nation's conscience: "Cristo te ama, Cógele el culo al prójimo, Libertad para los presos políticos, Carmen y Caco forever" (*Pez* 28; Jesus loves you, Fuck your neighbors, Freedom for political prisoners, Carmen and Caco forever). This brief list summarizes four important national tics: charismatic religious fervor, gritty and rude cynicism, *independentista* nationalism, and the jumble of Spanglish.

In "Dulce pesadilla, Abnel," once again, we have the allegory of the traffic jam standing in for the nation, but here it connects closely to the protagonist's unfulfilled desires. As she rides the bus, she is in agonies because being stuck in the traffic jam means that she won't make it back home in time to spy on her naked neighbor, the Abnel of the title:

> Las 5:50. La guagua vira vertiginosa la Loíza; todo parece ir bien. Pero de repente el vehículo se encuentra de frente con tremendo tapón. Pasan tres minutos . . . cuatro. La guagua no se mueve. Permanece encajada como un quiste putrefacto. 'Dios mío, ¿por qué me has abandonado?' piensa, suspirando. Las 6:05. ¿Qué sería de ella si la guagua no llega a tiempo? (*Pez* 29)

> 5:50 p.m. The bus turns vertiginously in Loiza Avenue; everything seems fine. But suddenly the vehicle hits smack into a tremendous traffic jam. Three minutes go by . . . four. The bus is not moving. It remains embedded like a putrefying cyst. 'My God, why hast thou forsaken me?' she thinks, sighing. 6:05. What would become of her if the bus does not arrive on time?

The traffic jam stifles movement as well as desire, that is to say, dreams of pleasure, connection, and fulfillment. In Santos Febres's story "Oso Blanco" (White bear), we find once again the same allegory of the nation as an existential traffic jam. This dystopian tale has elements of science fiction in which society is (again) broken and dysfunctional. Yet again we have a character in a car anxiously gazing at the horizon, which this time ends in a prison, "Guiar ansiosa, encontrarse de frente con una hilera interminable de carros y allá en la distancia, el presidio" (25; Driving anxiously, finding up ahead an endless row of cars and there in the distance, the prison). One character is trapped in a car, the other in a prison; both are bound together by the traffic jam. The female characters in the two stories live in urban settings from which they want to escape through eroticism, through passionate desire. In "Oso blanco," the illusory connection of the woman with a prisoner's arm seen through a window provides an incentive for her to live so that she eagerly drives by the prison and suffers the traffic jam in order to see it/him: "volar hacia el expreso, coger tapón, esperar, pasar frente al presidio, esperar [...] esperar en el tapón, la celda se despierta, sale el brazo, que salga el brazo y [...] reconozca el carro verdemonte destartalado y sonría" (29; flying to the expressway, taking the traffic jam, waiting, passing the prison, waiting [...] waiting in the traffic jam, the cell wakes up, out goes the arm, let that arm come out and [...] let it recognize the mountain green dilapidated car and smile). The prose's dismemberment is symptomatic of their lives and their island; chopped into pieces and the only ironic reference to the green of mountains is the rickety car. When, at the end of the story, the connection between the nameless woman and the prisoner (or rather, between their arms) is broken, the result is "el tapón más inmenso en toda la historia mundial de tapones en esta área del Caribe" (55; the biggest traffic jam in the entire history of the world in this area of the Caribbean).

Of course a people can be trapped in other places besides traffic jams; this is how Edgardo Rodríguez Juliá presents Puerto Rico in *El entierro de Cortijo* (from 1983). In the chronicle, he describes the pressure-cooker scene at a funeral as a suffocating mass of many clashing tribes. The people's social and personal identity is inflexibly bound to the social class to which they belong: politicians, musicians, project dwellers, writers, etc. These contending groups come together for the funeral of the famous musician Rafael Cortijo, whose music is one of the few things they all share. Carmen Dolores Hernández makes the connection between funeral and traffic jam clear when she writes about the stifling atmosphere at the funeral, with people yelling, pushing, fainting, and acting out. She says it is "labyrinths in which people are as trapped as in a traffic jam" (Hernández, *A viva voz* 270). The compacted messiness that is contemporary Puerto Rico, overdeveloped, crowded, confused, corrupt, with labyrinthine clashing politics, is the island on display in all these works.

Allegories of the nation as traffic jam, stories featuring cars, roads, and travel are now routine in Puerto Rican culture. For example, the following passage from a poem (from 2007) written by Eugenio García Cuevas offers another iteration of the suffocating vision of island life blasted by road noise and traffic jams:

> Qué triste el compás del vendedor
> de helados derritiéndose en la calle,
> las bocinas espantosas de los carros
> lo ahogan bajo el sol y ya los niños
> apenas descrifran su vieja afinación.
> Ya no hay muchachos en las calles,
> el disco sigue rayado y sus bocinas
> asfixiadas en desesperanza y llanto. (63)

> How sad the beat of the seller
> of ice creams melting on the street,
> the dreadful car horns
> drown him in the sun, and children
> barely decipher his old tune.
> There are no kids on the streets,
> the record is still stuck and its speakers
> smothered in despair and crying

In the 2007 film *Maldeamores*, directed by Carlos Ruiz Ruiz and Mariem Pérez Riera, we see another version of the trapped nation in a car, caught on the road to nowhere. The narrative frame that opens the film features a couple involved in the psychodrama of the war of the sexes while stuck in their car. The only escape is to jump from the moving car—that is to say to flee, to exit, whatever the cost may be.

And who wouldn't long to flee back to that once Lush Land now trampled by asphalt? Edgardo Rodríguez Juliá summarizes the *ubi sunt* lament inspired by this loss, "Todo el paisaje de mi infancia ha desaparecido" (*San Juan* 3; All the landscape of my childhood has disappeared). Even nowadays Puerto Rican writers leap from bemoaning the depredations of modernity to yearning for an agrarian lifestyle in the face of urban anonymity dominated by roads and traffic. Such is the case with Edwin Figueroa's short story "El amolador" (The grinder) (2000), which highlights the island's insufferable urban condition: "Sobre el alfalto húmedo otra vez el chirriar de la llanta [...] entre los mil ruidos de calles, avenidas y autopistas. La multitud se desplaza entregada al isócrono rito crepuscular tras la jornada del día. En cada atascadura la misma estridente,

FIGURE 5. Metropolitan area, 2009. (Photo by María Acosta Cruz)

frenética desesperación" (López-Baralt, *Antología* 472; On the wet asphalt again the squeaking tire [. . .] among the thousand sounds of streets, avenues, and highways. The crowd moves transported by the isochronous rite of twilight day after day. In each blockage the same shrill, frantic desperation). This lament will resonate with you if you've ever traveled the roads of San Juan and gotten caught in one of these.

Life in the San Juan of Eduardo Lalo's *Simone* takes place, "en el mismo centro de un embotellamiento, entre gases tóxicos y claxonazos, en esta mañana que es la misma desde que puedo acordarme" (63; In the very center of a traffic jam, between toxic gases and horns honking, this morning which is the same since I can remember). So that the traffic jam is not only toxic but an expected part of life, an everyday occurrence. As the narrator wanders around the dreaded but (to him) necessary cityscape, the urban streets are so inescapable that they have become the emotional center of his life: "Ni el exilio me libraría de la ciudad. Sencillamente sufriría dos veces: por la ciudad y por estar lejos de ella" (64; Not even exile would free me from the city. I would simply suffer twice as much: for the city and for being far from it).

When he dreams of the island's landscape, it is similar to but different from the traditional depiction: "Soñé con un área del centro de la isla que no existe. Muy montañosa (con montes mucho más altos que los de la Cordillera Central) y grandes precipicios de roca sin vegetación" (37; I dreamed of an area in the center of the island which does not exist. Very mountainous [with hills much taller than those of the Central Range] and large rock cliffs without vegetation).

The colonial condition has fried the land; it is full of empty gestures, consumerism, and traffic jams; he says, "Se me ha ido la vida en esta *Colony Economy*" (60; I've wasted my life in this *Colony Economy*). Far from a Lush Land, Puerto Rico is not even a touristy destination because the sun, that main attraction for visitors, is for the narrator as punishing that of Camus's *L'etranger*.

Could new forms of transport, for instance a more successfully planned version of the Tren Urbano, change the national allegory? Would we be sorry if efficient transportation eliminates the themes and images of roads and traffic jams which tap into national anxieties? As Diana L. Velez says, "Allegories all break down at some point," and so perhaps improvements to Puerto Rican transport systems, should they ever materialize, will swiftly take with them the allegory of the nation stuck in a traffic jam in an endless road.

But considering the *realities* of the island's present state of a landscape crisscrossed by the map of roads, what can a writer do? One option taken by writers like Eduardo Lalo above is to embrace the altered, degraded landscape and its urban reality, forgetting all that was green, forgetting all that was *campo*. Francisco Font Acevedo, for instance, whose short-story collection *La belleza bruta* (The brutal beauty) (2008) portrays Puerto Rico as an urban landscape filled with homicidal thugs, street gangs, prostitution, rampant sexuality and perversions, junk food, and nameless souls as is often seen in brutal realism. In Font Acevedo's eponymous short story, the car-ridden frenetic environment means that, "Nadie camina por caminar en esta ciudad desplazada por el fetiche de los carros y los centros comerciales" (44; No one walks just for the sake of walking in this city displaced by the fetish of cars and malls). He describes Río Piedras in acrid, urban-blight terms: "de día Río Piedras es una ciudad abandonada al sol, de edificaciones de pintura cuarteada y quincalleros desesperados por ganarse un peso; de noche, es territorio de putas, tiradores de drogas, vagabundos y estudiantes desorbitados por el alcohol o la yerba" (44; Río Piedras by day is a city abandoned in the sun, buildings with cracked paint and desperate hawkers out to make a buck, and at night, it's the land of hookers, drug shooters, tramps and students freaked out on alcohol or weed). The unifying element in the Río Piedras landscape is violence, which Font Acevedo calls a "river of blood under the city" that has become a "cohesive symbol" (85), the city's identifying trait. The nation's brand, its trademark, is now violence.

On the other hand, a person can, if so moved, ignore all the signs of overdevelopment, violence, and social strife and seek refuge in nostalgia. For instance, a blog entry titled "Oda a la tierra puertorriqueña" (Ode to the Puerto Rican land) in a major Puerto Rican news outlet shows the endurance of love for the Lush Land. Written by Ángel Cintrón Opio, a "cognition teacher" and blogger for *El Nuevo Día*, this ode to the mother country follows the tradition of José Gautier Benítez et al., romantically lauding an Edenic island, in 2009 no less. Cintrón Opio uses the familiar trope of the mother/nation, a nurturing mother-island that envelops the people in their beloved landscape, reeking of authenticity. Richard Koeningsberg stresses the protective slant of the mother/nation metaphor: "insofar as the nation is experienced, by the nationalist, as a projection of the omnipotent mother, the nationalist tends to feel that, as long as he is contained within the boundaries of the nation, he shall be shielded from the external world" (8). This trope has been used in Caribbean literature since at least the nineteenth century, when José Martí ferociously deployed the allegory for the larger homeland, Latin America, which is a suffering mother in "Nuestra América."

Like a twentieth-century Homer or Hesiod, Cintrón Opio calls upon the nation/muse for inspiration and then launches an unintentionally humorous comparison between that nation/mother and mother hens, "Que la falda de la Patria es amplia y cálida, como las plumas de las gallinas del país, que empollan sus huevos con orgullo y responsabilidad de madre impostergable" ("Oda"; That the *Patria*'s lap is wide and warm, like the feathers of the hens of the country, who hatch their eggs with the pride and responsibility of the inescapable mother). This strange yet morbidly sentimentalized view of the *patria* is then tied, in yet another throwback to nationalist sentiments of the nineteenth century, to a *religious* concept of the nation, "que la Patria es un regalo de Dios" (because the Homeland is a gift from God).

He uses stereotypical iconography of the nation such as flora (mango, tamarind, etc.), the beaches, and the sea as an ornate border to the nation without once alluding to the transformation of the landscape in modern times. No mention of the amazing number of roadworks, or congestion or overdevelopment; nary a Burger King in sight. Cintrón Opio is the florid heir to Gautier Benítez, and so the dream nation lives on. He is proof that people still want to sing odes to the motherland. Or, as he says, that "our tenors and sopranos are enough to sing the well-merited odes." Whither the *reggaetón*?

As we can see, there have been familiar, persistent patterns and literary tropes tied to the beautiful land since at least the seventeenth century. The destruction of such a land has produced its opposite: the allegorical map of the island lived on crisscrossing roads. Nationalist sentiments can work both sides of the symbolic divide. In either case, we can find the family/nation allegory, exceptionalist views of the island (and the inhabitants that represent it), and a stubbornly persistent dream nation.

In the next chapter, we will look at yet another literary/cultural mode of reworking the dream nation. How does history become a symbolic battleground, or better yet, the playing fields, for the (dashed) hopes for the nation? We examine authors such as Olga Nolla, Rosario Ferré, Magali García Ramis, and Edgardo Rodríguez Juliá, among others, who use heroic and antiheroic stories to refashion the meanings of the dream nation.

4 / Dream History, Dream Nation

A satisfying and long-standing cultural mechanism for those who regret that independence never came to pass is to rewrite/reinvent Puerto Rican history in order to recycle, reimagine, and reconstitute the bits of the past that relate to (dashed) hopes for an independent nation. From these arise interesting stories, fascinating heroes and heroines, and allegories full of significance. And even if you have doubts about the political viability of independence, its use as historical background can spice up stories.

The critic Silvio Torres-Saillant notes how Caribbean cultures have "inventive ways of looking at the past, including what Édouard Glissant has called a 'prophetic vision of the past'" (137). Glissant indeed spoke of how Caribbean cultures are obsessed with re-creating the past in order to correct, or at least forget, historical wrongs: "The past, to which we were subjected, which has not yet emerged as history for us, is, however, obsessively present. The only duty of the writer is to explore this obsession" (63–64). Many Puerto Rican writers have taken that duty to heart.

One of the most visible consequences of the nationalist context to Puerto Rican culture is, quite simply, mythmaking. José Rodríguez Vázquez says in very plain terms that "*Albizuist* national history was a mythologizing narrative" (236). In traditional nationalist thinking, the dream nation existed even before modern times, especially during the times of Borikén (before any invaders). A parallel belief is in the *authenticity* of Puerto Rican national identity under Spain's rule despite the fact that the island wasn't free in any sense (except that the United States had not set foot on it).

The island's history (real or made up) becomes fertile ground for stories and iconography that tie into the enduring popularity of struggles for liberty as well as to heroic figures. As we have seen before, the need for Puerto Rican heroes is long-standing; nineteenth-century Puerto Rican literature, for instance, is brimming with heroes, particularly those taken from Taíno mythology. The idealization of the Taíno, indeed, is commonplace in Puerto Rican culture, particularly graphic arts. (Indeed, the subject is too large for the scope of this chapter.) Suffice it to say that works from every era—starting in the sixteenth and seventeenth centuries—unabashedly worship the irreproachable and brave Taíno and paradoxically also his foe, the noble Spaniard. Forgotten in many of these tales is of course a third national component: the African slave.

Most notably there is the eye-catching persistence of Agüeybaná (or Agüeibana), the most famous Taíno cacique. His centrality as a "Puerto Rican"—he was no such thing since he lived in prenational times—hero begins at least with such sixteenth-century works of Juan de Castellano as "Arenga de Agüeibana" (Agüeibana's harangue) and "Muerte de Agüeibana" (Death of Agüeibana). The latter has the native chieftain full of "evil intent" to take arms against the Spaniards in revenge for the suffering they have caused his people. Castellano's "Elegía VI" (Elegy VI), which celebrates Juan Ponce de León, presents a more pathetic, peaceful Agüeybaná with an aging mother by his side. Castellanos, writing in 1589, portrays Ponce de León as a builder of a tranquil Puerto Rico and Agüeybaná as a noble, peaceful chieftain, a "varón prudente" (18; prudent man) whose son and heir will take up the fight against enslavement. Both Ponce de León and the Taíno leader became recurring characters in Puerto Rican literature—Ponce de León is, for instance, a dreamy administrator in Manuel Méndez Ballester's *Isla cerrera* (1937). The conquistador is also a source of inspiration for the lead character in Esmeralda Santiago's *Conquistadora* (2012). Reading the journals of her ancestor (who had come to the island with Ponce de León in 1508), Ana, the spunky heroine, "despaired that she was born female and centuries too late to be an explorer and adventurer" (16). She decides to leave her home in Spain and emulate her ancestor. Later, the novel features detailed planning for a celebration of the 355th anniversary of Ponce de León's first settlement in Puerto Rico, including the exhumation of his remains and his reinterment in the island's cathedral (330).

Clearly Agüeybaná also continues as literary inspiration well into the twenty-first century, for instance in Jalil Sued Badillo's *Agüeybaná el bravo* (2008). Sued Badillo's historiographical book about colonial times centers on the Taíno chieftain's epoch and illuminates the many sources that gave rise to his legend and his popularity as a literary character. Sued Badillo's aim is to debunk the image we see in Juan de Castellanos and other portrayals of the Taínos as long-suffering victims. Using anthropological and historical sources, Sued Badillo traces how the indigenous peoples' defeat was not without dignity and struggles: "the Indian of Borinquen did not disappear from his land without resistance, he did not merge with the invader without complaint, he did not die without lament" (197). After tracing many instances of resistance by the Taínos, Sued Badillo ends his book citing a poem by famous *independentista* writer Juan Antonio Corretjer. Titled "Agueibana," it paints a portrait of a fierce cacique whom Corretjer compares to a jaguar. The poem urges Puerto Ricans to follow the cacique's example and fight in defense of their homeland: "Ausculta, Puerto Rico, a tu jaguar dormido. A filo de machete es que hay que hacer la patria" (209; Listen, Puerto Rico, to your sleeping jaguar. On the edge of a machete is how one has to make the homeland). The nationalist poet, as is often the case, uses Agueibana as a symbol of the valiant quest for freedom *avant la lettre*. A hero born in a time before Puerto Rico was a Spanish colony, before the United States, before modernity stifled the island, and also a brave champion of liberty who foreshadows the struggle for independence that Corretjer yearned for. That's a lot of symbolism in just one hero.

Seva: The Invented Real History

Alternative history has proved a fruitful subgenre with which to explore the dream nation. The shining example is Luis López Nieves's 1983 story/novella *Seva*. This story of a fictional town that resists the U.S. invasion of 1898 to the death made a huge splash when it appeared and continues to be discussed, taught, and studied. In 2008, it was the subject of a documentary film, *Seva vive*, which takes as its starting point the story's initial impact and enduring popularity. The documentary features a debate among talking-head historians who argue about the importance of conventional heroism, violence, and sacrifice in the story's definition not just of Puerto Rican history but also of Puerto Ricanness itself. Juan Manuel García Passalacqua defends the story of Seva because, in his estimation, it redeems Puerto Ricans against the charge of docility.

Fernando Picó and Carlos Pabón, on the other hand, question the need for violent heroics, with Pabón pointing out that Puerto Rican daily life is already overflowing with everyday, banal violence. He also states that the story conflates heroism with victimhood: "Why the search for victimization, for that epic, for that tragedy?" (*Seva vive*).

Frances Negrón-Muntaner says that Puerto Ricans' sense of shame about their failure to become an independent nation—or to commit to statehood—makes Puerto Rican culture "a strategy for saving face" (*Boricua Pop* 5). In that regard, *Seva* deals with the shame, the wound that cannot be healed: the lack of resistance by the Puerto Rican population when the United States invaded the island in 1898. *Seva* offers a shot at redemption.

But what really happened in Puerto Rico when the Americans marched into town? Apart from scattered resistance, the real-life reception to the U.S. troops was positive, even joyful: "[U.S. general Nelson] Miles started disembarking his troops in Puerto Rico on July 25, 1898. They were joyously received. One of his companions called the invasion a *fête des fleurs*. Some newspapers referred to it as a 'military picnic.' There was no resistance to speak of, and the armistice was proclaimed on August 12" (Trías Monge 26). Because *independentismo* largely has had a binary view of Spain/good versus United States/bad, the lack of resistance in 1898 was ripe for López Nieves to rewrite; the tale of a dream nation that fights was needed to fill the *horror vacui*, the void of history.

Seva counteracts that historical story line of Puerto Ricans receiving the Americans with open arms with a categorically, exaggeratedly opposite fiction: a people who fought to the death. It was an instant *succés de scandale*, as critics such as Estelle Irizarry and Carmen Dolores Hernández have discussed. Hernández, indeed, calls the author an "enfant terrible" of Puerto Rican letters and highlights that *Seva* made López Nieves notorious (*A viva voz* 317). It was crucial that the story was published in the pro-independence flagship *Claridad*, which meant that López Nieves was preaching to the choir—since the likely readership was already primed for heroic tales of 1898, a year fraught with symbolic connotations for the newspaper's base. Mario R. Cancel argues that the destined public was "eager for arguments denouncing the cruelty of the colonial past" (*Literatura y narrativa* 13).

But is Seva a death or a birth? Martyrs and bloodshed help crystallize nations, at least according to the standard nationalist model. Blood and guts make for zippier tales of the nation's origins than other means to the birth of a nation; one hasn't often read a gripping tale of a nation being born by peaceful democratic processes. José Rodríguez Vázquez puts it succinctly: the standard nationalist, or *Albizuist*, nation-building project favors "the sacrificial model of blood shed in liberation struggles as the foundational act of nationhood *par excellence*" (216).

History in Puerto Rico made a very weak, collaborationist story in 1898. There was some scattered resistance to the United States, but logic says that if there was any mass resistance in that moment, it needed to have taken place in a remarkably short time since the U.S. troops marched in through Guánica on July 25 and the armistice that brought peace was signed on August 12.

This does not mean that there was no resistance at all. There were a few discrete pockets of uprisings. Mariel C. Marrero-García and Freddie Rodríguez's pro-independence documentary, *Dialogando sobre independentismos: Entre votos, consignas y trincheras, 1890–1959* (Talking about *independentismos*: Among votes, slogans, and trenches, 1890–1959), highlights the persistence of *independentismo* from the nineteenth century to 1959. It makes the case for significant resistance in 1898, stating that on August 13, 1898 (after the armistice); an uprising in the town of Ciales was led by a man called Ventura Casellas who had the support of between three hundred and four hundred *paisanos* who proclaimed the Republic of Puerto Rico. Another revolt happened in Mayagüez and was led by Juancho Bascarán; yet another took place in San Germán (with no leader of record). All of which begs the question, What did they want? Were all the would-be patriots defending a new republic of Puerto Rico, or were they defending Spain? In any case, no matter how many revolts there actually were, the United States didn't worry overmuch because it quickly *demilitarized* the area. Of the eighteen thousand troops the United States landed in July 1898, only three thousand remained by November 1899 (*Dialogando*).

By most accounts, the islanders did not put up much of a fight because they were divided. The historian Álvaro M. Rivera Ruiz states that people at the time fell into three camps: those who mourned the passing of Spanish control of the island; those who yearned for independence; and "the overwhelming majority of Puerto Ricans, especially the poorer sectors of the country, who saw with great hope the invasion of the 'good' empire of '98" (58). Many, such as the annexionists within the Partido Republicano and the Partido Federal, welcomed the United States because they thought that country would live up to its reputation for constitutional liberties and rule of law, as well as for the shelter of its emerging economic clout. These American achievements must have seemed very impressive to an island long oppressed by Spain—a monarchy with a less conspicuous belief in democracy (at the time). In fairness to the *independentistas*, the much-vaunted U.S. civil liberties took a while getting to the island; case in point, islanders did not become U.S. citizens until 1917.

Unconcerned with facts—and why should it be since it is literature?—*Seva* exaggerates the popular support against the American occupation forces in 1898. Carlos Pabón notes that "*Seva* . . . is a foundational myth invented to counter the support of large sectors to the U.S. invasion and the absence of a heroic epic in 1898" (242). The story brings the dream nation into its own by coming to the rescue of national pride.

In the imaginary town of Seva not only is there no shameful surrender, but when the Americans invade, the town is somehow ready for them (the story doesn't tell exactly how the townspeople prepared). In any case, Seva ambushes and humiliates the American forces. In the end, General Miles (whose fictional diary is the source of much of the tale) admits that the American forces succeeded only because of the betrayal of a Puerto Rican Benedict Arnold, whom the novel calls Luis M. Rivera (which is, of course, an allusion to a real historical figure, Luis Muñoz Rivera). After being defeated in Seva and heading to Guánica (the real-life disembarking place), the Americans attack Seva again; it offers a resistance that is, according to Miles, "feroz, organizada y heroica" (30; fierce, organized, and heroic). In the end, the American forces can only win by bombarding and massacring the township so that (nearly) every man, woman, and child is killed; later the entire area is razed and subsequently erased from historical memory. Ramón Duchesne labels the tale one of "martyr" resistance (review). So the story is more about memory and forgetting; its literary conceit is rescuing the pride in the dream nation through a lost (false) memory.

Punching up its impact is its breathlessly melodramatic tone. For instance, General Miles compares the month-long resistance of the town with the U.S. War of Independence and furthermore says it was worthy of Wellington or El Cid (this last, says Estelle Irizarry in *Seva vive*, should have been proof of the story's fictionality, since an American general probably wouldn't have heard of Spain's medieval hero). The only frame of reference Miles has is the heroism he had seen at Wounded Knee—thus establishing a genocidal background for him.

More than heroes, nations crave martyrs. López Nieves's weaving of fact and fiction hit a national nerve. The story's suspense is heightened because only one child escapes, and he is later traced by the historian character that investigates the forgotten town and devotes his life to organizing the (fake) data that comprise the story. The historian then suffers a satisfyingly mysterious end when he goes to infiltrate an American military base and is never heard from again (another martyr).

López Nieves's stated intent was not to create a ripping yarn but to question history and national origins; in order to do so he mixed real-life events and people into his fictional story. Furthermore, he published the story without saying it was fiction, indeed, refusing to allow publication unless the label "fiction" was removed. The publication caused a sensation reminiscent of Orson Welles's radio transmission of *War of the Worlds* in 1938 because many people thought the story was real. After it was exposed as a hoax, the author said it was "a literary gag" (Hernández, *A viva voz* 317), but even then pro-independence defenders went on wishing it were real.

Among the literary community, it caused a split along party lines according to their affiliation with or questioning of establishment *independentismo*. For pro-independence writers, the value of the work was self-evident. López Nieves basked in the adulation his work inspired, with Carmen Dolores Hernández telling him, "you created a foundational myth of heroism" (Hernández, *A viva voz* 318). With its gory bloodshed, *Seva* crystallized the yearning for a patriotic, massive heroic battle of resistance at a key symbolic event in dream-nation history. The book is still in print—the most recent edition is from 2006—proving that López Nieves's inventiveness fills a continuing emotional.

On the other hand, the venerable José Luis González proclaimed his confusion over the whole incident. Initially he thought López Nieves was satirizing "la mitomanía que ha plagado a un considerable sector del independentismo" (*Nueva visita* 120; the mythomania that has plagued a considerable sector of *independentismo*). González said he had taxed López Nieves with the matter and was disconcerted to hear *Seva*'s author affirm that he had indeed wanted to craft a new myth, "para fortalecer el orgullo nacional de los puertorriqueños" (*Nueva visita* 122; to strengthen Puerto Rican national pride). Like González, not everyone was enchanted with the new myth. Carlos Pabón counters that this new story is conservative, elitist, and oriented toward conspiracy theories and moreover that it follows hard-core *independentista* ideology: "*Seva* is nothing but the culmination of an elitist and moralist national discourse which has combined the notion of 'trauma' with a conspirational idea of history to justify why 'the people do not understand' the true implications of 1898 [which] is a narrative in the tradition of the Illustrated elitism of *independentismo*" (258).

Like it or not, by creating a new myth López Nieves connected in an almost Jungian way to what can only be called the collective unconscious of *independentistas* everywhere. Rafael Grillo buys into it and singles out López Nieves's inventive mix of styles and genres as key to the book's realism effect, "*Seva* is a mixture of letters, fragments of newspapers, testimonial sources, photos; that is how an investigative report is built. All that made a fictional story true."

History, it turns out—like the nation—is most popular when it hinges on dreams and imagination. After *Seva's* fevered reception, the author denied the *objectivity* of history itself as a field of knowledge, equating it with fiction: "I think history is fiction, I do not accept that it is a science, not even remotely. All history is interpretation and all countries create their own story. [. . .] We must shake off this negative view of ourselves which others have given us, and build our own positive vision of Puerto Rico" (Hernández, *A viva voz* 319–20). López Nieves follows this thinking to its logical (and brazen) conclusion, saying that stories that have symbolic value are as true as history: "I have no doubt that the story of Seva is true. Remember that writers work with symbols. It may not be literally true, but the story of Seva is a symbol of the way we have been invaded and dominated" (Hernández, *A viva voz* 320).

And at least one historian, Mario R. Cancel, has defended López Nieves's creativity on the grounds that nations and history are intertwined in complex ways: "*Seva* showed that, as suggested by Ernest Renan in 1882, the Nation also depended on 'historical mistakes.' Renan said that 'historical studies (are) often a danger for nationality'" ("*Seva*: Historia de una (re)lectura" ["*Seva*: History of a (re)-reading]). Cancel, however, edits Renan's emphasis on the forgetting of past *true* violence; Renan's full passage from "What Is a Nation?" reads: "Forgetting, I would even go so far as to say historical error, is a crucial factor in the creation of a nation, which is why progress in historical studies often constitutes a danger for [the principle of] nationality. Indeed, historical enquiry brings to light deeds of violence which took place at the origin of all political formations."

Writing the dream nation by means of a rip-roaring epic in fact involves a sleight-of-hand spin on Renan, who was pointing out how national formation works with forgetting of real past atrocities. López Nieves's argument in the interview previously cited is that history/fiction should be dexterously constructed to *forget* what really happened and to *persuade* by means of fiction, of emotion-laden storytelling. *Seva* tapped into the collective wish for a *substitute* history of 1898, which answered the desire for righting what was for many people a historical wrong (of not having really fought back) and inventing violence to save face. The story worked *because* of its hyperbolic boldness.

The force, persistence, and sheer stubbornness of the use of a dream nation was apparent later when López Nieves imagined a scene using a universally known stereotype of Puerto Ricanness, the *jíbaro*, to tell a story of popular support for Spain in 1898. He imagines how an average deep-country "peasant from Morovis," a *monarchist* who loved Spain, must have felt when he heard the news that the United States had taken over the island. This *jíbaro* (i.e., an authentic Puerto Rican) fresh from the mountain reacts with shocked dismay on being informed that, "la reina de España ya no manda aquí" (Hernández, A viva voz 321; the queen of Spain doesn't reign here anymore). López Nieves's microstory runs completely counter to everything history says about how ordinary Puerto Ricans reacted to the change of regime. One could argue that this bit of fiction plays with what Cancel has called "the senile fictions worked from within the Hispanophilic Cultural Nationalism domesticated by the culture of the most conservative populism" because of of its realiance on national stereotypes and the invented sympathy of the small-farmer class to Spain's rule over the island ("Seva: historia de una (re)lectura"). The opposite, in fact, of all that José Luis González had said about Puerto Rico's culture.

By way of contrast, Ángel Lozada's 1996 novel *La patografía* (The patography) features the opposite of the heroic town, since it focuses on a marginal character rejected by a unified people. Lozada's novel demolishes the notion of national heroism because in his story the townspeople are unheroic, hypocritical, oppressive, and hateful. His town, called Mayagüez like the real-life Mayagüez, is the anti-Seva; at the end of the novel, the unified town unites kills the gay protagonist. Lozada's magical realist novel presents Puerto Rico as a dystopia and Puerto Ricans as complicit with the worst domestic and social violence. Mayagüez, where most of the novel takes place, is a town that persecutes, tortures, and makes a martyr of a boy who has turned into a duck (the homophobic Puerto Rican slur is "pato"): "toda aquella ciudad patofóbica, [...] abrieron fuego por primera vez en la historia de aquella isla, como machos, valientemente, contra aquel niño inocente" (312; the whole patophobic city [...] opened fire for the first time in the history of that island, like machos, valiantly, against that innocent child). After they kill the *pato,* the people are

llenos de gozo, porque por primera vez el pueblo de Mayagüez se había unido en un solo pensar, en un solo espíritu, en una sola mente, para combatir el enemigo [. . .] aquel patocidio fue el único y más alto heroísmo, la única obra de valentía, la más alta defensa de los valores de la Isla del Cordero, y el más sublime acto de hombría que aquel pueblo mayagüezano cometió jamás. (313)

filled with joy because for the first time the town of Mayagüez had joined in one thought, one spirit, one mind, to fight the enemy [. . .] that *patocidio* was unique and highest heroism, the only work of courage, the highest defense of the values of the Isle of the Lamb, and the most sublime act of manhood that the people of Mayagüez ever accomplished.

Along with a critique of the macho-masculine bent of much heroism, Lozada's novel gets to the bitter heart of nationalist epics in which unity comes at the expense of minorities.

In 2005, López Nieves again told a story of 1898. A short story called "En la muralla de San Juan" (On San Juan wall) is a smaller-scale alternate history. In it, he imagines the life of a young woman called Verónica Toledo, a casualty of the (symbolic) shots fired when the Americans entered San Juan Bay. Lopez Nieves cannot help showing his true faith when he imagines a life for the dead girl. He uses the character to trace the ideal life-story arc of an *independentista* speculating that had she not been killed by the American forces, she would have been a standard-bearer for leftist causes: "Se habría hecho defensora de los pobres y de los perseguidos políticos y de las mujeres maltratadas, y como resultado natural de su crianza, de su época y de su grande inteligencia, es obvio que, a pesar de las protestas airadas de toda la familia, Verónica la Nieta habría salido independentista (She would have become a defender of the poor and of the politically persecuted and of battered women, and as a natural result of her upbringing, her time and her great intelligence, it is obvious that, despite the angry protests of the entire family, Granddaughter Veronica would have become an *independentista*) ("En la muralla de San Juan"). Of course.

Memory, as many thinkers have shown, is a slippery, thorny road. One popular postcolonial critic, Homi K. Bhabha, says that memory "is never a quiet act of introspection or retrospection. It is a painful remembering, a putting together of the dismembered past to make sense of the trauma of the present" (63). The pain and trauma involved in Puerto Rico's past becomes the stuff of fiction, national culture as therapy even if using false memories.

The Need for Heroes

López Nieves channeled what Édouard Glissant said, in *Caribbean Discourses*, is a *need* for heroes in the Caribbean: "the defeats of heroes are necessary to the solidarity of communities" (68). Glissant speaks of rescuing forgotten real heroes for the national memory; specifically those from Martinique, but also figures who impacted the wider Latin American community such as José Martí and Marcus Garvey. Glissant touches on two points that help explain the appeal of independence epics for Puerto Rican culture: (*a*) while Puerto Rican independence inarguably has been defeated at the polls, the heroes it created—the heroes whose vision of independence never became political reality—populate the Puerto Rican national imagination, both in highbrow and popular culture; and (*b*) that the presence of the hero bolsters a people's self-confidence and sense of dignity.

John D. Perivolaris discusses the implications of heroism in Puerto Rico because of its interconnectedness with Latin America: "In the context of an unfulfilled Puerto Rican (and Caribbean) nationalism, what is the place, if any, of heroism in recent discussions of Puerto Rico? Here I am referring to the fact that the validation of a patriotic sense of nationalism that emerged in other Latin-American countries, through successful Independence, and more recently, revolutionary struggles, has never been possible in Puerto Rico, where such struggles have been both stifled by the insufficient development of a powerful Creole elite and made less attractive to the population at large by the elitism and oppressive Hispanism of their leaders" (691). I don't agree with Perivolaris that all *independentista* leaders were/are Hispanophiles, but there is no disputing that successful independence validated the other Latin American nations, and Puerto Rico got left behind. Nevertheless, the need for authentication can be fertile ground—Glissant would note—for stories of failed heroes whose appeal is *heightened* by their defeats, for inventing the missing real-life epics. In *Seva*, which has not one hero but instead has a collective (town) hero, we find the fictional Puerto Rican *Fuenteovejuna*, a shared dream of righteous unity. And in *La patografía*, we have its opposite, the victory of the mob.

López Nieves offers the clearest example that the unrealized dream of independence can be deflected into fictions that, in revisiting, revising, and reinventing national history, write the dream nation outright. *Seva* also exposes the fundamental *neediness* of the dream of independence. López Nieves is a member of the generation of 1970 who often grappled with Puerto Rican history. Children born around the time of the newly constituted commonwealth, the ELA, these writers, when they reached adulthood, saw through the sham sovereignty of Muñoz Marín's construct and developed a literary tic for rewriting Puerto Rican history. Other members of that generation—as well as younger writers—have revisited the character, provenance, and gender of nationalist heroes to escape the grip of actual history. The most complicated narratives mix and match the past, questioning what Puerto Rico was and what it has become. The roster includes some of the most widely read Puerto Rican late-twentieth-century authors: Edgardo Rodríguez Juliá, Rosario Ferré, Magali García Ramis, Olga Nolla, Luis López Nieves, and Ana Lydia Vega.

Edgardo Rodríguez Juliá's historical novels, *La renuncia del héroe Baltasár* (The renunciation of the hero Baltasar) and *La noche oscura del Niño Avilés* (The dark night of the Niño Avilés), are in many ways reverse images of *Seva*. Both turn the search for heroes on its head and instead feature antiheroes, and yet both are written in such a way as to exaggerate and expose the sickening underbelly of the Spanish colony. *La noche oscura* features just as much violence and gore as *Seva* (and a lot more sexuality) and, like *La renuncia* and the nonhistorical reportage *El entierro de Cortijo*, gives the role of protagonists to Afro-Caribbean communities. In *La noche oscura*, Rodríguez Juliá pronounces the dream of history to be a nightmare: "Como los hombres sueñan, así también sueña ese oscuro esfuerzo humano que llamamos la Historia" (294; As men dream dreams, just so that dark human endeavor we call History also dreams).

La noche oscura, unlike *Seva*, features a multiplicity of cities and townships, therefore the nation has no symbolic center. The lost rebel city reportedly founded by the Niño Avilés, which is built on a swamp, is nowhere and anywhere at the same time. This watery environment is a city of "leyendas y canales" (9; legends and canals) that later disappears from history; it is described by one of the many unreliable narrators as having been suppressed by historical memory. Through its length the novel overflows with visions of cities such as a Nueva Venecia, Nueva Jerusalén, the city of God, the "Leviatán" city, various rebel and runaway towns, especially Yyaloide (a made-up rebel town like Seva), "la ciudad del vagar perpetuo" (225; the city of perpetual wandering), a "ciudad extraviada" (lost city) made of ships, a city with inverted towers (107), an invisible city, a "dark" city, visions of three cities in the air, Arcadia, Utopia, and, of course, the city around which all of these appear, the actual San Juan Bautista. These multiple cities that attempt to arise, do arise, and inevitably fall are all allegories for the decentered dream nation whose construction is never finished.

The instability of history and of the nation coagulates in the central allegory of a city built in a swamp by runaway slaves, which weaves in and out of the novel. It is also significant that the multiplying cities are inevitably all unfinished because "la ciudad humana es siempre un esfuerzo inconcluso" (243; the human city is always an unfinished effort). This is particularly true for the chimerical towns portrayed as being built on water: "La ciudad lacustre es un recinto precario" (302; The lake city is precarious ground). Unfinished, chimerical, precarious, dreamlike.

In *La noche oscura,* the figure of authority, Bishop Trespalacios, sums up the contrast between the messiness of a real city versus utopian fantasies: "Utopía lo que quiere decir es que no tiene espacio en el tiempo... —Pues esa ciudad está jodia... —Justo, y de ahí su pretensión maliciosa. Es la manía de querer encontrarse fuera de la historia. Ese es el verdadero sueño de Leviatán, la pesadilla nuestra" (320 [my italics]; What Utopia means is that it does not have a space in time... —Well, that city is fucked... —Just so, and hence its wicked pretension. It is the obsession of wanting to be outside of history. That is the real dream of Leviathan, our nightmare).

In this novel, Rodríguez Juliá paints an apocalyptic picture of history, as in *Seva,* but the two fictions differ in their literary intent since Rodríguez Juliá wasn't trying to fool anybody; his work is quite clearly intended to be regarded as a fiction that reinterprets Puerto Rican history as nightmare. López Nieves wrote a story that had instant popular reception; Rodríguez Juliá's is a more academic effort. They both use a mix of narrative techniques, but *La noche oscura* is a much more challenging book, in part because he takes his technique seriously and hews closely to the language and mannerisms of the eighteenth century as well as the mind-set of those days, for instance, the deep-rooted misogyny of the Catholic authorities as represented by Bishop Trespalacios. A further layer of difficulty is that at least one of the main characters is insane and rambles on about the construction of perfect cities. In addition, Rodríguez Juliá mocks the dreams of history and the construction of a nation at great length—the novel runs to 332 pages.

Why did Rodríguez Juliá transform Puerto Rico in both historical novels from the sleepy backwater of the Spanish empire that it was into apocalyptic dystopias exploding in sexual and racial conflagration? The novels' *literary* power lies precisely in their spectacular, over-the-top stories of the explosive mix of race, power, and gender in the colonial setting. The exaggerations make for *better,* more eye-catching stories that overtly mock power and hierarchies as well as nationalist heroics.

By comparison to *La noche oscura*, Rodríguez Juliá's novella *La renuncia del héroe Baltasár* is tiny and features one lone antihero, Baltasár Montañéz, who poses as a role model for the enslaved and downtrodden black population and later turns out to be a sham betrayer. *La renuncia* uses the allegory of a garden to represent the dreams of national history, just as the allegory of the city does in *La noche oscura*. In both cases, Rodríguez Juliá transforms history's dreams into nightmares. Many critics believe that anything other than leftist radicalism is a de facto neutral stance toward politics; Mario R. Cancel, for example, says that Rodríguez Juliá's ideological leaning is toward "de-politicized cultural nationalism" (*Literatura y narrativa* 16) but it seems to me, however, that the rejection of national heroism is very much a political choice, it's just not the *expected* choice, that is to say the habit of Puerto Rican writers for upholding as *the* central national story some wished-for campaign for freedom.

Many artists occupy the middle ground between veneration and cynicism about the glorious past linked to independence stories. One example is the *independentista* stalwart Jacobo Morales, whose films are often ambiguous about the past. For instance, *Linda Sara*, from 1994, has a simple plot: facing financial ruin, four brothers decide to sell all the valuables in their house, and to make the items more marketable they invent heroic historical significance for the family legacy. The film's grounding in nationalism is set at the beginning, which opens on a character visiting the tomb of Pedro Albizu Campos; then the camera pans out to the twin Puerto Rican flags (official and nationalist) waving overhead. The upper-class family fallen on hard times is an old set-up (reminiscent of René Marqués), and the background of the sugar/*hacienda* economy's downfall is the trigger for the story: "Since the sugar-processing plant closed all is finished [. . .] we're ruined," says Gustavito, who represents the landowning class.

They live not in the modern ubiquitous *urbanización* of post-*muñocista* Puerto Rico but in Old San Juan in a gracious, high-ceilinged manor like those of ruling-class nineteenth-century Puerto Rico. In fact, the secondary story, the romance between Sara and Alejandro, could have come out of a nineteenth-century novel, and their scenes are problematically represented in an upper crust whites-only environment (with only one token black woman). On the other hand, Puerto Rico's transnational situation is shown as the island family takes advantage of a Nuyorican niece whom they regard as a maid. The film shows the island's neocolonial dependency when Gustavito has to surreptitiously get the dreaded food stamps.

His brother Pablo (Jacobo Morales) comes up with the history-changing antique-selling scheme. His cynical logic is that reality and fiction are interchangeable so one may as well make a buck out of fictionalizing the past to heighten its heroic meaning. In order to sell an old relic, a heroic little story is invented: "The saber I saw in the attic may have belonged to Captain Don Fernando Defilló and Eychenique, who fought heroically against the Dutch in the Morro Castle in 1742." His brother Mayito, who is the family historian, objects that such a hero is a fraud, noting that "he was the first to surrender, and that in 1625," but Pablo prevails and invents the heroic, nationalistic stories that will bring up the price of the family relics. The film therefore has its cake and eats it too as it mixes high regard for the romantic fictions of *independentismo* with the selling of the dream nation.

A People of Many Houses

Rosario Ferré often uses the allegory of the house as a stand-in for the nation. Her *House on the Lagoon* is a shining example of how many dreams coexist in the national House. In an interview, Ferré talks about this complex and paradoxical symbol of nationhood: "*The House on the Lagoon* for example has two stories not four stories like those in José Luis González' essay. In the stories on top live the family which represents the mercantile bourgeoisie of San Juan, and below are the servants, who come from a town almost completely Afro-Caribbean which is called Loíza, then from this point of view the division in the island is shown into two classes, two ethnicities and two basic cultures which are the Spanish and the African" (Pino-Ojeda). The novel also explores variations on what constitutes history, writing, and truth. These human endeavors are filtered, as in all of Ferré's writing, through the lens of women's rights and gender issues.

The symbolic house on the lagoon is, again, a watery abode (as in Rodríguez Juliá and López Nieves, since Seva is a town by the sea). The novel swirls with the conflicts of the Family (itself a regular stand-in for the nation). Significantly, the titular house on the lagoon never stands for long; it changes and mutates, is reconstructed and destroyed. Kelli Lyon

Johnson summarizes its permutations saying that "each in turn represents a redefinition of the Mendizabal family and the country" (247). On a symbolic lagoon in a mangrove, the house is surrounded by a plant whose multifaceted symbolism (neither land nor water, endlessly twisty) is appropriately symbolic of Caribbean nations and their complicated histories.[1]

The split into two separate narrations features the main couple, Isabel and Quintín, exploring the writing of the nation. This couple is gendered in a manner familiar to Ferré's fiction: husband Quintín is conservative and pro-statehood, and he dismisses his wife Isabel's writing as "a feminist treatise, an *Independentista* manifesto" (386). He believes in the objectivity of history and assumes her *independentismo* with its patriotic sentiments will distort it. Isabel espouses fiction with its passionate creativity about the past; and her novel tries to reinstate the many forms of freedom usually denied to women.

Ferré's *House on the Lagoon* embraces Puerto Rican politics. Let's not forget she is the only major writer to come out in favor of statehood for the island; her intellectual background, on the other hand, is in *independentismo* which, moreover, is central to many of the characters; in fact, a character who is an *independentista destroys* the third house! The dueling narrators provide the novel with the appearance of giving voice to all sides; although in effect the wife's novel takes up most of the book; a sign that Ferré's *independentista* roots go very deep indeed and that *independentismo* is still appealing for the novelist because its fictions means de facto defying the bourgeoisie.

Part 4 of the novel, the section titled "The Country House in Guaynabo," is notable since it features independence and the nationalist forces of the Pedro Albizu Campos, who is powerfully described by an opponent as "dressed in black and spewing fire and brimstone, like the devil himself" (125). The real-life patriarch of the status quo, Luis Muñoz Marín, is also the subject of discussion by the characters: one of them thinks he has a smart take on how to use autonomy; the other says he's a turncoat.

The novel also dramatizes a central event for *independentismo*, the Ponce Massacre of 1937, which is taken up in chapter 13. The novel is thoroughly grounded in Puerto Rican history, with references to specific Puerto Rican political events such as the attack on the U.S. Congress by Lolita Lebrón and her cohorts, diverse plebiscites, 1960s activism, and many more since politics, and particularly the question of status, says Ferré, are "the national obsession" (329). Feminism, race, class, and

Puerto Rican migrations are also highlighted in the novel. The twisted roadmap of Puerto Rican history provided by the characters leads everywhere but not to *one* definitive reading of history.

The Spanish Colony Forever

Hispanophilia, the nostalgic longing for the dominion of Spain, is a theme that continually crops up in Puerto Rican literature, and as I've discussed, has been a source for fictions with deep links to the dream nation. It is a surprisingly resilient feature. Olga Nolla's 1996 novel, *El Castillo de la memoria* (The castle of memory), has an extensive treatment of the conquest of the Caribbean from the point of view of the Spaniards. Carlos Pabón takes note when he talks about the Spain-loving underpinnings of a novel in which, he says, "there is that Hispanophilic claim" (270).

Memory, the nominal theme of Nolla's novel, is centered on the mother country, Spain. The novel, which starts during the Spanish conquest, features as a symbol of national identity not a house but a castle—in fact, the family castle of the aristocratic Spanish founder of San Germán, Lope López de Villalba. On a visit back to Spain, Lope's mother shows him secret mosaics in the deeps of the family castle. They believe in a memory-laden racial/cultural heritage: "la memoria es un misterio vasto que se pierde en los orígenes de la raza" (126; memory is a vast mystery that is lost in the origins of the race).

Many scenes in the early part of the novel brim with nostalgia for the time and the values of the Spaniards on the island in the 1600s. The main characters are Lope and Juan Ponce de León—who achieves immortality after discovering the fountain of youth—and their descendants. The Spaniards are the center of the novel, which puts blacks and *criollos* on the periphery of the main story; there are no other storeys in this national house. The reverence accorded to the Spaniards is obvious in a Christmas scene that describes the cooking skills of a slave cook, Crucita, who serves doña Leonor (Lope's wife) and cooks all day, her labors aided by two nameless "esclavas negras" (black slaves). Their efforts to feed the family result in Christmas scenes within a symbolic grid that has the family at the center of the town's plaza, with the twin authorities of church and government on either side., The *criollo* neighbors play their Spanish musical instruments and show due reverence to their social superiors, the Spaniards.

Nolla's novel uses heroism at its most blatantly nostalgic and Hispanophilic when it describes the male Spanish descendants chasing escaped slaves. These passages are so over-the-top in the depiction of the blithe brutality of the Spaniards that any implicit denunciation of the slave-owner mentality lacks punch since it is buried in the facsimile of the style of the times. The lack of any point of view except for that of the Spanish descendants tilts the story in their favor; we don't hear from the slave or the runways, who remain (symbolically) nameless.

The essentialist theme of racial memory reappears at the end of the novel, when Ponce de León remarks with admiration that the descendants of the noble families "heredan el recuerdo como se hereda el color del cabello y el tamaño de la nariz" (419; inherit memory like one inherits hair color and size of nose). It is hard to think that passages like these are tongue-in-cheek because of the cumulative effect and the humorlessness of the descriptions.

One of the top sites of trauma for the dream nation, 1898, appears in the last part of Nolla's novel. The point of view is still Juan Ponce de León's, who finally dies defending his *país* (meaning Puerto Rico governed by Spain), but Nolla goes the opposite way of *Seva*: she presents the tension between her heroes (all descendants of Spanish noble families) and ordinary Puerto Ricans, who resent Spain (as they did in real life). The latter receive the Americans with open arms: "La entrada de los invasores a Mayagüez pareció entonces más un carnaval que una guerra" (436; The entrance of invaders in Mayagüez then seemed more a carnival than a war). But the novel's viewpoint is still that of the descendants of Spanish noble families; the narrator, a Spanish ghost, and his ghost wife note the responses of their own social class: "las casas de las familias más prominentes permanecieron cerradas" (436; the houses of the most prominent families remained closed).

José Luis de la Fuente, an admirer of both López Nieves's and Nolla's rewriting of history, sums up the intent of the two writers to reaffirm the dream nation: "they also agree on the objectives of their work by offering Puerto Rico a new history, one equipped with mythical, mysterious, and heroic components" (72). He takes the genre of the historical novel with its mythification of nationalist epic struggles as a substitute, not just a rewriting, of Puerto Rican history.

Luis López Nieves's stories in *La verdadera muerte de Juan Ponce de León* (The real death of Juan Ponce de León) are equally Hispanophilic and present Spanish conquistadors comparable to Nolla's. The first story is titled "El gran secreto de Cristóbal Colón" (The great secret of Christopher Columbus), and it comes down unabashedly on the side of the Admiral. The story starts in the hours before Columbus's historical collision with the so-called New World, and at landfall, without a trace of irony, the sailors *kneel* before the Admiral and beg his forgiveness for having doubted him. Then, at the end of the story, when Columbus meets the (symbolically) nameless indigenous people, their oldest representative kneels before him, respectfully lowers his head and in a low voice says, "¡Maestro, al fin has regresado!" (17; Master, you have finally returned!), giving the story a science-fiction twist ending. The second story, called "El Conde de Ovanda" (The Count of Ovanda), is heavily weighted toward Eurocentrism and follows a similar path to alternative historical fiction; it is set during the seventeenth century. The lead characters, a count and his daughter, are cast as philosophers and scientists in the Enlightenment/Romantic mold; in point of fact, the count's atheism is derived from Voltaire, about whose cultural importance López Nieves wrote a novel, *El corazón de Voltaire* (Voltaire's heart). The short story is a bodice-ripper (see the account of the daughter, Doña Isabel de Ovando y Portilla, riding her magnificent Spanish horse in the first two pages) with a dash of the Marquis de Sade in the descriptions of both the clearly incestuous overtones of the count's relationship with his daughter and the torture of the daughter at the end. Torture is big in this story; the count sadistically torments slaves as a form of experimental science. Is this an indictment of the Europeans? It's hard to say since (like in Nolla) the Spaniards are the protagonists, and the reader sees only their viewpoint. The Puerto Ricans are a nameless mass who can only rubberneck when the count and the ecclesiastical authorities have a violent confrontation over the body of the daughter.

Short of the notoriously costly *Faro a Colón* monument in the Dominican Republic, it is difficult to imagine a more mythologizing homage not only to Columbus but to Europe as the stories in *La verdadera muerte*, with their belief in the civilizing effect of the historical clash of Spain and the peoples of the Americas. As a point of contrast, the polar opposite appears in the work of another Caribbean author, the Cuban Alejo Carpentier, whose Columbus is a foul-mouthed, lying, whoring cheat for whom his crew are the enemy (and vice versa) in "La llegada de Colón" (The arrival of Columbus) in *El arpa y la sombra* (The harp and the shadow).

More recent writers are less interested in Spanish colonial times or in 1898. In the twenty-first century, many intellectuals aren't as focused on the past, being concerned with multicultural and minority issues, climate change, the wealth gap and educational inequalities, and many other causes. The days when narrators limited themselves to just the island setting are gone. Mayra Santos Febres writes: "Creo que hay que escribir cada vez más novelas globales, donde el Caribe muestre su cara migratoria, donde la gente esté en distintos lugares, en Chicago, Mérida, Brasil, que se mueva como nos movemos nosotros" (Rivera and Celis 264; I think we should write novels that are increasingly global, where the Caribbean shows its migratory face, where people are in different places, in Chicago, Merida, Brazil, where people move around as we move around).

López Nieves, the author of *Seva* himself, has followed suit, in *El corazón de Voltaire*, the peripatetic lead character, who is French and goes from Europe to Argentina, Puerto Rico, and Mexico in search of DNA proof of the authenticity of a relic. This novel is a contemporary reworking of the epistolary novel, telling its story through e-mails as well as purported eighteenth-century correspondence, which includes Voltaire's.

Magali García Ramis's novel *Horas del sur* (Hours of the south) also takes the reader on a global tour that follows a roaming protagonist from small-town Puerto Rico to the United States and Europe throughout the twentieth century. And yet, her fictional character gets involved in the failed 1930s nationalist turmoil. The protagonist, Andrés Estelrich, restates the old nationalist ortodoxy in a pro-independence letter: "la gente necesita no sólo el pan, la justicia y la libertad, lemas del nuevo partido que impulsaba el país hacia el progreso, sino la dignidad. ¿Dónde se encuentra si no en la soberanía?" (246; people need not only bread, justice, and freedom, the new party's slogans which urged the country to progress, but dignity. Where can it be found if not in sovereignty?). His life offers a panoramic view of Puerto Rican history balanced by his peripatetic cosmopolitan experiences of many cultures. Nevertheless he retains love of *patria* so that at the moment of the (real-life) uprising in Jayuya, he races with a trunk full of pistols and fusils to join the nationalist sympathizers, but alas he passes out en route to that push for independence. When he regains consciousness, the revolt is over. He never even gets there! He bemoans where history went, specifically the incomplete revolutionary effort to rouse the masses: "creían que tendrían el poder para convocar a las masas a través de la lucha armada. Parece que mucha gente pensaba así, pero no tanta como para poder triunfar contra la Guardia Nacional y la Policía estatal" (246; they thought they would have the power to summon the masses through armed struggle. It seems that many people thought so, but not enough to succeed against the National Guard and the state police).

The novel strives for a balanced social picture without falling into the old dichotomy of United States–bad/Puerto Rico–good since it features complicit Puerto Ricans as well as the selfless American nuns who run a small school in the mountains where Andrés goes to spend the rest of his life at the end of the novel, since education, not revolution, becomes for him the force for greater good. Also important for the novel's historical effect is that the educational benefits come through a feminist/activist character called Carmen Ocasio, who defends the new system that allows poor children to study in a coed environment.

Mayra Santos Febres also has dabbled in history. Her *Nuestra señora de la noche* (Our lady of the night) paints a broad sociohistorical panorama of Puerto Rico through the lens of a character based on a famous twentieth-century black prostitute. This is the same historical character featured in Rosario Ferré's famous short story "Cuando las mujeres quieren a los hombres" (When women love men) from the 1970s. Santos Febres gives a broad historical overview of the era of Puerto Rico she depicts. When a lead character, Luis Arsenio Fornarís, and his upper-class friends are going to the famous Isabel's whorehouse, they given a summary of the island's political situation, specifically the presence of the American "new masters" (*Nuestra señora* 27). Black American soldiers and the issue of miscegenation and exploitation of the prostitutes are part of the novel's depiction of Puerto Rico's colonial condition and highlight what critic Nadia Celis Salgado sees as a "link between sexual exploitation and the expansion of the U.S. military empire" (143). The matter of U.S. culpability is complicated, however, because the lead character, Isabel Luberza, herself profits from and is complicit with the military and social power structures and their abuses while at the same time undermining and threatening the society she lives in merely by virtue of being a powerful black woman. As the novel goes back and forth in time throughout Luberza's life, it revisits the politics of early- to mid-twentieth-century Puerto Rico and the Caribbean (particularly leftist and nationalist events) with references to many issues such as the threat posed by Puerto Rican nationalists, famous pro-statehood leader José Celso Barbosa, the assassination of Colonel Riggs, unionization and Luisa Capetillo, and Rafael Leonidas Trujillo. The novel, however, is concerned with more than just rewriting history because in terms of long-established sexual politics what is more important is a commanding black woman whose brothel, "el Elizabeth's," upsets the balance of power in society, "En el Elizabeth's otro era el son al que se movían los cuerpos, y otras las leyes que regían las costumbres" (84; At el Elizabeth's the moving bodies danced to another tune, and other laws governed customs). Juan Pablo Rivera and Nadia V. Celis stress that the novel's (and the novelist's) interests lie in the portrayal of alternative histories, "of transvestites, prostitutes, slaves, and all sorts of outcasts" (20).

Even though literary critics consider the generation of 1970 as central to historical fiction, by no means has the interest in history disappeared from Puerto Rican literature; recent fictions continue to explore the island's past. For instance, Gina González de Freytes's 2010 novel *De porcelana y acero* (On porcelain and steel) stands out because it retells a broad sweep of Puerto Rican history using nationalist events, even though the thrust of the story is socially conservative.

A telltale sign of the importance of notions of national sovereignty is González de Freytes's use of the capitalized word *Isla* to refer to Puerto Rico. Her novel is in many ways a profoundly conservative work that uses the well-worn trope of the family as microcosm of the nation. It stands out because, even though published in the twenty-first century, it has at its center a white, well-off, Catholic family, there are no black characters of any note. When there is an incident involving a rebellious black character—Yare-Yare, a liberated black who kills a town mayor—his story is told through exposition (from one white character to another) instead of being dramatized or enacted (254). The family's women cling to traditional gender stereotypes; a woman's virginity is imperative and marriage even more so since it is entirely a heterosexual environment. Does all this signal a new openness in Puerto Rican literature for writers who diverge from leftist tradition? Not necessarily because the novel also uses (although it does not dramatize) significant events ripped from the nationalist tropes checklist in order to give added depth and authenticity to the Puerto Rican historical panorama behind the family saga.

Notably, the novel features representatives for all three status options, a rarity in Puerto Rican letters. Some of its main characters are pro-statehood, some are pro-independence, and in addition, in the 1940s the main couple, Carlos and Emi, join the pro-commonwealth party, the PPD. González de Freytes's novel, however, is a wholly conventional family saga. The "steel" of the title initially refers to the bayonet factory that the original French family owned; "porcelain" is repeatedly used to describe its women, for instance, the great-grandfather's description of his soon-to-be wife as "a porcelain virgin" (14). In fact, all the main characters are descendants of steely/porcelain white, well-off families, and the author uses a peculiarly retro view of gender stereotypes; the grandfather describes his own mother as being "loyal, self-sacrificing, and strong as steel" (22), and the novel has a plethora of self-sacrificing women who devote their lives to caring for their families, reverting to stereotypes of the devoted mother.

Oddly enough, for a woman writer from an island with a strong tradition of feminist and postfeminist writers such as Rosario Ferré, Ana Lydia Vega, Mayra Montero, and Mayra Santos Febres, González de Freytes has written a novel that completely shies away from female (or male) sexuality. The description of the founding couple's long union, for instance, is quite chaste and sex-free. A lead character alludes to the matter only when he says that his wedding night was "fiery" (39). Since so much of the novel follows conventional romance novel storytelling, it is unusual that it is missing the titillating conventions of that genre.

In the end, the enactment of national history is necessary window dressing for the saga of a well-off white family. Delia, a daughter of the family, delights in talking about the Grito de Lares, but neither she nor any of the other characters takes part in it (89). Another event that is also a touchstone of nationalism, the Ponce Massacre of 1937, is told at a distance; the news reaches the characters in Añasco, the small town where they live. Pedro Albizu Campos appears—reaffirming the fascination of Puerto Rican culture with the nationalist hero—but, *De porcelana* being what it is, Albizu is not present in the action; he is at a distance, someone the characters have heard of and who frightens them. The main character at that particular time, Emi, frets about what might happen if Albizu wins but decides—in a way that summarizes the novel's conservative ideology—that she's powerless, "What can I do? If I'm only a simple woman? I cannot change anything in this country; what I have to do is work and take care of my family; nothing else!" (308).

González de Freytes's characters, particularly the women, tend to be quite conservative; as a matter of fact, one of the few female characters who is an *independentista* sympathizer gets raped and killed by working-class rebels. Whatever else can be said about the novel, González de Freytes proves that independence is *paradoxically* necessary when narrating the dream nation, even if you disagree with its aims. The struggle for independence and its signal nationalist events and heroes make for good backdrop to the novel because the events are exciting, far-off tales; their high suspense adds drama even though the main saga remains tied to a romance-novel template.

We will see this phenomenon again in the next chapter when we look at the work of Esmeralda Santiago, a prominent Latina writer. It also features an appraisal of Puerto Rican writers in the United States to explore how they look back at/to the complex Puerto Rican dream nation. We will explore the Latinos' relationship to dream nation symbols and stories, to Puerto Ricans' paradoxical wavering between ideas of cultural independence and the realities of political dependency. Can Puerto Ricans in the States ever fully harmonize the complexities of their own lives lived between Puerto Rico and the United States? Would they want to?

5 / Dreaming in Spanglish

If the only Nuyorican writers you have read are the Nuyorican Poets Cafe and Esmeralda Santiago—among the most popular and anthologized of Latino writers—you would think all Puerto Ricans everywhere wish for the island's independence. Nevertheless, there is a divide between writers like Santiago, who use romanticized notions of La Isla, and writers like lesser-known Judith Ortiz Cofer, who embraces a more realistic and paradoxical view of the island seen through bicultural Latina eyes.

The historical context of the Nuyorican intellectuals is that the most visible literary figures were steeped in independence from the get-go. Juan Flores has argued that from early on Puerto Rican culture in the United States leaned solidly for independence. Why? He says because the first important writers were all *independentista* exiles ("Puerto Rican Literature in the United States" 55). Edna Acosta-Belén and Carlos E. Santiago document in their book, *Puerto Ricans in the United States*, that New York City was a refuge for Puerto Rican nationalists between the 1930s and the 1950s: "Among the most prominent Puerto Rican Nationalists living in New York during this period were Corretjer [the iconic nationalist poet]; his wife, Consuelo Lee Tapia, who helped administer and occasionally wrote for *Pueblos Hispanos*; feminist poet Julia de Burgos, a regular columnist for the newspaper; and avant-garde poet Clemente Soto Vélez, a regular contributor to many New York Spanish-language newspapers" (177). Even earlier émigrés like Eugenio María de Hostos and Bernardo Vega were independence crusaders.

As I've argued elsewhere in this book, Puerto Rican writers in the United States, such as the 1970s generation (which featured the noted writers Miguel Algarín, Miguel Piñero, Sandra María Esteves, Pedro Pietri, Victor Tato Laviera, and Piri Thomas) have had a complicated relationship with Puerto Rico and with their own Puerto Ricanness. Often, though, their works signal a rapprochement to *independentismo* as a vehicle to channel more *authentic* forms of Puerto Ricanness. The notion of a far-off verdant land where people fight for freedom is itself very appealing and has the added attraction of being antibourgeois. This embrace of the dream nation leads to cultural products with the same blind spots we saw in earlier literature from the island, especially with one-sided views of the political reality of the past fifty years without reference to the will of the public.

The Nuyorican/Latino writers' have had varied experiences of life on the island. Many were born on the island but came to the United States with their families as children or teenagers; some were born in the United States. Their cultural connection to La Isla also varies. Initially a stumbling block to their popularity on the island was that most of their works are written in either English or Spanglish, which meant rejection by many island *independentista* culture critics for whom Spanish is the sine qua non of Puerto Ricanness. The bicultural, bilingual diversity of the Nuyorican writers has resulted, on occasion, in personal angst, but it also has fueled creative works that spring from what Román de la Campa calls "the complex narrative of the Nuyorican subject," leading to, he says, "an unexpectedly refreshing sense of belonging nowhere, except in the verbal agility and poetic movement" (378).

As everyone knows, Puerto Ricans on the island are not the *only* Puerto Ricans. There are more self-identified Puerto Ricans in the United States than on the island itself. As Angelo Falcón writes: "One of the most striking recent developments in the Puerto Rican experience was the realization in 2003 that the stateside Puerto Rican community was larger than that of the island for the first time. According to the latest U.S. Census estimates, in 2005 there were about 3,780,000 Puerto Ricans living in the States compared to about 3,670,000 in Puerto Rico" ("The Diaspora Factor"). The reterritorialization of Puerto Ricanness—the one memorialized by "La guagua aérea"—has become a reality.

Yet many Nuyorican writers look back and bring into play Puerto Rico (the island) as a dream nation, a Puerto Rico of the imagination, of remembrance and nostalgia. This they often bolster with themes, stories, and images that come from and resonate with the kinds of hard-core

Puerto Rican nationalism we've explored before. Moreover, some of the Nuyorican writers specifically allude to independence as if it were the collective dream of all Puerto Ricans (see the preface to this book). In this disregard for island realities, they are, of course, identical to many of their island brethren. Except that unlike most island writers, many Nuyorican writers have a thorny love-hate relationship with their national identity and with the Puerto Rico/United States divide.

Nuyoricans in the 1970s, when many of the writers discussed below came to prominence, were fiercely focused on the social issues and experiences of Puerto Ricans in the United States. Among these were the experience of racism; the politics of the times, especially the 1970s, with issues such as Vietnam; their community's sociopolitical issues; and a passionate immersion in minority issues with an increased awareness of women's oppression by both the Puerto Rican and the U.S. cultures. The culture they produced is therefore deeply linked to life in the States, particularly New York and its environs.

The works of the writers prominent in the 1970s also appeared at a time of progressive radicalism, which coincided with the rise of the Puerto Rican demographic in New York City. As Francisco L. Rivera-Batíz notes, the Puerto Rican migration to New York City had its greatest expansion from 1940 to 1970, "when the Puerto Rican population of the city grew by close to 750,000 people" (108).

The 1960s and 1970s were not only a time of general leftist radicalism but also specifically a time of significant activism for the Puerto Rican community in New York itself. Angelo Falcón describes the numerous grassroots organizations and institutions of Puerto Ricans in New York City at that time, from the highly radicalized Young Lords organization to the founding of the Museo del Barrio in East Harlem in 1969. The matter of Puerto Rico's independence was in the air because, as Falcón states, the 1968 election in Puerto Rico resulted in a pro-statehood government that led to "the movement of a significant number of pro-*independentista* intellectuals and activists to New York" ("From Civil Rights" 89). Many broad social activist groups coincided with Puerto Rican militancy and "gave expression to a revitalized and reconfigured nationalist/left movement in the Puerto Rican community [in the New York area]" (89). Falcón acknowledges that the independence movement on the island failed to garner support [in fact it lost support], but he states "these movements had a profound impact on the political and cultural sensitivities of the

Puerto Rican leadership and youth in New York and elsewhere. Opinion surveys indicated that by the 1980s, a significant portion of Puerto Rican leaders supported the independence of Puerto Rico, although the large majority of the community supported the status quo of commonwealth" (93). The split between the intelligentsia and the public at large follows the same pattern as on the island.

Without a doubt, writers of consequence, such as the members of the Nuyorican Poets Café, were firmly on the side of independence. That is clearly visible when certain topics appear or are alluded to in their works, topics such as heroes and patriotism, Puerto Rican history, and nostalgia for the Lush Land—in sum, all the markers of the dream nation. The connection in some Latino works to Puerto Rican nationalism, however, at times is similar to the literature on the island but at other times is distant from the uncritical patriotism of many nationalists on the island.

Poetry remains the best-known literary product of the 1970s Nuyorican writers' movement, and although the present book focuses on prose, I want to illustrate the tenor of their use of the themes of independence by looking at some of the ways in which the dream nation (i.e., a verdant land in which a unified people fight for freedom) shows up in this specific generation of poets.

Take Pedro Pietri's famous "Puerto Rican Obituary." His Puerto Ricans in New York are, above all, oppressed: "they never spoke back / when they were insulted / they worked / they never took days off / that were not on the calendar / they never went on strike [. . .] They worked / ten days of the week / and were only paid for five" (Stavans 1358). The long poem traces the staccato rhythm of their painful lives amid hatred, poverty, racism, and death. Yet despite their disillusionment and oppression, they search for meaning, and the one source of redemption that stands out (in caps) is that "PUERTO RICO IS A BEAUTIFUL PLACE / PUERTORRIQUEÑOS ARE A BEAUTIFUL RACE" (Stavans 1363).

Miguel Piñero, as much as any poet at the height of the 1970s, had a love-hate relationship with the island. He wanted to represent the spirit not of Puerto Rico but of New York City's Lower East Side; this is clear in his emblematic "A Lower East Side Poem" in which the poet asks that his ashes not be scattered in Puerto Rico but on the Lower East Side. Piñero embodied the torn feelings of anger his generation felt toward the island, and therefore he was not exactly idealizing the lost land in his poem "This Is Not the Place Where I Was Born," in which he distances himself from the island, stating that "puerto rico 1974 / this is not the place where I was born." Even so, he gives in to nostalgia for an olden Puerto Rico: "I was born on an island where to be puerto rican meant to be / part of the land & soul" (Stavans 1395). His patriotic feelings about the blessings of island life are blurred, however, by the bitterness he feels when the Lush Land rejects him and other Nuyoricans:

> this sun drenched soil
> this green faced piece of land
> this slave blessed land
> where nuyoricans come in search of spiritual identity
> are greeted with profanity
>
> (Ibid.)

The feelings about such a betrayal were vividly dramatized in the biopic about his life (starring Benjamin Bratt) in the scene where the poet performs before the island academic intelligentsia and is accused by a professor (who is considerably whiter than he is) of not being Puerto Rican enough.

One of the core principles of *independentismo*, a Spanish-only culture that anchors the dream nation, is profoundly at odds with the literature produced by the diasporic Puerto Ricans. Here was perhaps *the* conundrum for island *independentismo* in the early years of the Nuyorican movement: How do you establish a rapport with people who self-identify as Puerto Ricans yet write in English?

As a result of the inherent tension, the return to the island of those who had gone abroad became a fractious topic. Characters in literature often experience that return as one of surprise, regret, disorientation, and disillusionment. Arturo Sandoval says that these characters are imprisoned by the kind of nationalism that predetermines their failure; that is to say, their identities are defined by nationalist notions that exclude *them*. He uses as examples Eduardo, the protagonist of Pedro Juan Soto's novel *Ardiente suelo, fría estación* (Hot land, cold season), who returns to the island and discovers he is out of place. He also notes that in one of Ana Lydia Vega's most famous short stories, "Pollito Chicken," the protagonist returns to Puerto Rico as a tourist, as someone who doesn't belong.

As the portmanteau title states, Tato Laviera's "AmeRícan" is a riff on the "Rican" brand. This poem harks back directly to the nationalism-laden vision of La Isla. (The use of the capital letter for the "Island" is always a dead giveaway of the dream nation.) Laviera connects the identity of his people in the United States to the Lush Land, which he associates with the island and its inherent treasures: "we gave birth to a new generation, / AmeRícan, broader than lost gold / never touched, hidden inside the / puerto rican mountains" (Stavans 1401).

As often as not, when the island appears in the Nuyorican poets—as much as with island writers—the visual imagery refers to a shared dream of a beautiful landscape, a pure land that inspires feelings of love and nostalgia. Aurora Levins Morales uses such nostalgia for the remembered Lush Land in contrast to the U.S. landscape: "the mulberry trees of Chicago, that first summer, had looked so utterly pitiful beside her memory of flamboyan and banana and. . . . No, not even the individual trees and bushes but the mass of the, the overwhelming profusion of green life that was the home of her comfort and the nest of her dreams" (Stavans 984).

The connection to the island appears not just as treasured pictorial images but as faithfulness to traditional (therefore regarded as authentic) gender roles in Sandra María Esteves's famous poem "My Name Is Maria Cristina." The poem channels the lost land through gender roles for Puerto Rican women that date back to the culture of the early to mid-twentieth century. This is the voice of a traditional woman, one connected to the original culture, one who affirms "I do not complain about cooking for my family / because abuela taught me that a woman is the master of fire" (Kanellos 267). In a poem titled "Here," Esteves goes into full-on nostalgia mode for the remembered island when she brings up, once again, the dream landscape: "I may never overcome / the theft of my isla heritage / dulce palmas de coco on Luquillo / sway in windy recesses I can only imagine / and remember how it was / but that reality now a dream" (Stavans 1397–98).

Miguel Algarín writes about how Nuyorican poets explicitly sympathize with nationalist historical events, saying they take sides in favor of independence in response to the "aggression" that Puerto Ricans face on the island and in the United States. He uses as an example Martín Espada's poem about the Ponce Massacre, a key nationalist event. Written on the fiftieth anniversary of that event, it is called "Rebellion Is a Circle of a Lover's Hands." Algarín also makes the explicit connection between Nuyorican poets and *independentismo* when he reminisces about a recital by José Brandon of a poem about the same key nationalist event (Algarín and Holman, *Aloud* 10–11). An "epic poem" is what Sandra María Esteves calls "Grito de Lares" by Louis Reyes Rivera; she also looks at Lucky Cienfuegos's "Lolita Lebrón, recuerdos te mandamos" [sic] (Lolita Lebrón, we send you memories) and "Ambivalencia o activismo" (Ambivalence or activism) (197). Nationalist events and heroes like these touchstones shared by Nuyorican culture in the 1970s as much as they were on the island.

Nevertheless, the revolutionary/nationalistic fervor of the Nuyorican writers did not end with the 1970s; it can be found in the twenty-first century in well-worn slogans and leftist mottos. For instance, Jaime "Shaggy" Flores's poem "When Tito Plays" (2000) has lines that could have been written in 1970: "'QUE BONITA BANDERA' vs. / IMPERIALISM, / COLONIALISM, / AND CAPITALISM [. . .] PALANTE MI GENTE! / PALANTE . . . / DESPIERTA." (Matos Valldejuli and Flores 63). He expresses nationalist solidarity through key terms from *independentismo* (the flag, denunciations of imperialism and colonialism) as well as identifying with the slogans of two rebellious ancestors: the Young Lords ("palante") and Los Macheteros ("despierta"). He therefore establishes kinship to the kind of counterculture that became almost automatic for *independentismo*.

For a good, old-fashioned *independentista* tirade one need look no further than Giannina Braschi's 2011 *United States of Banana*, the second part of which is an agitprop play. In its strident denunciation of American imperialism, it uses an everything-but-the-kitchen-sink approach to topical matters such as Iran, Iraq, the fall of the Twin Towers, the banking system, pesticides, and Starbucks among many, many others. The main force of the attacks is against American capitalism and in defense of Puerto Rican independence: "I want to liberate my island" (97), "I want independence" (97), and "I want the secession of Puerto Rico from the U.S. of Banana" (98). Braschi's extended rant against the United States vis-à-vis Puerto Rico relishes the slogans as well as the aims of traditional *independentismo* (anti-Americanism, anticapitalism) as well as a more up-to-date solidarity with sexual minorities and women.

Esmeralda Santiago and the Selling of Puerto Ricanness

If her latest work, *Conquistadora*, is any indication, Esmeralda Santiago, who is probably the most famous Puerto Rican writer in the United States, has found a winning formula, and she intends to stick to it. In this novel, her oeuvre's closeness to genre romance novels reaches its apex, but, as in her previous works, it is still in service to a dream nation. The formula features at its center a feisty heroine who overcomes her circumstances, finds love and lust in equal measure, and in the end conquers her part of the world. In *Conquistadora*, it is a Spaniard in the 1800s who comes to Puerto Rico. Yet at the heart of the story is once again the island identity that had been lost in Santiago's best seller, her memoir *When I Was Puerto Rican*. What makes Santiago notable is that the recipe so obviously hinges on more than a dash of a nostalgic dream nation, Puerto Rico seen through independence-minded eyes with particular affinity for the Lush Land agrarian world.

Before I comment on this latest historical novel, I want to set the stage of this Latina writer's use of the dream nation by revisiting my main arguments in the article "Esmeralda Santiago in the Marketplace of Identity Politics," kindly published by *Centro Journal*. As I stated in the article, Santiago's publication history proves that her formula sells. This is due in part to what Ellen McCraken calls "successful 'minority commodities,' versions of the Latino Other that mainstream publishing companies authorize, market, and even, to some degree, foment" (5). In chapter 2, we saw José Luis González denounce an element that is key to the identity formation of Santiago's Puerto Rico, a paradoxically conservative *independentismo*. Works like *When I Was Puerto Rican* and *America's Dream* fall into the cultural category that he labeled *jibarismo literario* (*El país de cuatro pisos* 37). As I have noted, González was sternly critical of this kind of mythification of small-town Puerto Rico and its agrarian setting.

The impact (through massive marketing and exposure) of Esmeralda Santiago's vision within a Latino search for roots is that for those large numbers of high school and college students in the United States who read her memoir (or the parts of it in anthologies), Puerto Rico is perpetuated as a 1950s agrarian lost land that fights for its freedom. All of the island's complexity is also lost.

In her famous memoirs, the tone of nostalgia for the island's old-timey ways is set by the epigraph, a paean to the land written by the nineteenth-century Land-worshipping poet Luis Lloréns Torres: "El bohío de la loma / bajos sus alas de paja, / siente el frescor mañanero / y abre sus ojos al alba" (The *bohío* on the hill / under its straw wings, / feels the cool morning / and opens its eyes to the break of dawn).

Another famous Latina memoirist, Sonia Sotomayor, also uses a Romantic poet prominently, José Gautier Benítez, in much the same way, to allude to visions of a dream nation, which help make the hard migrant life of her family and friends bearable.

Santiago's narrator is tied directly to *independentismo* through her father, whose teachings explain, for instance, why Americans are imperialists and why, as he says, "they expect us to do things their way, even in our country" (73). His view of the world, and of history, is summarized by the statement that "Puerto Rico was a colony of Spain after Columbus landed here [. . .] In 1898, los Estados Unidos invaded Puerto Rico and we became their colony" (72–73). His is a traditional definition of nationhood, not just about a language but about food, music, and "the things you believe in" (72–73). The prologue to the memoir, called "How to Eat a Guava," sets the symbolic value of authenticity of Puerto Ricanness (of food and cultural identity) when the narrator compares the acrid guava at a Stop & Shop in the States to the juicy and fragrant fruit of memory, "my last guava the day we left Puerto Rico" (4).

The memoir also features a chapter that showcases the general ideological attitude of *independentismo* toward the United States. Heavy-handedly called "The American Invasion of Macún," it centers on school and family, two important areas of any nation's life. The narrator and the townsfolk confront the vast cultural divide between who they are as Puerto Ricans (and what their heritage is) through the foreignness of donated American food. This happens during a U.S.-led session for Puerto Rican parents on what the Americans consider proper nutrition and hygiene, presenting American food charts and donated foods. American fare such as powdered eggs, white bread, canned juice, margarine, and other equally insipid and foreign-seeming provisions seem disgusting to the townsfolk when compared to fresh native Puerto Rican produce, which is so plentiful it falls from the trees. At the core of this Manichaean comparison is the authenticity and closeness to the land via the native foods as contrasted to the foreignness and artificiality of the donated, canned goods, which rankle precisely because they are viewed as charity, which causes the shame of dependency.

The truth-value or authenticity of any memoir is debatable because the genre relies on the vagaries of individual memory. However, if we focus on her first pure fiction novel, *América's Dream*, we see the repercussions of Santiago's portrayal of Puerto Rico and Puerto Rican identity even when not directly linked to autobiography. If the memoirs take place roughly from the late 1940s to the early 1970s, in *América's Dream* the time frame shifts to the 1990s, although not much about Puerto Rico changes.

América's Dream, though entirely cast as fictional, characterizes Puerto Rico in the same terms as the author's first two memoirs (the second of which is called *Almost a Woman*), which avow to represent the real Puerto Rico. For example, in the novel's acknowledgments, Santiago states, "while this is a work of fiction, it takes place in Vieques, which is real," which connects the novel to nationalist political action, though one that occurs only in the distance since none of the characters is an activist.

The novel has a dichotomous structure: the tale told on the island transfers midway to the concrete jungle of the United States. Her presentation repeats and solidifies a specific picture of Puerto Rico: a patriarchal agrarian paradise spoiled by modernity from which an abused but beautiful working-class woman living in a cycle of oppression runs away (to the United States), only to be pursued by the macho man she sought to escape. The novel's strategic underpinning, a mix of melodrama and naturalism, allows Santiago to revisit not just América's dream but the dream nation itself.

Far from presenting a varied picture of Puerto Rican society at the end of last century (when it was published), in *América's Dream* Santiago depicts a Puerto Rico bound by strict divisions of class and educational level, and the working-class protagonist is as isolated from contact with other classes as any subcontinental untouchable. Santiago's portrayal of Puerto Rico suffers from cultural essentialism, which Uma Narayan explains this way: "culturally essentialist feminist representations of 'Third World cultures' sometimes depict the practices and values of privileged groups as those of the 'culture as a whole'" (84).

Crucial to this representation is how Santiago interprets Puerto Rican history: through the prism of romantic nostalgia, a telluric imaginary of the sort we have seen before in nineteenth- and early-twentieth-century Puerto Rican literature. Her memoirs and novels present Puerto Rico as agrarian and pure. She repeats that formula again in great detail in *Conquistadora*—which is her first purely historical novel.

América's Dream uses a neo-*jíbara* identity that rejects the political realities of the island. Tied to this ideology is the portrayal of the island itself; Puerto Rico is a nostalgic dreamland where a utopian landscape is being replaced by the evils of modernity. When América remembers her Vieques neighborhood, she recalls how in her childhood, "every house was set back behind broad yards, surrounded by mango, breadfruit, and avocado trees. Before urbanization. They didn't have running water then, or electricity" (25). Vieques is the setting for a reenactment of the conditions that permeated the Puerto Rico of *When I Was Puerto Rican*, an agrarian, dirt-poor, underprivileged setting fit for Santiago's underdeveloped Puerto Ricans.

A strategic linchpin to the far-awayness of Santiago's Puerto Rico is the lack of references to contemporary Puerto Rican or U.S. culture. (In *Conquistadora*, she will abandon contemporary Puerto Rico altogether and place the action in the nineteenth century.) Most remarkable is the lack of allusions to that all-consuming Puerto Rican pastime: politics.

One of the few examples of a real-life cultural reference point is when the novel refers to then current gender/culture issues, mentioning an unnamed *merengue* about a man whose "wife went to New York and now that she's back, she won't do his laundry, won't cook his meals, and won't have sex with him unless he speaks to her in English" (71). The novel, however, does not explore the connections between misogyny and popular music, or between language and identity. It also refers to 1990s TV shows such as Cristina Saralegui's (U.S.-based) talk show and mentions that América's mother watches *telenovelas*. In a brief nod to the media's distortions of everyday Puerto Rican life, at the end of the novel Ester herself achieves celebrity when she appears on Cristina's show about domestic violence and its effects on family members. The reality of the interconnectedness of the United States and Puerto Rico through mass culture is nevertheless tossed aside when América rides her first train in the United States yet has no point of reference to contemporary life there: "her image has been formed by the iron black locomotives in westerns" (180). This kind of deliberate ignorance about life in the United States repeats the novel's avoidance of the greater world out there and its centeredness on a dream nation uncontaminated by U.S. culture.

Santiago's lack of attention to mass or popular culture is a phenomenon that speaks to her refusal to acknowledge Puerto Rico's contemporary reality, particularly its politics, which would give the lie to the protagonist's claim that her people are fighting for independence. In part this is also motivated by the characters' attachment to the microcosm of La Familia and to the fact that their world begins and ends in a small-town view of the nation and the world.

Santiago's portrayal of women is key to understanding the continued mass-market appeal of her work. The protagonist, named resonantly (if strangely accented on the first but not the last name) América Gonzalez, has the traits of the docile Puerto Rican: she is undereducated, poor, and, in a new feminist twist, a battered common-law wife. Genealogy—a long line of women as victims—structures the fate of the female characters on the island. This kind of fatalism represents a cult of victimhood that sells well in the mass market (cf. any *telenovela*), but as Gloria E. Anzaldúa points out in *This Bridge We Call Home*, "Buying into victimhood forces you/them to compete for the coveted prized of the walking wounded" (5).

The novel's reductive simplification of women's nature is symbolized by the hedge of roses that surrounds Ester's house; América and Ester are constantly restrained by the "tunnel of spiny rose branches" (81), as they are mired in their womanhood with its supposed limitations—in their case due more to a collusion of sociocultural forces such as lack of education, poor working conditions, and a definition of femininity that centers on relations with men. Proof of the emphasis on the limitations of so-called natural gender is that América's lover Correa is unaffected by the restraining flowers (84). Equally essentializing is the women's notion of destiny; this is obvious in the scene where América, after staring at a placid cow (which reflects her own situation in life), "heads not toward Esperanza, but away from it, toward Destino" (15).

To further deepen the portrayal of women's life of despair on the island, this novel deals openly with domestic violence. It realistically presents an abusive relationship: the brutal macho, the submissive woman who swallows her rage, an irrational pattern of swift and blinding violence, a society that acquiesces with and reinforces gender stereotypes, a direct connection between alcohol and aggression (including sexual violence), and an ineffectual law system. The social acceptance of domestic violence hinges on turning a blind eye even to public abuse since Correa slaps América in public several times. However, again bypassing the real island and its legal and political reality, the novel doesn't mention the Puerto Rican Ley Núm. 54, the groundbreaking law against domestic violence passed in 1989, making Puerto Rico the first Latin American nation to pass such a law.

The character is, to put it mildly, not very self-analytical either about her own life or about the island's situation. When her acquaintance, a Guatemalan nanny called Adela, points out the benefits of a legal Social Security card, América realizes her U.S. citizenship allows her to bypass worries about a green card or opening a bank account. Of course, América's situation looks enviable to the undocumented maids, who congratulate her on being an American citizen. The chapter "Las Empleadas" is the most fully realized presentation in the novel of the complicated lives of working-class Latinos (since Santiago doesn't dwell on Latinos from other social classes). For example, their training is going to waste: back in their home countries they were nurses, bank tellers, schoolteachers, etc., but now all are nannies and maids. Santiago presents a realistic vision of the nonexistent American Dream through the cultural chasm the maids suffer.

America's Dream is also set in Vieques, a key place for *independentismo*. Early in the novel there is a telling description of Vieques that is worth analyzing in detail: "Once these lowlands were a sea of sugarcane, which elegant señores oversaw atop sprightly Paso Fino horse. But when the U.S. Navy appropriated two-thirds of the island for its maneuvers, the great sugar haciendas disappeared and the tall stacks that dotted the island were bulldozed out of the way. This is history, and América doesn't think about it" (17). The conspicuous paradox of a maid who comes from a line of servants being nostalgic for graceful patriarchal life is nonsensical unless one places it within the ideology of Hispanophilic independence. The reference—without apparent irony—to the proud and tall stacks of that old iconic standby, the sugar *central,* is the opposite of José Luis González's view of the island's dependency on and exploitation by the sugar industry. As he never tired of explaining, the "hateful" *haciendas* (both sugar and coffee plantations) had emerged from an oppressive subculture created by European migrants (*Nueva visita* 150). He adds that the *haciendas* were never telluric or homegrown economic engines but a foreign economic system created to put profit into the hands of the few and to exploit the workers. Santiago's retro vision of the *haciendas* as a noble part of the very *landscape* and of the island's *history* is due to her use of what José Luis González called conservative *independentismo* and its mythified view of the island and its history (*El país de cuatro pisos* 25).

As to the reference in the passage quoted earlier to "the sprightly *Paso Fino* horses," González identified precisely the same animal as symbol of a class, landowners (and their supporters), who produced a culture filled with antiquated notions of Puerto Rican identity: "quienes ya no pudieron seguir 'volteando la finca' a lomos del tradicional caballo, se dedicaron a hacerlo a lomos de una décima, un cuento o una novela" (*El país de cuatro pisos* 33; those who could no longer "go around the homestead" riding a traditional horse, devoted themselves to doing so atop a *décima*, a story or a novel).

Juan Flores agrees with González's fundamental critique of the uses of a nostalgic ersatz island, writing that a certain brand of Puerto Rican nationalism is a vehicle for conservative "moral Puritanism, elitism, patriarchy, and heterosexism" (*Bomba* 33). Santiago's novel holds fast to an old-timey presentation of identity (national, class, and gender-based), over which América's old-guard patriotic *independentismo* presides as a key conceptual instrument of Puerto Rican identity. Santiago adds second-wave feminism to the story, making it palatable to late-twentieth-century audiences, both Latinos and other readers interested in reading minority-themed literature.

Santiago's one-sided depiction of Puerto Rico is in part due to rah-rah nostalgia for the homeland felt by diasporic Puerto Ricans. Flores notes the heightened patriotic sense of belonging experienced by Puerto

Ricans in the mainland: "people, say in Guaynabo [. . .] take their culture for granted, while others in Philadelphia defend it passionately" (52). He uses as the quintessential example of this cultural quirk the famous *casitas*, the little houses in the Bronx and Brooklyn that look and are built like those found in the mountains of Puerto Rico in olden days.

The *obiter dicta*, the words that give the game away (as Tom Wolfe would say), appear explicitly when América flees to the United States and tells her Latina friends that "where she comes from people are fighting to win independence from the United States" (253). América's dream, it turns out, is the dream nation.

With *Conquistadora* (2012), Santiago repeats her formula for *manufactured* Puerto Ricanness; in fact, this historical romance is steeped in the Hispanophilic sensibility straight from old-fashioned *independentismo*. The novel has a chapter called "Miguel Gets Alivio" devoted to separatism in the mid-1800s. By setting the novel in the nineteenth century, she avoids the murkiness and fragmentation of *independentismo* in the twentieth and twenty-first centuries. The chapter presents Puerto Rican men who want to be free of Spain at a time of censorship in which "liberal ideals were nearly impossible to disseminate" (321). Independence is therefore seductively clandestine since the men's discussions would be considered seditious by the Spanish authorities. Men like the teacher, the pharmacist, and the young men of means meet to discuss independence at the drugstore owned by a fourth-generation resident, making him an *authentic* (i.e., Puerto Rican) leader.

What is also fundamental to the novel's dream of a verdant nation where people fight for freedom is the existence, pre-1898, of a *national conscience*, a unified Puerto Rico seen in the intent of the group leader "to create the Puerto Rico for Puerto Ricans that he envisioned yet was unable to realize" (322). The chapter goes into great detail about how the inequities of Spain's rule (taxation, lack of infrastructure, few schools, high illiteracy rate, nepotism, and, of course, slavery itself) riled up the *criollos*. During the separatist meetings, talk turns to one of the great *independentista* and abolitionists of the time, Ramón Emeterio Betances, who is not, however, part of the action; he is only described from a distance as a fiery orator who is encouraging armed revolt to achieve Puerto Rico's freedom.

The two young male characters have no interest in the polite meetings of the good people of society; what they really want is the *frisson* of furtive underground gatherings of manly men seeking freedom: "the truly secret societies didn't meet in the easy to infiltrate *tertulias* of poets, apothecaries, and known liberals. They met in small groups and members' homes [. . .] on the *fincas* that dotted the landscape near rivers and harbors, on the *estancias* where men came together to ride and race horses, watch bullfights, enjoy a bloody cockfight, to drink, gamble, and plot" (324). So even though Santiago makes clear that independence notions of the time were linked to abolitionist aspirations, what the lead characters want is grounded in melodrama and the enjoyment of traditional masculine pursuits. The novel accurately diagnoses the problem of achieving independence without the popular, mass support of the *jíbaro*; popular support was then (and is now) the stumbling-block to reaching the lofty ideal of sovereignty: "The question at the forefront of the leaders' discussions was how to motivate the average *campo*-dwelling, poor Puerto Rican to rise against the oppression that was so obvious to the upper class *criollos* leading the nationalist movement" (324–25). Since the novel is a historical romance, it is only fitting that when Miguel joins the nationalist movement he sees *la lucha* in terms of melodrama and heightened emotion: "Miguel floated along the margins, trying to find his place in the glorious mission. He was enamored of the romance of *patria, igualdad, libertad*, and believed he'd found something worth dying for" (325).

The matter of slavery is a thorny one in *Conquistadora* because the protagonist, Ana, her two husbands, and her son are plantation owners who use slave labor. Ana is not really very conflicted about owning slaves; she buys into the standard defense of slavery, considering herself a good master to her people: "She'd show him [her son] how well she cared for her people, how they were housed, clothed, and fed, given important work, and provided for in every respect" (367). Her son Miguel tries to liberate the slaves when he inherits his grandfather's property, but he is not allowed to do so because of a stipulation in the will.

Conquistadora is grounded in the same view of Puerto Rico as the rest of Santiago's oeuvre. She has continued the trajectory of her first success by presenting the dream nation as if it were a solid fact. Not *when* she was Puerto Rican, but always a *dream* Puerto Rican.

Judith Ortiz Cofer: The Shifting Memories

In contrast to Santiago, this Latina writer presents her recollections of Puerto Rico by first noting that memory is an imperfect tool that leads to self-exploration but not to historical or cultural truth. Her approach to the island stems from Virginia Woolf's impact on her thinking,

> I was afraid to begin writing this autobiographical work thinking, "How can I trust my memory? They will call me a liar because what I remember is not necessarily what other people remember." And Virginia Woolf would say, no, it's your childhood, you reconstruct and re-create it any way that suits you, because memory is mostly fiction. [. . .] She opened my eyes to that truth, that my memories were as valid for art as anybody's memories. As long as I didn't delude myself into thinking that they were historical facts.
>
> (Ocasio 732)

This distinction between self and history is key to why Ortiz Cofer's presentation of Puerto Rico is so different from Santiago's even though both write bildungsromans about roughly the same time, the 1950s and 1960s. The separation of self and history is clear from her title, *Silent Dancing: A Partial Remembrance of a Puerto Rican Childhood*, which already labels memory as partial or imperfect, casting doubt on its truth value. Santiago's best seller *When I Was Puerto Rican*, by contrast, stakes a claim to truth, to certainty about knowing what a Puerto Rican is.

Ortiz Cofer states that her memories are not just family history since "memory for me is the 'jumping off' point; I am not, in my poetry, in my fiction writing, a slave to memory" (12). At one point, when she tries to remember the day her father returned from Panama, the narration stops and she says, in italics, "I may have imagined this" (46). The author has stated that she aims for a kind of storytelling that leads to poetic truth; however, Bridget Kevane says that Ortiz Cofer is careful to not misrepresent the island: "Ortiz Cofer never publishes a novel or a poem about Puerto Rico without consulting her friends who are historians and literary critics" (117–18).

Ortiz Cofer's detailed descriptions of growing up bilingual and bicultural are mediated by the Freudian overtones implicit in her misremembering of one childhood incident. She states several times that she had unfocused memories about getting burned in an open fire during a family party as a very young child; later, in her mother's recollection, it turns out that it was a bilingual dictionary that was burned in the fire, not the child herself. Therefore, as the mother points out, she does not bear physical scars, only the troubled recollections of what growing up bicultural, bilingual was like.

Silent Dancing proves that when recalling distant events, even external memories are faulty because the past and its meanings can never be fully recaptured by any means. When Ortiz Cofer talks about scenes from the five-minute home movie that gives the book its name—the "silent dancing" that is both "comical and sad" (95)—she says that even when she's looking at the home movie, memory interferes to rearrange the picture. She can never be an impartial observer; for instance, she remembers things that are not in the movie, "the linoleum floor is light blue, and if it was subjected to the spike heels as it was in most places, there were dime-sized indentations all over it that cannot be seen in this movie" (89). Instead of a hard-edged demarcation of the past, the silent figures only open the floodgates for what is clearly a dream sequence that reinvents the past.

Ultimately Ortiz Cofer is searching for Puerto Ricanness (like Santiago), although she is critical of rote nationalism on the island. She has mentioned how her Puerto Rican literary friends who are *independentistas* complain of being deprived of a Latin American identity because they are U.S. citizens and how she finds their attitude puzzling because "[i]t is important to have a literary identity, but what about economic and political issues?" Literary concerns are not, for her, reason enough to seek independence (Ocasio 740). Elsewhere she has said that she is "a writer, not a political activist" and that, furthermore, by writing her memoirs she was not "standing on a soapbox" (Acosta-Belén and Cofer, "*MELUS* Interview" 85). She also feels very strongly that she has every right to consider herself a Puerto Rican despite writing in English (Acosta-Belén and Cofer 90).

Silent Dancing features her family's comings and goings from Puerto Rico to the mainland due to her father's job in the U.S. Navy. The family's nomadic existence—in a six-month rotation back and forth—leads her to define herself as a "Navy brat" who turns into a "cultural chameleon" navigating both cultures. The migratory pattern, instead of being an impediment, becomes the opportunity for growth and multiple possibilities *along with* the pains of a bicultural life: "one part of life stops and waits for you while you live another for a while—and if you don't like the present, you can always return to the past" (52). Even though her first memories of Puerto Rico are related to a woman's world centered on her grandmother with storytelling skills and knowledge of herbs, the young girl is sometimes unprepared for the return trip to life in a rambunctious extended family, "Mamá's tribe," which is, above all, loud.

The fluidity and open-endedness of the family's transitions between island and mainland makes for a portable Puerto Ricanness: "the idea of home on [their] backs from house to house" (138), which helps her to overcome and in fact to capitalize on the mix of racial and class distinctions, sexual mores, and national identities. This is particularly true of her bilingual abilities; she speaks humorously of her "two-way accent: a Spanish accent when I spoke English; and, when I spoke Spanish, I was told that I sounded like a 'Gringa'" (17).

Ortiz Cofer and Santiago are eerily similar in the symbolic attachment to guavas that, as we saw in chapter 1, appear in the prologue to Santiago's memoirs as the fruit symbolic of authenticity. Like in *When I Was a Puerto Rican*, the Americans' misunderstanding of and cluelessness about Puerto Rican culture is symbolized in *Silent Dancing* by fruit, apples, oranges, and grapes flown in from the States during a Christmas of her childhood; the fruit is needlessly, obliviously sent to a place where anyone can just pick fruit from the mango or guava trees. The magical link to the fruitful land is further apparent when Ortiz Cofer narrates one of the María Sabida stories she invented as a child and the guava is a miraculous medicine. When reminiscing about the fruit of her childhood, she says that the guava cannot be compared to anything else; it has a privileged place in her memories of the island.

But there is an symbolic difference in how Ortiz Cofer and Santiago remember the island's fruitful bounty; two paragraphs later, Ortiz Cofer remembers with equal fondness the American sweets of her childhood (Old Colony soda, Mary Jane candies, Bazooka gum, boxes of Chicklets). She gives transnational foodstuffs (definitely colonial food) comparable status in her memories.

So that she is constantly navigating the difficulties of two cultures at once, not one at a time like Santiago. When her family lives in New Jersey, she feels that she is constantly crossing "the border of two countries" (125). One of these is the *dream* of Puerto Rico that her mother nourishes—going so far as to not learn English in order to go back "pure" to her island—and the other country is the America outside of their apartment. Of course, the American view of life keeps erupting into the family's life through the television that her father had buys.

Nostalgia is important to reconstructing the distant homeland in *Silent Dancing* because of her mother's constant yearning for her Island and resistance to assimilation to U.S. life. The mother "never adopted the U.S., she did not adapt to life anywhere but in Puerto Rico" (41). When they live in El Building and are surrounded by Puerto Ricans, she can at least construct a "reasonable facsimile" of her Puerto Rico by using cultural reference points: language, music, and "the strong aroma of red kidney beans boiling" (90). But during one of the family's many sojourns in the United States, when they live in more affluent West Paterson, she feels like a real exile because "we heard no Spanish, no loud music, no fathers yelling at children, nor the familiar ¡Ay, bendito! the catch-all phrase of our people. Mother lapsed into silence herself, suffering from *La Tristeza*, the sadness that only place induces and only place cures" (64). Nostalgia is like a religion: "my mother carried the island of Puerto Rico over her head like the mantilla she wore to church" (127). Her simulacrum of the island in their apartment leads to something neither here nor there, a "twilight zone."

Ortiz Cofer's remembered father is diametrically opposed to Santiago's in *When I Was Puerto Rican*, who is identified as being an *independentista* and therefore treasures that brand of Puerto Ricanness. Ortiz Cofer's father feels no longing "to return to the Island that held no promise for him" (129). Teresa Derrickson states that the parents in the memoir "embody the extremes of the disparate cultures they straddle" (128) and faults Ortiz Cofer for falling into easy binaries: "Not only is there an overarching emphasis on the gendered contrast between the father and the mother, but the passage also pits ethnic 'paleness' against ethnic 'darkness,' intellect against beauty, and restraint against effusion" (128). But the memoir ends not in the irreconcilable ideological split of the parents but in the life of their daughter, who creatively blends both cultures.

In the end, nostalgia and the dream nation are defeated by the passage of time. When Ortiz Cofer's mother finally returns to stay in Puerto Rico, even her small town has changed: "the original town remains as a tiny core [. . .] but surrounding this postcard scene there are shopping malls, a Burger King, a cinema. And where the sugar cane fields once extended like a green sea as far as the eye could see: condominiums, cement blocks in rows, all the same shape and color. My mother tries not to see this part of her world. The church bells drown the noise of traffic; she feels safe—under the shelter of the past" (151–52).

Ortiz Cofer and Santiago are not always so far apart in their views of the island. Ortiz Cofer also bemoans the colonial conditions of the United States/Puerto Rico relationship when she talks about how her parents as children were forced to learn English in public schools. She is also critical of how her family's position is viewed in the society of her little town of Hormigueros, where "status is judged by unique standards in a culture where, by definition, everyone is a second-class citizen" (56).

The biggest difference between the two Latina authors is that Ortiz Cofer accepts, acknowledges and critiques the broader changes the island has been through. It is evident that the speed and pace of the colonial working conditions are never quite right for the town and its people. This is symbolized by the way the sugarcane from the American-owned La Central is transported; first by superloaded ox-drawn carts that delay traffic because they are too slow, later in open-back trucks—also loaded to the limit with sugarcane—"traveling the roads of the Island at sixty or seventy miles per hour, granting no other vehicle (except police cars) right-of-way" (77). She sees both eras, both modes of transport (past and present) as equal menaces to local society because of the island's colonial underdevelopment.

Sotomayor also carefully weighs the prism of memory; she remembers Puerto Rico through her mother's stories about growing on the island in the 1930s, her own bucolic memories during vacations on the island as a child, and compares them to the beloved yet discordant island she visits as a grown-up.

Sotomayor, Ortiz Cofer, and Santiago show the possibilities for Latina remembrance of Puerto Rico. Ortiz Cofer shows that one can remember Puerto Rico, and be a Puerto Rican, without grasping for a romanticized view of the island governed by a dream nation. On the other hand, Santiago's memoir, which has been immensely popular and sold many more books, proves that the dream nation, a verdant land that fights for independence, sells better. Justice Sotomayor, admittedly not with "literary" intent, combines Romantic poetry and personal remembrance to her analysis of how Puerto Ricans in the States channel their nostalgia. In any case, memory, sweet or sour, constantly seeks to re-create the emotional resonance of the nation.

Conclusion

Culture, as is evident and well-known, is most compelling when it finds stories and tropes that explore, capture, and summarize significant, shared emotions from the personal, sociopolitical, and economic stew from which it arose. The dream nation—the fiction of Puerto Rico as a Lush Land where a valiant people continue to fight for freedom—is sometimes nostalgic decoration, sometimes wishful thinking. It can be a sign of willful forgetting of painful and necessary realities, particularly the Puerto Rican preference for dependency. It can also signal the vitality of the push-pull of contradictory impulses in Puerto Rican hearts and minds. A dependent reality versus dreams of independence: this constant paradox churns up writers, artists, songwriters, filmmakers, and other culture producers because tradition connects us to bygone pictures of a verdant land; reality is the traffic jam that awaits outside the door.

 I have looked at how the fictions of independence have both enriched and stifled Puerto Rican culture. As I said before, the only way to avoid the issue of independence in Puerto Rican literature—particularly pre-twenty-first century—is to not read it. Yes, there are other consequential ideas, themes, and allegories in Puerto Rican culture, but the dream nation made a deep mark with its fictions of a beloved land both lush and blighted, with its constant call to heroism, with its invention and retelling of a glorious past (true and false) in tribute to national pride. In the first chapter, we saw how a whole century's worth of literature proves how deep the traces go, along with the evidence of a dearth of literary representations of the other two status options, those that are actually chosen by the majority at the polls. Then, in chapter 2, we saw how a valiant few rose up against the academic orthodoxy and proclaimed that there was something wrong with the emperor's fashion choices. In the third and fourth chapters, we looked at emblematic ways of processing independence (or lack thereof) in interpretations of landscape and history. By the last chapter, we were looking at the coexistence of romanticized versus realistic images of Puerto Rico in Latino writers.

Despite the early signs of negative *independentista* beliefs (Hispanophilia being the most notable), its countercultural *cool* and *je ne sais quoi* allure have offered a potent cocktail that still draws in even hip-hop stars. The dream nation that culture built and whose foundations have the imprint of independence is still a seductive image, a well-known song, even when it moves to the beat of reggaeton. And the complicated culture that the dream nation nurtured helped define Puerto Rico as a cultural nation despite its perpetual political dependency.

The fictions of the dream nation bring many things treasured by Puerto Ricans:

- heroes galore
- compelling stories retelling the past
- images recalling a beloved landscape
- a therapeutic outlet for the shame of dependency
- a channel for moral indignation against colonialism
- a call of love for land
- a trove of marketable stories and icons that sell

In an island where two pro-U.S. parties dominate, it seems like independence has stood for something *different*, giving it the potential for enhancing (or at least varying) the national conversation. Do the emerging poststatus parties have a future? How will this brave new world of Puerto Rican politics be reflected in literature and culture? And how will the future culture reflect the twenty-first-century exodus, with 576,000 Puerto Ricans migrating to the United States from 2000 to 2011?

We have also seen that there are signs that high-end culture producers are abandoning the dream nation; in fact, the much-heralded demise of the "problema identitario" (identity problem) may signal an end in Puerto Rican culture to the centrality of the hope, anger, and sorrow about failed independence. In any case, the culture at large has moved from status issues to more complex ideas of the Puerto Rican nation.

Some views reveal a fractious, consumerist majority that listlessly roams the overcrowded landscape but other views portray sides that had not been represented, such as the LGBT contingent. Rooms are being shuttered just as others are added to the house of the nation.

But the *independentista* brand, call it indomitable spirit or infinite capability for delusion (whichever you prefer), resurfaced again after the nonbinding ballot question in the 2012 elections in which "no" to the current status received 53.99 percent of the vote. This, claimed PIP leaders, proved that *el pueblo* had rejected the island's colonial status. The old-guard spokesman for the PIP, Ruben Berríos, didn't mention that only 5.53 percent voted *for* independence, saying instead: "we crushed the attempt to maintain the colonial regime. It sends a message to the whole world that colonialism by consent is over." This will to *spin*, to redefine reality, means that the appeal of independence may continue to feed Puerto Rican culture as it has, and to exist side by side with the reign of dependency.

The island's paradoxical and conflicted feelings about dependency versus independence are the mix, the brew, the *burundanga* from which rise stories, themes, and images that power up the culture. These are the fictions of the dream nation.

Biographical Appendix

The following is a list of writers who appear in López-Baralt's biographical notes as having direct ties to independence (sometimes political, often cultural). For a fuller picture, I've supplemented information regarding major figures with data from other sources; this is indicated by an asterisk.

Rafael Acevedo (1959–) collaborates with *Claridad.*
Ramón Luis Acevedo (1947–) wrote a book about independence activist Pachín Marín.
Ernesto Álvarez (1937–) published a book on Lares, the famous revolutionary town.
Margot Arce de Vázquez (1904–1990). López-Baralt calls her an "indefatigable" defender of independence.
Marina Arzola (1939–1976) was honored posthumously by the journal *Guajana*, which was devoted to revolutionary poetry.
Emilio Belaval (1903–1972), as a lawyer, participated in the investigation of the Ponce Massacre.
Tomás Blanco (1897–1975) was an activist in various causes allied to independence, such as the Comité de Derechos Civiles, picketing the Anti-American Investigations Committee on the island.
*Julia de Burgos (1917–1953). Some of her poems are fiercely patriotic, especially in her first collection. She was firmly pro-worker. *Enciclopediapr.org* calls her "cantora de la patria" (songstress of the motherland).
Antonio Cabán Vale (1941–) wrote "Verde luz," the alternative nationalist hymn. He was a member of *Guajana*.

Francisco Manrique Cabrera (1908–1978) was one of the founders of the Movimiento Pro Independencia (Pro-Indepencence Movement) as well as founding member of the Partido Socialista Puertorriqueño (Puerto Rican Socialist Party).

˙Nemesio Canales (1878–1923) was a member of the Partido Autonomista (Autonomist Party).

Andrés Castro Ríos (1942–2006) was a founding member of *Guajana*.

Juan Antonio Corretjer (1908–1984), a towering figure of independence, was a follower of Albizu Campos and went to prison numerous times for his militancy.

Ángela María Dávila (1944–2003) was a member of *Guajana*.

Virgilio Dávila (1869–1941) was famous for his eulogies of the Land, a favorite nationalist trope.

Abelardo Díaz Alfaro (1917–1999) was a nativist writer who exalted agrarian Puerto Rico.

˙Emilio Díaz Valcárcel (1929–) stated that he had been involved with the nationalist movement in his youth, clarifying that: "Yo no era nacionalista activo, aunque participé en piquetes y cosas así. Pero el nacionalismo me sirvió para insuflarme fuerza, me dio un motivo por el cual escribir" (Hernández, *A viva voz* 55; I was not an active nationalist, even though I took part in strikes and such. But nationalism helped infuse me with strength; it gave me a reason to write).

˙José de Diego (1866–1918) was a founding member of the Partido Unionista and is still an icon for *independentismo*.

˙Rosario Ferré (1938–) favored independence in her youth, particularly during the days of the journal *Zona Carga y Descarga*, a short-lived left-wing magazine she cofounded in the early 1970s. Ferré later supported statehood.

José Ferrer Canales (1913–2005) was expelled from the UPR-RP for his militancy.

˙Hjalmar Flax (1942–) says that although he was rejected by *Guajana* (for not being folkloric enough), he was a militant *independentista* as a youth (Hernández, *A viva voz* 160–61).

˙Magali García Ramis (1948–) admits she was "ultrapolitizada" (ultrapoliticized) as a leftist during her youth (Pérez Rivera).

˙José Luis González (1926–1996) broke ranks with die-hard independence, though he remained a militant Marxist.

Josemilio González (1918–1990) was a member of the Nationalist Party.

Eugenio María de Hostos (1939–1903) was a famous patriot and defender of independence. He was the founder in exile of the Liga de Patriotas Puertorriqueños (League of Puerto Rican Patriots), which sought independence.

˙Enrique Laguerre (1906–2005). His novels focus on the island's economic and social ills, usually with a working-class component.
Edgardo López Ferrer (1943–) was a founding member of *Guajana*.
Luis López Nieves (1950–) wrote *Seva*, the most spirited blurring of historical fact and fiction in support of *independentismo*.
Carmen Lugo Filippi (1940–) writes for *Claridad*.
Luis Llorens Torres (1878–1944) wrote a play about the Grito de Lares.
Hugo Margenat (1933–1957) founded the student pro-independence group FUPI.
˙René Marqués (1919–1979). His plays and his famous essay "El puertorriqueño dócil" are nostalgic for Spain's rule of the island and bemoan the island's Americanization—key terms of customary *independentismo*. However, he was critical of the PIP.
Rosendo Matienzo Cintrón (1855–1913) cofounded the Partido Autonomista.
Francisco Matos Paoli (1915–2000) served in the Nationalist Party with Albizu Campos and went to prison for it.
Ramón Felipe Medina (1935–) wrote a book about the nationalist poet Juan Antonio Corretjer.
Joserramón Meléndez (1952–) wrote a book about Juan Antonio Corretjer.
Graciany Miranda Archilla (1910–1993) cofounded the nationalist poetry group La Atalaya.
˙Mayra Montero (1952–) publishes in *Claridad*.
Luis Muñoz Marín (1898–1980) was pro-independence in his youth; he later recanted and founded the ELA.
Olga Nolla (1938–2001) cofounded the journal *Zona Carga y Descarga* with her cousin Rosario Ferré.
˙Luis Palés Matos (1898–1959) was an orator in the 1920s for the Alianza Puertorriqueña, which defended independence.
Antonio S. Pedreira (1898–1939) wrote a book on Hostos, but also one on José Celso Barbosa, a noted early-twentieth-century pro-statehood activist.
Edwin Reyes (1944–2001) was a founding member of the journal *Guajana*.
˙Evaristo Ribera Chevremont (1896–1976) wrote many poems with nationalist themes ("El jíbaro" [The *jíbaro*]; "La décima criolla" [The creole song]; "Noches de Puerto Rico" [Puerto Rican night]; "Paisajes en nuestro cielo" [Landscapes in our sky"]).
Lola Rodríguez de Tió (1843–1924) was a famous nationalist who wrote the lyrics to the revolutionary hymn "La Borinqueña."

*Edgardo Rodríguez Juliá (1946–) recalls, in *A viva voz*, attending the UPR-RP at the height of the Marxist-*independentista* 1960s. Widely considered a centrist; wrote a book about Luis Muñoz Marín.

Vicente Rodríguez Nietzsche (1942–) was a founding member of *Guajana*.

Juan Sáez Burgos (1943–) was a founding member of *Guajana*.

*Luis Rafael Sánchez (1936–) is a supporter of independence.

*Esmeralda Santiago (1948–) states that Puerto Ricans seek independence in her novel *America's Dream*.

*Mayra Santos Febres (1966–) writes about defiantly "declaring" herself *independentista* at thirteen (*Sobre piel y papel* 206).

Wenceslao Serra Deliz (1941–) was a founding member of *Guajana*.

*Pedro Juan Soto (1944–) is a renowned *independentista*.

Clemente Soto Vélez (1905–1993) cofounded the poetry group "La Atalaya"; a militant nationalist in the 1930s, he served nine years in prison.

José Manuel Torres Santiago (1940–) was a founding member of *Guajana*.

*Ana Lydia Vega (1946–) is an outspoken defender of independence.

Bernardo Vega (1885–1916) was a "socialist and *independentista*."

Nilita Vientós Gastón (1903–1989) as a lawyer achieved designation of Spanish as the national language by the Puerto Rican Supreme Court.

Manuel Zeno Gandía (1855–1930) in 1912 helped create the Partido de la Independencia de Puerto Rico.

Notes

Introduction

1. The struggles for independence differ wildly. The BBC summarized the Chechnian situation saying, "Rebel fighters want independence, or at least self-rule, and they almost got it after 1996" ("Q&A: The Chechen Conflict"); Russia has been fighting them ever since. The independence movements in Cataluña and Scotland are pushing for referenda to decide whether their regions will return to their status as independent sovereign states. A quick summary of the far more splintered, and peaceful, Quebecois movement can be read at CBC News, "Quebec Sovereignty Debate Settled: Poll" (www.cbc.ca/canada/montreal/story/2010/05/18/mtl-poll-national-question-crop.html).

On the other hand, the results of the Tamil Tiger pro-independence movement were far more bloody; the *New York Times* (9 Sept. 2010) estimates that sixty thousand people died and perhaps 1 million were displaced between 1983, when the Tamil separatists took up arms, until 2010, when, after the government defeated them in 2009, the Tamil Tigers downgraded their call from "independence" to "self-rule" (http://topics.nytimes.com/top/news/international/countriesandterritories/srilanka/index.html?scp=1-spot&sq=sri percent201anka&st=cse).

2. In the 2012 election, a (disputed) majority (44.9 percent) preferred statehood in an (albeit muddled and nonbinding) ballot initiative/referendum while at the same time rejecting the pro-statehood party. The ballot had two parts; the first asked voters if they wanted to retain the present status (commonwealth) and "no" won the most votes, with 934,238, while "yes" took 796,007. The second part gave voters three options: statehood (which won with 809,652 votes or 44.9 percent); an (ill-defined) sovereign commonwealth (441,505 or 24.5 percent); or, finally, independence (73,362 or 4.1 percent). Complicating matters was the high number of blank ballots, 472,674, on the second part.

3. Rafael Bernabe, for instance, analyzes differences in contemporary *independentismo*, particularly that of the group called Taller de Formación Política (13).

Mariel C. Marrero-García and Freddie Rodríguez's *Dialogando* is also a nuanced take on the contending sides of the movement throughout the twentieth century. In a similar vein, Mario Ramos Méndez's *Posesión del ayer* looks at the different versions of a contending status option, pro-statehood.

4. Memes are the cultural counterpart of genes: "A cultural unit (an idea or value or pattern of behavior) that is passed from one person to another by non-genetic means (as by imitation)" (wordnetweb.princeton.edu/perl/webwn).

5. In Puerto Rico, "nationalist" is synonymous with *independentista* because the mid-twentieth-century Partido Nacionalista was an important force for independence.

6. "La calle al revés," *El Nuevo Día* 15 Jan. 2012.

7. The blogger and critic Ivette Romero-Cesareo affirmed at the time of Lebrón's death that "in recent years, Lebrón tempered her support for violent struggle. 'I think times have changed, and there is no need now to kill for freedom,' she told *El Mundo* newspaper in 1998. 'I would not take up arms nowadays, but I acknowledge that the people have a right to use any means available to free themselves.'"

8. *Claridad* also published a more pointedly explicatory item titled "Lolita Lebrón championed the struggle for independence without violence in one of her last interviews" (*Claridad* 2 Aug. 2010).

9. Edgardo Rodríguez Juliá wrote an acclaimed book on Muñoz (as that political leader was popularly known) titled *Las tribulaciones de Jonás* (1981) that reimagines and dramatizes the history and politics of Puerto Rico in Muñoz's time. Rodríguez Juliá uses a New Journalistic style that mixes memories and experiences of that time (Rubén González 46).

10. Guadeloupe, which had been a colony of France, became an overseas department of France in 1946; in 1974, it converted into an administrative region. Its deputies sit in the French National Assembly in Paris. Martinique also became an official department of France in 1946 and an administrative region in 1982.

11. Prominent *independentistas* in the discussion were Juan Manuel Carrión Morales, Michael González Cruz, Ángel Israel Rivera, and Rafael Bernabe.

12. The word refers to a class of people, the country folk of yore; they are a long-standing symbol of the nation.

13. Nathaniel L. Córdova, in "In His Image and Likeness: The Puerto Rican Jíbaro as Political Icon," provides an in-depth analysis of the process of co-option of the *jíbaro* by the PPD.

14. A member of the Movimiento Hostosiano, an *independentista* group named after Eugenio María de Hostos. The *hostosiano* movements are a variant on *independentismo* cofounded by the late Juan Mari Brás, a stalwart of the independence movements of the twentieth century.

15. I use Néstor García Canclini's definition of the term "globalization": "globalization develops in the second half of the twentieth century, when the convergence of economic, financial, communication, and migration processes enhances the interdependence of almost all societies and generates new flows and structures of supranational interconnection" (2).

16. www.pueblotrabajador.com/propuestas/programa-del-partido-del-pueblo-trabajador.html.

17. http://abcnews.go.com/ABC_Univision/Opinion/puerto-rico-status-plebiscite/story?id=17674719#.UJ5oMuS7PWR.

18. Héctor Martínez Ramírez has written on the influence of Pentecostal activist organizations on the general elections of 1992 and 1996.
19. http://soberaniapuertorico.blogspot.com/ [7 Jan. 2010].
20. "Their Day in the Sun," *Economist* 15 July 2011, 43.
21. www3.weforum.org/docs/WEF_GCR_Report_2011–12.pdf.
22. According to the Associated Press, 13 June 2011.
23. The others members of the group proposing radical statehood were Juan Duchesne Winter, Chloé Georas, Agustín Lao, Pedro Angel Rivera, and Aurea María Sotomayor (Ramos Méndez 160–68).
24. He's quoting Muñóz Marín from Edgardo Rodríguez Juliá's *Las tribulaciones de Jonás*, 32 (Torres-Saillant 146)
25. http://independencia.net/entrada.html [7 Jan. 2010].
26. www.youtube.com/user/jrbaspr?gl=ES&hl=es [7 Jan. 2010].
27. http://piprincon.blogspot.com/ [7 Jan. 2010].
28. http://cienciaeindependencia.blogspot.com/ [7 Jan. 2010].
29. http://lugaresimaginarios.wordpress.com/2011/05/12/seva-relectura/.
30. http://elvuelodelagarza.blogspot.com/ [7 Jan. 2010].
31. www.vozdelcentro.org/ [8 Jan. 2011].
32. For instance: www.laesquinadekarde.8k.com/catalog.html [8 Jan. 2011] and http://members.tripod.com/~Mictlantecuhtli/Albizu/concna13.html [8 Jan. 2011].
33. Puerto Rico's economic situation became dire in the aftermath of 2008. In order to balance the budget in 2009, the government enacted the largest layoffs in government workers yet; starting November 2010, that meant 16,970 lost their jobs and 40 government agencies, out of 134, ceased to exist.
34. "The isle of enchantment" is a popular and Chamber of Commerce moniker for Puerto Rico.

1 / Literary Tradition and the Canon of Independence

1. Pro-independence newspapers.
2. I use the categorization of "generations" because it is useful and traditional but note the objections to this method of periodization. Juan G. Gelpí, for instance, says that the division of literature into generations is paternalistic because these are often structured around a *caudillo* and therefore subordinate multiplicity to unity and exclude difference (López-Baralt, *Antología*160).
3. Beyond Martínez Masdeu and Melon's two-volume *Antología general*, there are several anthologies that give a panoramic sweep: Josefina Rivera de Álvarez and Manuel Álvarez Nazario's *Antología general [. . .]*, vol. 1 (covering the sixteenth through early twentieth centuries); Ramón Luis Acevedo Marrero's *Antología crítica* (covering the sixteenth to the nineteenth centuries); Hilda E. Quintana, María Cristina Rodríguez and Gladys Vila Barnés's *Personalidad y literatura puertorriqueñas*; Mayra Santos Febres's *Mal(h)ab(1)ar. Antología de nueva literatura puertorriqueña*, which, as the title states, features writers of her generation (roughly the 1980s and 1990s). Recently, we've seen anthologies geared to contemporary interests such as LBGT and so-called diasporic themes such as David Caleb Acevedo, Moisés Agosto Rosario and Luis Negrón's *Los otros cuerpos. Antología de temática gay, lésbica y queer desde Puerto Rico y su diáspora*. There have also been many anthologies by genre (short stories and poetry seem most popular).

4. The serious tone is in contrast to the charmingly light style of her cultural reminiscences in *Llévame alguna vez entre flores*.

5. Frustratingly, the anthology dates the piece by the edition of 1977, not by the date of publication.

6. On the twenty-fifth anniversary of its publication, in 2011, *El Nuevo Día* reported that it had been reprinted eleven times, translated into many languages, and that overall 120,000 copies had been sold (Pérez Rivera).

7. Varo's *Consideraciones antropológicas y políticas en torno a la enseñanza del Spanglish en Nueva York* (Anthropological and political considerations regarding the teaching of Spanglish in New York) opposes the teaching of a course on Spanglish; another book, *Puerto Rico: Radiografía de un pueblo asediado* (Puerto Rico: X-ray of a besieged country) deals with the island's colonial condition.

2 / Breaking Tradition

1. Soto's recollections on Laguerre are muddled since, after asserting that Laguerre was secretly a conservative, he affirms that the same writer "se vino a descubrir ahora como independentista" (Hernández, *A viva voz* 30; came now to be discovered as an *independentista*).

2. In the interview titled "Rosario Ferré: Familia e historia nacional" with Walescka Pino-Ojeda.

3 / From the Lush Land to the Traffic Jam

1. Ana Lydia Vega defines the term as an assimilationist betrayal of *independentista* patriotism: "servilismo imitativo apodado 'pitiyanquismo'" ("El PNP y el inglés"; imitative servility nicknamed "pitiyanquismo").

2. www.tendenciaspr.com/Publicaciones/transporte/tapon.html [updated 16 Sept. 2008].

4 / Dream Nation, Dream History

1. The use of "rizomal" as a modifier for culture was developed by philosophers such as Édouard Glissant (in the Caribbean) and Gilles Deleuze and Félix Guattari. For instance, a conference of Caribbeanists in 2009 at the University of Puerto Rico, Mayagüez, called "Rethinking the Mangrove" used the plant as an overarching metaphor with which "to reconceptualize Caribbeanness beyond the limitations of nation, language, and culture, focusing on the crosscurrents that traverse the multiple and overlapping spaces and subjectivities of the Caribbean. The roots of the mangrove, which hang above the water, evoke a Caribbean alternative to an ethnolinguistically monolithic ideal of identity symbolized by the terrestrial root" (http://blogs.uprm.edu/mangroveuprm).

Works Cited

Acevedo Marrero, Ramón Luis. *Antología crítica de la literatura puertorriqueña. Desde los mitos taínos hasta Zeno Gandía.* San Juan, Puerto Rico: Cultural, 2005. Print.

Acosta Cruz, María. "Esmeralda Santiago in the Marketplace of Identity Politics" *Centro: Journal of the Center for Puerto Rican Studies; Hunter College, CUNY* 27.1 (Fall 2006): 170–87.

Acosta-Bélen, Edna, and Judith Ortiz Cofer. "A *MELUS* Interview: Judith Ortiz Cofer." *Poetry and Poetics.* Spec. issue of *MELUS* 18.3 (Autumn 1993): 83–97. JSTOR. Web. 3 April 2009.

Acosta-Belén, Edna, and Carlos E. Santiago. *Puerto Ricans in the United States: A Contemporary Portrait.* Boulder and London: Lynne Rienner, 2006. Print.

Aldama, Frederick Luis. *Why the Humanities Matter: A Commonsense Approach.* Austin: University of Texas Press, 2008. Print.

Algarín, Miguel. *Survival. Superviencia.* Houston, TX: oustoArte Público Press, 2009. Print.

Algarín, Miguel, and Bob Holman. *Aloud: Voices from the Nuyorican Poets Cafe.* New York: Holt, 1994. Print.

Alonso, Manuel Antonio. *El Gíbaro: Cuadro de costumbres de la isla de Puerto Rico.* Juan Oliveres, 1849. Google Book Search. Web. 17 Feb. 2009.

Álvarez, Eric. "Las tribulaciones nacionalistas del escritor Edgardo Rodríguez Juliá." *Cuantum de la cuneta (blog).* Web. 20 Nov. 2010.

Álvarez Curbelo, Silvia. "La patria desde la tierra: Pedro Albizu Campos y el nacionalismo económico antillano." Carrión et al. 83–95.

Amar Sánchez, Ana María. "Héroes, vencedores y derrotados o 'la banalidad del mal' en la narrativa latinoamericana." *Foro hispánico. Para romper con el insularismo: Letras puertorriqueñas en comparación*. Ed. Efraín Barradas and Rita de Maeseneer. Amsterdam and Atlanta: Rodopi, 2006. 9–26. Print.

Anazagasty Rodríguez, José. "Más sobre las carpetas y la era de la disculpa." *80Grados*. Web. 4 May 2012.

Anderson, Benedict. *Imagined Communities*. London: Verso, 1991. Print.

Anselin, Alain. "West Indians in France." *French and West Indian: Martinique, Guadeloupe, and French Guiana Today*. Ed. Richard D. E. Burton and Fred Reno. Charlottesville: University of Virginia Press, 1995. Print.

Anzaldúa, Gloria E. "(Un)natural bridges, (Un)safe spaces." *This Bridge We Call Home*. New York: Routledge, 2002. 1–6. Print.

Arroyo, Carmen. "Literatos endosan la independencia." *El Nuevo Día*. Web. 26 Jan. 2007.

Barradas, Efraín. *Para leer en puertorriqueño: Acercamiento a la obra de Luis Rafael Sánchez*. Río Piedras, Puerto Rico: Cultural, 1981. Print.

———. *Partes de un todo. Ensayos y notas sobre literatura puertorriqueña en los Estados Unidos*. San Juan, Puerto Rico: Universidad de Puerto Rico, 1998. Print.

Bayrón Toro, Fernando. *Elecciones y partidos políticos de Puerto Rico 1809–2000*. Mayagüez, Puerto Rico: Isla, 2003. Print.

Bernabe, Rafael. *Manual para organizar velorios*. Puerto Rico: Huracán, 2003. Print.

Bhabha, Homi. *Nation and Narration*. London: Routledge, 1990. Print.

Blanco, Tomás. "Reflexiones finales del prontuario histórico de Puerto Rico." Mari Brás 205–15.

Bobes, Marilyn, Pedro Antonio Valdéz, and Carlos Roberto Gómez Beras, eds. *Los nuevos caníbales. Antología de la más reciente cuentística del Caribe hispano*. 2nd ed. Havana, Cuba: Unión, 2004. Print.

"Bosnia and Herzegovina." 27 Nov. 2010. *Encyclopædia Britannica*. 2010. Encyclopædia Britannica Online. Web. 9 July 2011.

Braschi, Giannina. *United States of Banana*. Kindle eBook. 2011.

Brookhiser, Richard. "The Nation: Unmanifest Destiny—What to Do with Puerto Rico." *National Review* 52.11. Web. 19 June 2000.

Brown, Emma. "Lolita Lebrón, Jailed for Gun Attack at U.S. Capitol in 1954, Dies at 90." *Washington Post*. Web. 2 Aug 2010.

Burgos, Julia de. *Obra poética*. San Juan, Puerto Rico: Instituto de Cultura Puertorriqueña, 1961. Web. http://ufdc.ufl.edu/UF00076943/00001.

Caleb Acevedo, David, Moisés Agosto Rosario, and Luis Negrón. *Los otros cuerpos. Antología de temática gay, lésbica y queer desde Puerto Rico y su diáspora*. San Juan, Puerto Rico: Tiempo Nuevo, 2007. Print.

Cámara Fuertes, Luis Raúl. *The Phenomenon of Puerto Rican Voting*. Gainesville: University Press of Florida, 2004. Print.

Cámara Fuertes, Luis Raúl, and Olga I. Rosas Cintrón. "Social and Ideological

Bases of Status Support in Puerto Rico." *Caribbean Studies* 32.2 (July–Dec. 2004): 145–78. Web. 3 Mar. 2010.

Campa, Román de la. "Latin, Latino, American: Split States and Global Imaginaries." *Comparative Literature* 53.4 (Autumn 2001): 373–88. JSTOR. Web. 6 Dec. 2008.

Cancel, Mario R. *Anti-figuraciones: Bocetos puertorriqueños.* Mario R. Cancel, 2003. Google Book Search. Web. 16 Sept. 2008.

———. *Literatura y narrativa puertorriqueña: La escritura entre siglos.* San Juan, Puerto Rico: Pasadizo, 2007. Print.

Cancel Sepúlveda, Mario R. "Miradas al treinta: Del Aliancismo al Nacionalismo." *8ogrados.* 11 May 2012. Web. 13 May 2012.

———. "Seva: historia de una (re)lectura." *lugaresimaginarios.* 12 May 2011. Web. 17 May 2011.

Carpentier, Alejo. *El arpa y la sombra.* Madrid: Siglo XXI, 1999. Print.

Carrión, Juan Manuel. "Etnia, raza y la nacionalidad puertorriqueña." Carrión et al. 3–18.

Carrión, Juan Manuel, Teresa C. Gracia Ruiz, and Carlos Rodríguez Fraticelli, eds. *La nación puertorriqueña: Ensayos en torno a Pedro Albizu Campos.* San Juan, Puerto Rico: Universidad de Puerto Rico, 1993. Print.

Carrión Morales, Juan Manuel. *Voluntad de nación: Ensayos sobre el nacionalismo en Puerto Rico.* San Juan, Puerto Rico: Nueva Aurora, 1996. Print.

Castellanos, Juan de. "Arenga de Agüeibana" and "Muerte de Agüeibana." Acevedo Marrero 33–38.

———. "Elegía VI. A la muerte de Juan Ponce de León." Rivera de Álvarez 16–20.

Celis, Nadia V., and Juan Pablo Rivera, eds. *Lección errante. Mayra Santos Febres y el Caribe contemporáneo.* San Juan, Puerto Rico: Isla Negra, 2011. Print.

Chamoiseau, Patrick, and Édouard Glissant. "Los muros. Acercamiento a los azares y a la necesidad de la idea de identidad." *Revista Casa de las Américas* 249 (Oct.–Dec. 2007): 92–97. Print.

Cintrón Opio, Ángel. "Oda a la Tierra Puertorriqueña." *El Nuevo Día.* Web. 8 Jan. 2009.

Colón López, Joaquín. *Puertorriqueños pioneros en Nueva York. 1917–1947.* Houston, TX: Arte Público Press, 2002. Print.

Colón Solá, Aura. "Lo más cercano a la libertad." *Claridad.* Web. 25 Sept. 2010.

Cooper, Helene. "In Visit to Puerto Rico, Obama Offers (and Seeks Out) Offers (and Seeks Out) Support." *New York Times.* Web. 14 June 2011.

Córdova, Nathaniel L. "In His Image and Likeness: The Puerto Rican Jíbaro as Political Icon." *Centro Journal* 17.2 (Fall 2005): 170–91. Web. 17 Aug. 2007.

Corretjer, Juan Antonio. *Alabanzas.* www.centropablo.cult.cu/libros_descargar/alabanzas.pdf. Web. 4 Sept. 2008.

———. *La lucha por la independencia de Puerto Rico.* 1949. Ciales, Puerto Rico: Casa Corretjer, 1995. Print.

Coss, Luis Fernando. *La nación en la orilla (respuesta a los posmodernos pesimistas).* Puerto Rico: Punto de Encuentro, 1996. Print.

Coss, Papo. "La renovación del independentismo 2009." *RedBetances.com.* 2 May 2009. Web. 13 May 2009.

Council on Hemispheric Affairs (COHA). "Guadeloupe: Out of Sight, but Not Out of Mind." *coha.org.* 2 Mar. 2009. Web. 9 Mar. 2009.

Dávila, Arlene M. *Sponsored Identities: Cultural Politics in Puerto Rico.* Philadelphia: Temple University Press, 1997. Print.

Delgado, José A. "En ocho minutos." *El Nuevo Día..* Web. 15 June 2011.

———. "Obama nombra otro boricua." *El Nuevo Día.* Web. 31 Mar. 2009.

———. "Sotomayor y el status." *El Nuevo Día.* Web. 30 May 2009.

Derrickson, Teresa. "'Cold/Hot, English/Spanish': The Puerto Rican American Divide in Judith Ortiz Cofer's *Silent Dancing.*" *Haunted by History.* Spec. issue of *MELUS* 28.2 (Summer 2003): 121–37. Web. 21 June 2012.

Devine, Susan. "La meta-historia de Puerto Rico en *Maldito amor* de Rosario Ferré." *Divergencias. Revista de Estudios Lingüísticos y Literarios* 2.2 (Fall 2004): 73–80. Web. 8 Feb. 2010.

Díaz Quiñones, Arcadio. *Conversación con José Luis González.* 2nd ed. Río Piedras, Puerto Rico: Huracán, 1977. Print.

Duany, Jorge. *The Puerto Rican Nation on the Move: Identities on the Island and in the United States.* Chapel Hill: University of North Carolina Press, 2002. Print.

Duchesne, Juan Ramón. *Ciudadano insano. Ensayos bestiales sobre cultura y literatura.* San Juan, Puerto Rico: Callejón, 2001. Print.

———. Review of *Seva. Revista de Crítica Literaria Latinoamericana* 11.21/22 (1985): 256–59. Web. 18 May 2010.

Duchesne Winter, Juan. "Escritor, idioma, literatura: 'Defensas' que no ayudan." *Sololiteratura.com.* Web. 30 July 2012. http://sololiteratura.com/fer/ferescritor.htm

———. "Metafísica narrativa de la nación albizuista." Carrión et al. 19–31.

"El camino hacia la independencia. Editorial." *Claridad..* Web. 25 Sept. 2009.

Encyclopedia of Contemporary French Culture. Ed. Alex Hughes and Keith Reader. London and New York: Routledge, 1998. Print.

Encyclopedia of Nationalism: Leaders, Movements, and Concepts. Oxford: Elsevier Science and Technology, 2000. *Credo Reference.* Web. 15 January 2009.

Esteves, Sandra María. "Ambivalencia o activismo desde la perspectiva poética de los Nuyoricans." *Imágenes e identidades: el puertorriqueño en la literatura,* edited by Asela Rodríguez de Laguna. Río Piedras, Puerto Rico: Huracán, 1985. Print.

Falcón, Angelo. "The Diaspora Factor: Stateside Boricuas and the Future of

Puerto Rico." *NACLA Report on the* Americas 40.6 (Nov.-Dec. 2007): 28–31. Web. 7 April 2009.

———. "From Civil Rights to the 'Decade of the Hispanic': Boricuas in Gotham, 1960–1990." *Boricuas in Gotham: Puerto Ricans in the Making of Modern New York City. Essays in Memory of Antonia Pantoja.* Ed. Gabriel Haslip-Viera, Angelo Falcón and Félix Matos Rodríguez. Princeton, NJ: Markus Wiener, 2004: 107–30. Print.

Ferrao, Luis Ángel. *Pedro Albizu Campos y el nacionalismo puertorriqueño 1930–1939.* Río Piedras, Puerto Rico: Cultural, 1990. Print.

Ferré, Rosario. *The House on the Lagoon.* New York: Plume, 1995. Print.

———. *Las puertas del placer.* Puerto Rico: Alfaguara, 2005. Print.

———. "Puerto Rico, U.S.A." *New York Times.* 19 Mar. 1998. Web. 5 Aug. 2010.

Flores, Juan. *From Bomba to Hip-Hop: Puerto Rican Culture and Latino Identity.* New York: Columbia University Press, 2000. Print.

———. "Puerto Rican Literature in the United States: Stages and Perspectives." *Recovering the U.S. Hispanic Literary Heritage, Volume 1.* Ed. Ramón A. Gutiérrez, and Genaro M. Padilla. Houston: Arte Público Press, 1993. 53–68. Google Book Search. Web. 18 Jan. 2010.

———. *The Diaspora Strikes Back: Caribeño Tales of Learning and Turning.* New York: Routledge, 2009. Print.

Font Acevedo, Francisco. *La belleza bruta.* San Juan, Puerto Rico: Tal Cual, 2008. Print.

Franco, Jean. *An Introduction to Spanish-American Literature.* Cambridge: Cambridge University Press, 1994. Print.

Fuente, José Luis de la. "El castillo de la memoria de Olga Nolla: De la inmortalidad a la identidad." *Murales, figuras, fronteras: Narrativa e historia en el Caribe y Centroamérica.* Ed. Patrick Collard and Rita de Maeseneer. Madrid: Verveurt, 2003. 65–92. Print.

García Canclini, Néstor. "La globalización: ¿Productora de culturas híbridas?" *Actas del III Congreso Latinoamericano de la Asociación Internacional para el Estudio de la Música Popular.* Bogotá, 2000. hist.puc.cl. Web. 16 Oct. 2007.

García Cuevas, Eugenio. *Descendientes del sonido.* San Juan, Puerto Rico: Isla Negra, 2007. Print.

García Passalacqua, Juan Manuel. "Prólogo." Ramos Méndez 13–17.

García Passalacqua, Juan M., and Néstor R. Duprey Salgado. *Conversaciones en el convento: La visión de Luis Muñoz Marín a mediados del siglo XX.* Madrid: EMS, 2006. Print.

García Ramis, Magali. *Felices días, tío Sergio.* Puerto Rico: Antillana, 1992. Print.

———. *Las horas del sur.* San Juan, Puerto Rico: Callejón, 2005. Print.

Garsd, Jasmine. "Puerto Rican Hip-Hop Icon Tego Calderon Mixes Prose and Politics." *NPR.org.* 8 Feb. 2013 Web. 9 Feb. 2013.

Genocchio, Benjamin. "Three Artists, an Island's History and Botany." *New York Times* 25 Mar. 2007. Web. 3 April 2009.

Gil, Carlos. "Intellectuals Confront the Crisis of Traditional Narratives in Puerto Rico." *Social Text* 38 (Spring 1994): 97–104. JSTOR. Web. 6 Nov. 2006.

Glissant, Édouard. *Caribbean Discourse: Selected Essays*. Trans. J. Michael Dash. Charlottesville: University Press of Virginia, 1989. Print.

González, José Luis. *Antología personal*. 2nd ed. Río Piedras: Universidad de Puerto Rico, 1998. Print.

———. *Cuentos completos*. Mexico City: Alfaguara, 1997. Print.

———. *El país de cuatro pisos y otros ensayos*. 7th ed. Río Piedras, Puerto Rico: Huracán, 1989. Print.

———. *Nueva visita al cuarto piso*. 2nd ed. Santurce, Puerto Rico: Flamboyán, S.B.P., 1987. Print.

González, Rubén. *La historia puertorriqueña de Rodríguez Juliá*. Río Piedras: Universidad de Puerto Rico, 1997. Print.

González Cruz, Michael. *Nacionalismo revolucionario puertorriqueño (1959-2005). La lucha armada, intelectuales y prisioneros políticos y de guerra*. San Juan/Santo Domingo: Isla Negra, 2006. Print.

González de Freytes, Gina. *De porcelana y acero*. San Juan/Santo Domingo: Isla Negra, 2010. Print.

Grillo, Rafael. "Las extrañas ucronías de Luis López Nieves. O la verdadera 'subversión.' A propósito de la publicación en Cuba de los libros *Seva* y *El corazón de Voltaire*." *El Caimán Barbudo*. ecured.cu. no. 356. Web. 4 Dec. 2010.

Grosfoguel, Ramón. *Colonial Subjects: Puerto Ricans in a Global Perspective*. Berkeley: University of California Press, 2003. Print.

———. "The Divorce of Nationalist Discourses." Negrón-Muntaner and Grosfoguel 57–76.

———. "La estadidad desde una perspectiva democrática radical." *Diálogo* (1997): 30–31. Print.

Guillory, John. *Cultural Capital: The Problem of Literary Canon Formation*. Chicago: University of Chicago Press, 1993. Print.

Guzmán, Robert. "Critical Mass." puertorican.com. Web. 6 Jan 2010.

Hernández, Carmen Dolores. *A viva voz. Entrevistas a escritores puertorriqueños*. Bogotá: Norma, 2007. Print.

———. "La breve y maravillosa carrera literaria de Junot Díaz." *El Nuevo Día*. Web. 3 Mar. 2009.

———. *Puerto Rican Voices in English: Interviews with Writers*. Westport, CT: Praeger, 1997. Print.

Hernández Cabiya, Yanira. "Ola de cesantías arropa la isla." *El Nuevo Día*. Web. 26 Sept. 2009.

Hintz, Suzanne S. "La palabra, según Rosario Ferré." ensayistas.org. 8 April 2009. Web. 15 May 2010.

Hodges, Kenneth. "Why Malory's 'Launcelot' Is Not French: Region, Nation, and Political Identity." *PMLA* 125.3 (May 2010): 556–71. Print.
Irizarry, Estelle. "Historiografía novelada: Redescubrimiento de *Isla cerrera* de Manuel Méndez Ballester."*Ciudad Seva* 4 Feb. 2010. Web. 5 Aug. 2010.
———. "La "Leyenda urbana" en la narrativa de Luis López Nieves." *Hispania* 86. 1 (Mar. 2003): 32–42. JSTOR. Web. 19 May 2010.
Irizarry Natal, Federico. *Kitsch*. San Juan, Puerto Rico: Isla Negra, 2006. Print.
Janer, Zilkia. *Puerto Rican Nation-Building Literature: Impossible Romance*. Gainesville: University Press of Florida, 2005. Print.
Johnson, Kelli Lyon. "Writing Home: Mapping Puerto Rican Collective Memory in *The House on the Lagoon*. Torres-Padilla 239–55.
Kanellos, Nicolás. *Herencia: The Anthology of Hispanic Literature of the United States*. Oxford and New York: Oxford University Press, 2002. Print.
Kevane, Bridget. *Latino Literature in America*. Bridgeport, CT: Greenwood, 2003. Print.
Kevane, Bridget, and Juanita Heredia. *Latina Self-Portraits: Interviews with Contemporary Women Writers*. Albuquerque: University of New Mexico Press, 2000. Print.
Klor de Alva, Jorge J. "Aztlán, Borinquen, and Hispanic Nationalism in the United States." *The Latino Studies Reader: Culture, Economy, and Society*. Ed. Antonia Darder and Rodolfo D. Torres. Malden, MA: Blackwell, 1998: 63–82. Print.
Koenigsberg, Richard. *The Nation: A Study in Ideology and Fantasy*. Charlotte, NC: Information Age Publishing, 2007. Web. Google Book Search. 3 May 2009.
La Torre Lagares, Elidio. *Correr tras el viento*. Viejo San Juan, Puerto Rico: Terranova, 2011. Print.
Lalo, Eduardo. *Simone*. Buenos Aires: Corregidor, 2011. Print.
Lao, Agustín. "Islands at the Crossroads: Puerto Ricanness Traveling between the Translocal Nation and the Global City." Negrón-Muntaner and Grosfoguel 169–88.
Lass, Rolf. "'Nigrescent Ganesh' Cultural Nationalism and the Culture of Writing in Chen, Glissant, and V. S. Naipul." *Writing the Nation: Self and Country in Post-colonial Imagination*. Ed. John C. Hawley. Amsterdam and Atlanta: Rodopi, 1966. 1–22. Print.
Laviera, Tato. *Mixturao*. Houston, TX: Arte Público Press, 2008. Print.
"Lolita Lebron, Puerto Rican Independence Activist; at 89." Obituary. *Boston Globe*. 2 Aug. 2010. Web. 2 Aug. 2010.
López Adorno, Pedro. "Making the Decolonized Visible: Puerto Rican Poetry of the Last Four Decades." *Centro Journal of the Center for Puerto Rican Studies; Hunter College, CUNY* 18.2 (2006): 5–23. Print.
López-Baralt, Mercedes. "Estudios Hispánicos no se rinde." *8ogrados*. 24 Jan. 2011. Web. 24 Jan. 2011.

———. *Literatura puertorriqueña del siglo XX: Antología*. Río Piedras, Puerto Rico: Universidad de Puerto Rico, 2004. Print.

———. *Llévame alguna vez entre flores*. San Juan, Puerto Rico: Isla Negra, 2006. Print.

López Bauzá, Juan. "Rosario Ferré: El debate del idioma, los escritores de ayer y hoy." *Palique* 19 Feb. 1999. Web. 21 Oct. 2008.

López Nieves, Luis. *El corazón de Voltaire*. Bogotá: Norma, 2005. Print.

———. "En la muralla de San Juan." www.ciudadseva.com. 27 Jan. 2005. Web. 17 April 2009.

———. *La verdadera muerte de Juan Ponce de León*. Bogotá: Norma, 2006. Print.

———. *Seva*. 5th ed. San Juan, Puerto Rico: Cordillera, 1987. Print.

Lozada, Ángel. *La patografía*. México: Planeta, 1996. Print.

———. *No quiero quedarme sola y vacía*. San Juan, Santo Domingo: Isla Negra, 2006. Print.

Luis, Leopoldo. "*Seva* en Casa." *El Caimán Barbudo*. ecured.cu. no. 344. Web. 16 Dec. 2011.

Lyon Johnson, Kelli. "Writing Home: Mapping Puerto Rican Collective Memory in *The House on the Lagoon*. Torres-Padilla 239–55.

Macherey, Pierre. *A Theory of Literary Production*. Trans. Geoffrey Wall. London: Routledge, 1978. Print.

Macías de Yoon, Claudia. "Historia de arroz con habichuelas de Ana Lydia Vega, ¿una alegoría del pasado?" *Espéculo* 45. Web. 4 Mar. 2011.

Mari Brás, Juan, comp. *En busca de una estrella. Antología del pensamiento independentista puertorriqueño: De Betances a Filiberto*. Mayagüez, Puerto Rico: Causa Común, 2007. Print.

Marqués, René. *El puertorriqueño dócil y otros ensayos (1953–1971)*. 3rd ed. San Juan, Puerto Rico: Antillana, 1977. Print.

Marrero-García, Mariel C., and Freddie Rodríguez, dirs. *Dialogando sobre independentismos. Entre votos, consignas y trincheras. 1890–1959. Parte I*. Producciones Zaranda (zaranda.com), 2006. DVD.

Martí, José. "Nuestra América." ciudadseva.com. 10 Nov. 2010. Web. 14 Jan. 2011.

Martínez Masdeu, Edgar, and Esther M. Melon, eds. *Literatura puertorriqueña. Antología general. Tomo II—Siglo XX*. 2nd ed. Río Piedras, Puerto Rico: Edil, 1972. Print.

Martínez Ramírez, Héctor M. "Pentecostal Expansion and Political Activism in Puerto Rico." *Caribbean Studies* 33.1 (Jan.–Jun. 2005): 113–47. JSTOR. Web. 29 Aug. 2009.

Matos Valldejuli, Jorge, and Juan Flores. "New Rican Voices: Un muestrario/A Sampler at the Millennium." *Centro Journal of the Center for Puerto Rican Studies; Hunter College, CUNY* 12.1 (Fall 2000): 49–95. Print.

McCracken, Ellen. *New Latina Narrative: The Feminine Space of Postmodern Ethnicity*. Tucson: University of Arizona Press, 1999. Print.

Miranda, Maria. "Anniversary of US Invasion of Puerto Rico." *Daily Sun*. Web. 25 July 2011.
Morales, Ed. *Living in Spanglish. The Search for Latino Identity in America*. New York: St. Martin's Press, 2002. Print.
———. "Puerto Rico's Simulated Self-Determination." *Edmorales.net.*. Web. 11 Nov. 2012.
Morales, Jacobo, dir. *Linda Sara*. 1994. DVD.
Mujica, Barbara. "Teaching Literature: Canon, Controversy, and the Literary Anthology." *Hispania* 80.2 (May 1997): 203–15. Web. 17 Oct. 2012.
Musgrave, Thomas D. *Self-Determination and National Minorities*. Oxford: Oxford University Press Oxford Monographs in International Law, 1997. Print.
Narayan, Uma. "Essence of Culture and a Sense of History: A Feminist Critique of Cultural Essentialism." *Decentering the Center: Philosophy for a Multicultural, Postcolonial, and Feminist World*. Ed. Uma Narayan and Sandra Harding. Bloomington: Indiana University Press, 2000: 80–100. Print.
Negrón, Luis. *Mundo cruel*. Río Piedras, Puerto Rico: La Secta de los Perros, 2010. Print.
Negrón-Muntaner, Frances. *Boricua Pop: Puerto Ricans and the Latinization of American Culture*. New York: New York University Press, 2004. Print.
———. "English Only Jamás but Spanish Only Cuidado: Language and Nationalism in Contemporary Puerto Rico." Negrón-Muntaner and Grosfoguel 257–85. Print.
Negrón-Muntaner, Frances, and Ramón Grosfoguel. *Puerto Rican Jam: Rethinking Colonialism and Nationalism*. Minneapolis: University of Minnesota Press, 1997. Print.
Negrón-Muntaner, Frances, and Raquel Z. Rivera. "Reggaeton Nation." *NACLA Report on the Americas* 40.6 (Nov.–Dec. 2007): 35–40. Print.
Ocasio, Rafael. "The Infinite Variety of the Puerto Rican Reality: An Interview with Judith Ortiz Cofer." *Callaloo* 17.3 (Summer 1994): 730–42. Print.
Oquendo, Ángel R. "Liking to Be in America: Puerto Rico's Quest for Difference within the United States." *Duke Journal of Comparative & International Law* 14 (2004): 249. law.berkeley.edu. Web. 22 Dec. 2008.
Ortiz Cofer, Judith. *Silent Dancing: A Partial Remembrance of a Puerto Rican Childhood*. Houston, TX: Arte Publico Press, 1990. Print.
Pabón, Carlos. *Nación postmortem. Ensayos sobre los tiempos de insoportable ambigüedad*. San Juan, Puerto Rico: Callejón, 2002. Print.
Padgett, Tim. "Puerto Rico: Obama Visits a Commonwealth's Uncommon Problems." *Time*. Web. 13 June 2011.
Palau de López, Awilda. *Veinticinco años del periódico independentista Claridad y su visión de 68 problemas sociales puertorriqueños*. Río Piedras, Puerto Rico: Universidad de Puerto Rico, 1992. Print.
Paravisini-Gebert, Lizabeth. "Unchained Tales: Women Prose Writers from the

Hispanic Caribbean in the 1990s." *Bulletin of Latin American Research* 22.4 (2003): 445–64. Print.

———. "Women against the Grain: The Pitfalls of Theorizing Caribbean Women's Writing." *Winds of Change: The Transforming Voices of Caribbean Women Writers and Scholars*. Ed. Adele S. Newson and Linda Strong-Leek. New York: Peter Lang, 1998: 161–68. Print.

PEN Club de Puerto Rico, Certamen literario anual del. *Penclubpuertorico. blogspot.com*. Web. 24 Mar. 2009.

Pérez Rivera, Tatiana. "Feliz cumpleaños, tío Sergio." *El Nuevo Día*. Web. 13 Mar. 2011.

Perivolaris, John D. "Heroes, Survivors, and History: Edgardo Rodríguez Juliá and Puerto Rico's 1898." *Modern Language Review* 94.3 (Jul. 1999): 691–99. JSTOR. Web. 19 May 2010.

Pino-Ojeda, Walescka. *Sobre castas y puentes: Conversaciones con Elena Poniatowska, Rosario Ferré y Diamela Eltit*. Santiago, Chile: Cuarto Propio, 2000. Print.

"PIP se solidariza con la clase artística del País." Press release. *piprincon. blogspot.com*. Web. 1 June 2009.

"Proclama de Panamá. Congreso Latinoamericano y Caribeño por la Independencia de Puerto Rico." www.copppal.org.mx/doc-procla-pan.htm. Web. Nov. 2006.

"Q&A: The Chechen Conflict." *BBC News*. Web. 10 July 2006.

"Quebec Sovereignty Debate Settled: Poll." *CBC News*.. Web. 18 May 2010.

Quintana, Hilda E., María Cristina Rodríguez, and Gladys Vilá Barnes. *Personalidad y literatura puertorriqueñas*. 2nd ed. Madrid: Playor, 1986. Print.

Quiñones, Ernesto. *Bodega Dreams*. New York: Vintage, 2000. Print.

Raheja, Lauren. "The Future of Puerto Rico's Independence Movement." *City Limits* 29 July 2010. Web. 30 Oct 2010.

Ramos-Collado, Lilliana. "¿Arte queer? Ahora lo ves . . . ¡y ahora también lo ves!" *bodegonconteclado.wordP.com*. Web. 6 Feb. 2012

———. "Escritores, fin de siglo: un documento." *revistacruce.com*. n.d. Web. 27 Jan. 2013.

Ramos Méndez, Mario. *Posesión del ayer: La nacionalidad cultural en la estadidad*. San Juan, Puerto Rico: Isla Negra, 2007. Print.

Renan, Ernst. "What Is a Nation?" cooper.edu/humanities. Web. 25 Oct. 2007.

Ríos Ávila, Rubén. *La raza cómica: Del sujeto en Puerto Rico*. San Juan, Puerto Rico: Callejón, 2002. Print.

———. "Queer Nation." Caleb Acevedo et al. 293–307.

Ríos Cordero, Hugo. *A lo lejos el cielo*. Puerto Rico: Isla Negra, 2010. Print.

Rivera, Ángel Israel. *Puerto Rico ante los retos del siglo XXI*. San Juan, Puerto Rico: Nueva Aurora, 2007. Print.

Rivera-Batíz, Francisco L. "Puerto Rican New Yorkers in the 1990s: A Demographic and Socioeconomic Profile." *Boricuas in Gotham: Puerto Ricans in the Making of Modern New York City. Essays in Memory of Antonia Pantoja.* Ed. Gabriel Haslip-Viera, Angelo Falcón, and Félix Matos Rodríguez. Princeton, NJ: Markus Wiener, 2004. 106–25. Print.

Rivera de Álvarez, Josefina, and Manuel Álvarez Nazario. *Antología general de la literatura puertorriqueña.* Vol. 1. Madrid: Partenón, 1982. Print.

Rivera Ruiz, Álvaro M. *Aguadilla: El pueblo que le dio la espalda al mar.* San Juan/Santo Domingo: Isla Negra, 2007. Print.

Rivera Santana, José E. "Mensaje del MINH el 11 de enero de 2009." *redbetances.com.* Web. 13 May 2009.

Rodó, José Enrique. "Ariel." *analitica.com.* Web. 26 Jan. 2009.

Rodríguez, Pedro Juan. "Rafael Cancel Miranda." *NACLA Report on the Americas* 31.1 (July–Aug. 1997): 50 (2). Print.

Rodríguez Alcalá, Hugo. *Literatura de la independencia.* Madrid: La Muralla, 1980. Print.

Rodríguez de Tió, Lola. *Mi libro de Cuba.* Imprenta La Moderna, 1893. Google Book Search. Web. 17 Jul. 2008.

Rodríguez-Frese, Marcos. "Décimas de la estadidad." Web. 20 June 2012. borinquenliterario@gruposyahoo.com on behalf of guajana@coqui.net.

Rodríguez Juliá, Edgardo. "De la necedad a la suciedad." *El Nuevo Día.* Web. 10 July 2011.

———. "¿De qué país estamos hablando?" *El Nuevo Día.* Web. 14 Nov. 2010.

———. *El entierro de Cortijo.* Río Piedras, Puerto Rico: Huracán, 1983. *Print.*

———. "La calle al revés." *El Nuevo Día.* Web. 15 Jan 2012.

———. *La noche oscura del Niño Avilés.* Río Piedras, Puerto Rico: Huracán, 1984. Print.

———. *La renuncia del héroe Baltasar* 2nd ed. San Juan, Puerto Rico: Cultural, 1986. Print.

———. "No culpable." *El Nuevo Día.* Web. 10 April 2010.

———. *San Juan. Ciudad soñada.* San Juan, Puerto Rico: Tal Cual; Madison: University of Wisconsin Press, 2005. Print.

Rodríguez León, Mario A. "El altar de la Patria." *Claridad* (12 June 2013). Web. 13 June 2013.

Rodríguez Vázquez, José. *El sueño que no cesa: La nación deseada en el debate intelectual puertorriqueño.* San Juan, Puerto Rico: Callejón, 2004. Print.

Romero-Cesareo, Ivette. "Famed Puerto Rican Pro-Independence Activist Lolita Lebrón Died Today." *Repeating Islands blog.* Web. 1 Aug. 2010.

Rosado, José Angel. *El cuerpo del delito, el delito del cuerpo: La literatura policial de Edgar Allan Poe, Juan Carlos Onetti, Wilfredo Mattos Cintrón.* San Juan, Puerto Rico: Callejón, 2012. Print.

Rosaldo, Renato. *Culture and Truth: The Remaking of Social Analysis.* Boston: Beacon Press, 1993. Print.

Roy-Féquière, Magali. *Women, Creole Identity, and Intellectual Life in Early*

Twentieth-Century Puerto Rico. Philadelphia: Temple University Press; 2004. Print.

Ruark, Liz. "Rosario T. Ferré '60." *wellesley.edu*. 28 May 2001. Web. 8 April 2009.

Ruiz Ruiz, Carlitos, and Mariem Pérez Riera, dirs. *Maldeamores*. 2007. DVD.

Said, Edward. *Humanism and Democratic Criticism*. New York: Columbia University Press, 2008. Print.

Salgado, Nadia Celis. "Heterotopías del deseo: Sexualidad y poder en el Caribe de Mayra Santos Febres." Celis and Rivera 132–52.

Sánchez, Luis Rafael. "La guagua aérea." *No llores por nosotros, Puerto Rico*. Hanover, NH: Ediciones del Norte, 1998. 11–22. Print.

———. *La guaracha del Macho Camacho*. Buenos Aires: De la Flor, 1976. Print.

———. "Preguntas con ton y con son" *El Nuevo Día* 1 Mar. 2009. Web. 17 Mar. 2009.

———. "Vivir para chismear." *El Nuevo Día*. Web. 21 May 2008.

Sandoval, Arturo. "¡Mira, que vienen los nuyoricans!: El temor de la otredad en la literatura nacionalista puertorriqueña." *Revista de Crítica Literaria Latinoamericana* 23.45 (1997): 307–25. Print.

Santiago, Esmeralda. *América's Dream*. New York: HarperCollins, 1996. Print.

———. *Conquistadora*. New York: Vintage, 2012. Print.

———. *When I Was Puerto Rican*. New York: Vintage, 1994. Print.

Santiago Caraballo, Yaritza. "Al encuentro del Caribe francés." *El Nuevo Día*. Web. 22 Mar. 2010.

Santos Febres, Mayra. "Albizu." Carrión et al. 241–49.

———. *El cuerpo correcto*. San Juan, Puerto Rico: R&R Editoras, 1998. Print.

———. *Mal(h)ab(l)ar. Antología de nueva literatura puertorriqueña*. Puerto Rico: Fundación Puertorriqueña de las Humanidades, 1997. Print.

———. *Nuestra señora de la noche*. Madrid: Espasa Calpe, 2006. Print.

———. *Pez de vidrio*. Puerto Rico: Huracán, 1996. Print.

———. *Sobre piel y papel*. Puerto Rico: Callejón, 2005. Print.

———. *Urban Oracles*. Trans. Nathan Budoff and Lydia Platon Lázaro. Cambridge, MA: Lumen, 1997. Print.

Serrano, Francisco. *Seva vive*. 2008. DVD.

Sotomayor, Aurea María. "La imaginería nacionalista: De la historia al relato." Carrión et al. 251–71.

Sotomayor, Sonia. *My Beloved World*. New York: Knopf, 2013.

Stark, Lucy, Luke Lecheler, and Dyan Anunson. "Rosario Ferré." *Voices from the Gaps*. voices.cla.umn.edu. 8 Apr. 2009. Web. 10 Aug. 2009.

"Status Change Means Dutch Antilles No Longer Exists." *BBC News* 10 Oct. 2010. Web. 12 Oct. 2010.

Stavans, Ilan, ed. *The Norton Anthology of Latino Literature*. New York and London: Norton, 2011. Print.

Tapia y Rivera, Alejandro. *Mis memorias: O, Puerto Rico como lo encontré y*

como lo dejo. Puerto Rico: Editorial Edil, 1979. Google Book Search. 7 Mar. 2011.
Thomas, Piri. *Down These Mean Streets.* New York: Vintage, 1997.
Torres, Daniel. *Cabronerías o historias de tres cuerpos.* San Juan, Puerto Rico: Isla Negra, 1995. Print.
Torres Caballero, Benjamín. "Puerto Rico." *Concise Encyclopedia of Latin American Literature.* Ed. Verity Smith. London: Routledge, 2000. Credo Reference. Web. 31 Dec. 2010.
Torres-Padilla, José L., and Carmen Haydée Rivera. *Writing Off the Hyphen: New Perspectives on the Literature of the Puerto Rican Diaspora.* Seattle: University of Washington Press, 2008. Print.
Torres-Saillant, Silvio. *An Intellectual History of the Caribbean.* New York: Palgrave Macmillan, 2006. Print.
Trías Monge, José. *Puerto Rico: The Trials of the Oldest Colony in the World.* New Haven: Yale University Press, 1997. Print.
Van Haesendonck, Kristian. *¿Encanto o espanto? Identidad y nación en la novela puertorriqueña actual.* Madrid and Frankfurt: Iberoamericana and Verveuert, 2008. Print.
Vargas-Ramos, Carlos. "Migration and Political Resocialization: The Impact of Political Environment Change on Political Orientations among Puerto Rican Return Migrants."*Centro Journal of the Center for Puerto Rican Studies; Hunter College, CUNY* 23.1 (Spring 2011): 125–61. Web. 11 June 2012.
Varo, Carlos. *Consideraciones antropológicas y políticas en torno a la enseñanza del Spanglish en Nueva York.* Río Piedras, Puerto Rico: Librería Internacional, 1971. Print.
———. *Puerto Rico: Radiografía de un pueblo asediado.* Puerto Rico: Puerto, 1973. Print.
Vega, Ana Lydia, ed. "El PNP y el inglés." *PIP Rincón blog.* Web. 3 Feb. 2009.
———. *El tramo ancla.* Río Piedras, Puerto Rico: Universidad de Puerto Rico, 1989. Print.
———. *Encancaranublado y otros cuentos de naufragio.* Río Piedras, Puerto Rico: Antillana, 1983. Print.
———. *Falsas crónicas del sur.* Río Piedras, Puerto Rico: Universidad de Puerto Rico, 1991. Print.
———. "La pelona tiene la palabra." *El Nuevo Día* 3 July 2011. Web. 5 July 2011.
———. "Marejada de los muertos." *El Nuevo Día.* Web. 3 July 2011.
———. *Mirada de doble filo.* San Juan, Puerto Rico: Universidad de Puerto Rico, 2008. Print.
———. *Pasión de historia y otras historias de pasión.* Buenos Aires: De la Flor, 1987. Print.
———. "Visita de médico." *El Nuevo Día.* Web. 11 Feb. 2010.
Velázquez, Brunymarie. "Plantean medidas para frenar el éxodo de boricuas." *El Nuevo Día* 27 Jan. 2013. Web. 27 Jan. 2013.

Vélez, Diana L. "We Are (Not) in This Together: The Caribbean Imaginary in 'Encancaranublado' by Ana Lydia Vega." *Puerto Rican Women Writers*. Spec. issue of *Callaloo* 17.3 (Summer 1994): 826–33. Print.

Vicioso, Sherezada, and Lizabeth Paravisini-Gebert. "Julia de Burgos: Our Julia." *Puerto Rican Women Writers*. Spec. issue of *Callaloo* 17.3 (Summer 1994): 674–83. Print.

Villanueva Collado, Alfredo. "René Marqués, Ángel Lozada and the Constitution of the (Queer) Puerto Rican National Subject." *Centro Journal of the Center for Puerto Rican Studies; Hunter College, CUNY.* 19.1 (2007): 178–91.

Wallace, David Foster. *Consider the Lobster*. New York: Back Bay Books, 2007. Print.

Index

80Grados, 51, 108

Abkhazia, 19
Acevedo Marrero, Ramón Luis, 185n3
Acosta-Belén, Edna, 156
Agüeros, Jack, 118
Agüeybaná, 133–34
Albizu Campos, Pedro, 7; "Camp," 108–9; cult of, 5, 42, 86; documentary on, 41; graphic images of, 6, 41; in literature, 12, 41, 42, 147, 154; on elections, 32; on heroism, 4–5, 132, 136; online, 41, 42; reappraisal of, 5, 64, 86, 87, 102; repression of, 5, 30; street names, and 41
Aldama, Frederick Luis, 19
Alegría, Ricardo, 51
Algarín, Miguel, 21, 115, 157, 161
Alonso, Manuel, 120
Álvarez Curbelo, Silvia, 114
Anazagasty Rodríguez, José, 31
Anderson, Benedict, 20
Anthology, definition of, 53–54
Anzaldúa, Gloria, 66, 166
Aponte Alsina, Marta, 77
Arce de Vázquez, Margot, 119
Arriví, Francisco, 51
Aruba, 38
Ateneo Puertorriqueño, 26, 40, 50, 51

Balderston, Daniel, 81

Barradas, Efraín, 123
Barsy, Kalman: *Naufragio*, 78; "jardín, El," 72
Bayrón Toro, Fernando, 25–26
Belaval, Emilio, 22, 48
Bello, Andrés, 110–11
Benítez, María Babiana, 111–12
Bernabe, Rafael, 14, 183n3
Berríos, Rubén, 7, 178
Betances, Ramón E., 21, 40, 169
Bhabha, Homi K., 141
Blanco, Tomás, 22, 48; "Elogio de la plena," 60
Bolaño, Roberto, 105
Bonaire, 38
Braschi, Giannina, 162
Brookhiser, Richard, 23
Burgos, Julia de, 21, 22, 48, 116

Cabiya, Pedro, 52
Calderón, Tego, 4
Caleb Acevedo, David, 185n3
Calle 13, 3–4, 6, 99
Cámara Fuertes, Luis Raúl, 23–25, 28
Campa, Román de la, 157
Canales, Blanca, 104
Canales, Nemesio, 59
Cancel, Mario R., 42, 62, 87, 135, 139, 140
Cancel Miranda, Rafael, 10, 32, 94
Cancel Sepúlveda, Mario, 31

Caribbean Context, 8, 35–38
Carpentier, Alejo, 150
Carpeteo, 30
Carrión, Juan Manuel, 83
Castellanos, Juan de, 133, 134
Castillo, Jorge Luis, 78
Castro Pereda, Rafael, 64
Cataluña, 1, 20, 183n1
Celis, Nadia V., 152
Cerro Maravilla, 30
Chechnya, 1, 183n1
Cienfuegos, Lucky, 161
Cintrón Opio, Ángel, 130–31
Claridad, "En Rojo," 14, 21, 103; online, 42; publication of *Seva*, 135
Colectivo Homoerótica, 50
Collado Schwarz, Ángel, 14, 42
Colonial condition, 100; allegory of, 45, 174–75; compared to DOMs, 9; historical overview, 22–23; pragmatic considerations, 37; reputed effects of, 32, 33; UN anti-colonial stance, 40
Commonwealth, 1, 3, 23, 31. See also ELA
Córdova, Nathaniel L., 184n13
Corretjer, Juan Antonio, 22, 32–33, 48, 115–16, 134
Coss, Papo, 15–16
Cuba, 35–36, 37, 48, 70, 81–82
Curaçao, 38

Dávila, Arlene M., 15, 16–17
Départements d'Outre-Mer, 9–10; modernity in, 121
Derrickson, Teresa, 174
Díaz Alfaro, Abelardo, 48; "Josco, El," 63–64, 70
Díaz Quiñones, Arcadio, 50; "De cómo y cuándo bregar," 69–70; José Luis González interview, 10, 83–93 passim
Díaz Valcárcel, Emilio, 49, 51; *Figuraciones en el mes de marzo*, 76
Diego, José de, 21, 30, 48, 58, 62; "En la brecha," 63
Diego Padró de, José, 81; *En babia*, 76
Duchesne, Ramón, 137
Duchesne Winter, Juan, 95
Dutch Caribbean islands, 38

Echavarría Ferrari, Arturo, 77
Economy, 14, 18, 23, 33–34, 42, 185n33; as security issue, 28; failed, 24

Editorial Isla Negra, 52
ELA, 1, 3, 14; attachment to, 25; and cultural symbols, 33; definition of, 23; party of, 15, 24
Elections, 23–28, 178, 183n2
En la Orilla: Una virtual experiencia de la joven literatura puertorriqueña, 51
"En Rojo." See *Claridad*
Espada, Martin, 161
Esteves, Sandra María, 21, 157, 161

Facebook, xii, 41
Falcón, Angelo, 157
Ferrao, Luis Ángel, 5, 87
Ferré, Luis A., 15. See also Pro-statehood party (PNP)
Ferré, Rosario, 22, 48, 51, 56, 93–98, 154; bilingual identity, 94–95; controversy with Ana Lydia Vega, 2, 96–97; "Cuando las mujeres quieren a los hombres," 71, 152; *Eccentric Neighborhoods*, 94; *House on the Lagoon, The*, 94, 97, 98, 118, 146–48; *Maldito Amor*, 98; *Papeles de Pandora*, 97; support of statehood, 11, 93, 95; *Zona de Carga y Descarga*, 93
Ferrer Canales, José, 58; "José Martí y José de Diego," 61–62
Figueroa, Edwin, 73–74, 127
Flores, Jaime "Shaggy," 162
Flores, Juan, 3, 14, 35, 36–37, 156, 168–69
Font Acevedo, Francisco, 129–30
Franco, Jean, 21
Francophone Islands, 8–10
French Caribbean Islands. See Francophone Islands
Fuente, José Luis de la, 149
Fuster Lavin, Ana María, 7, 108

García Canclini, Néstor, 184n15
García Cuevas, Eugenio, 105, 126–27
García Passalacqua, Juan Manuel, 134
García Ramis, Magali, 41; *Felices días, tío Sergio*, 76–77; *Horas del sur*, 151–52
Gautier Benítez, José, 21, 30, 48, 112–13, 131, 163
Gelpí, Juan G., 49, 185n2; "Literatura y paternalismo en Puerto Rico," 65
Generación del '30, 21, 48, 49
Gil, Carlos, 10

Glissant, Édouard, 4, 132, 186n1; on the need for heroes, 142
González, José Luis, 14, 22, 25, 33, 48, 70, 71, 102, 103, 162, 168; on Albizu Campos, 8, 86–87; critique of independentismo, 64, 82–89; on de Diego, 84; denunciation of "telurismo," 84–85, 114–15; on Ferré, 96; on López Nieves, 138; *País de cuatro pisos, El*, 60, 64, 89–93 passim; short stories, 89–93
González Cruz, Michael, 33
González de Freytes, Gina, 153–54
Gran Familia Puertorriqueña, La, 7, 39, 43, 75, 123, 146
Grillo, Rafael, 139
Grito de Lares, 12–13, 18, 28, 40
Grosfoguel, Ramón, 8, 14, 31, 37, 39, 44; *Puerto Rican Jam*, 10, 101–3
Guadeloupe, 8–9, 184n10
Guajana, 3, 48, 101
Guillory, John, 53
Guyana, 103

Hernández, Carmen Dolores, 50, 51; *A viva voz*, 95, 126, 135, 138; "Escribiendo en la frontera," 66
Heroes, ix, x, 4–8, 14, 100, 133; in literature, 12–13
Hispanophilia, 61, 62, 76, 88, 90, 142, 148, 168–69, 177
Hodges, Kenneth, 20
Homar, Lorenzo, 51
Hostos, Eugenio María de, 21, 30, 31, 48, 52, 57, 62, 156

Independentismo, 15, 22, 50, 51, 62; as counter-culture, 38; González, José Luis and 82–89, 168; harassment of, 28, 31; hip-hop and, 4; Nuyoricans and, 157, 161; questioning of, 82–89, 106; religious overtones, 58, 62, 83–85; Spanish-only attitude 160, 164, 177–78
Independentistas, 9, 17, 26, 184n5; and culture 29; violence against 28, 30. *See also* Albizu Campos; Independentismo
Instituto de Cultura Puertorriqueña (ICP), 15, 50
Instituto Soberanista Puertorriqueño (ISP), 14, 51

Irizarry, Estelle, 135
Irizarry Natal, Federico: "Camp," 108–9

Janer, Zilkia, 16
Jíbaro, 16; adulation of jibarismo, 84; estadidad jíbara, 15; jibarismo literario, 70, 163; in literature, 89–92, 124, 140, 165; migration of, 34

Kevane, Bridget, 95
Klor de Alva, J. Jorge, 120
Kosovo, 20

La Torre Lagares, Elidio, 52; *Correr tras el viento*, 105; "Unicornio," 74
Laguerre, Enrique, 81; *llamarada, La*, 75–76
Lalo, Eduardo, 52, 80, 105; invisibility, notion of 23; *Simone*, 106, 128–29
Lao, Agustín, 38
Laviera, Tato, 21, 157; "AmeRícan," 160
Lebrón, Lolita, 4, 6–8, 12, 147, 184n7
Levins Morales, Aurora, 161
Ley de la Mordaza, 30
Ley Núm. 54, 167
LGBT movement, 26, 45, 56, 71, 103, 105, 178; support in culture production, 14
Lloréns Torres, Luis, 21, 163; "Canción de las Antillas," 88
López Adorno, Pedro, 55
López Alemán, Ramón, 42
López Baralt, Luce, 67–68
López Baralt, Mercedes, 50, 53–54
López Bauzá, Juan, 95
López Nieves, Luis, 72; *corazón de Voltaire, El*, 150, 151; "En la muralla de San Juan," 141; "lado oscuro de la luna, El" 72; *Seva*, 13, 67, 134–41, 142, 144, 146; *verdadera muerte de Juan Ponce de León, La*, 149–50
López Rivera, Oscar, 18, 40
Lozada, Ángel, 105; *No quiero quedarme sola y vacía*, 105–6; *Patografía, La*, 34–35, 140–41, 142
Lyon Johnson, Kelli, 146

Macheteros, Los, ix, 6, 104, 162
Macías de Yoon, Claudia, 96
Maldeamores (2007), 127
Maldonado, Adál, 42

Mari Brás, Juan, 7, 26, 41, 184n14; on voting, 32
Marín, Pachín, 21
Marqués, René, 10, 32, 48, 51, 71, 82; *Carreta, La*, 115
Marrero García, Mariel C., 32, 136, 183n3
Martí, José, 53, 62; "Nuestra América," 30, 63, 130
Martínez Maldonado, Manuel, 78
Martínez Masdeu, Edgar, 54, 55, 62, 185n3
Martínez Ramírez, Héctor, 185n18
Martinique, 23, 151, 175, 184n10
Matienzo Cintrón, Rosendo, 59
Matilla, Alfredo, 78
Matos Paoli, Francisco, 48
McCraken, Ellen, 163
Meléndez, Concha, 51
Meléndez Muñoz, Miguel, 70
Meme, 3, 41, 184n4
Méndez Ballester, Manuel, 76, 133
Miranda, Lin-Manuel, 3
Modernity, 22, 31, 111, 115–19, 134, 165; comparison to DOMs, 121; definition of, 19
Montero, Mayra, 3, 39, 57, 105; *Púrpura profundo*, 78
Morales, Ed, 20, 25, 58
Morales, Jacobo, 3; *Linda Sara*, 145–46
Movimiento Independentista Nacional Hostosiano, 15–16, 17, 184n14
Movimiento Unión Soberanista (MUS), 24
Mujica, Bárbara, 55
Muñoz Marín, Luis, 9, 37, 143; portrayal in literature, 147, 184n9
Museo del Barrio, 118, 158

Narayan, Uma, 165
National allegories, 7, 40, 43, 58, 63, 65, 116, 120, 126, 129. *See also* Gran Familia Puertorriqueña, La
National imagination, 44, 52, 109, 110, 111, 113, 121, 142; definition of, 20
Nationhood, 19; cultural definition of, 15–16, 19; symbols of, 1, 2, 7, 8, 9, 15, 16, 17, 21, 33, 42, 43, 52, 57, 63, 65, 67, 72, 74, 120, 123, 134, 148
Nationalists. *See* Independentistas
négritude, 88
Negrón, Luis, 105; *Mundo Cruel*, 106–7
Negrón-Muntaner, Frances, 10, 14, 37; *Puerto Rican Jam*, 101–3; on Puerto Rican shame, 135
Negrón-Portillo, Mariano, 102
Nolla, Olga, 93; *castillo de la memoria, El*, 115, 148–49, 150
Nostalgia, 2, 43, 45, 57, 60, 71, 84, 87, 89, 100, 103, 111, 113, 117, 120, 122, 130; Hispanophilic, 90, 148, 157, 159, 161
Nuyorican Poets Café, 21, 156–62
Nuyoricans, 95

Obama, Barack, 27, 40, 99
Ojeda Ríos, Filiberto, 6
Oller, Francisco 111; "Camino a la Hacienda Aurora," 117–18
Oquendo, Ángel R., 17, 29
Ortiz Cofer, Judith, 45, 159; *Silent Dancing: A Partial Remembrance of a Puerto Rican Childhood*, 170–75

Pabón, Carlos, 11, 41, 135, 138
Pagán, Dilcia N., 104
Paisajismo, 111
Palau Islands, 103
Palés Matos, Luis, 60, 81
Palestine, 19
Paravisini-Gebert, Lisabeth, 97, 116
Partido del Pueblo Trabajador (PPT), 24
Partido Independentista Puertorriqueño (PIP), 23, 27, 29, 39, 40, 51, 178; criticism by René Marqués, 82; internet presence, 41–42
Partido Nuevo Progresista (PNP), 17, 24; representation in literature, 106–7
Partido Popular Democrático (PPD), 15, 17, 24, 31, 35; and cultural symbols, 33
Partido Puertorriqueños por Puerto Rico (PPR), 24
Peace of Westphalia (1648), 19
Pedreira, Antonio S., 22, 48, 59–61; *Insularismo*, 10
Pérez, René, 3–4
Perivolaris, John, 5, 81; on implications of heroism, 142
Picó, Fernando, 135
Pietri, Pedro, 21, 157; "Puerto Rican Obituary," 159
Piñero, Miguel, 21, 157, 159–60
Plebiscites, 27, 80
Political Prisoners, ix. *See also* López Rivera, Oscar
Ponce de León, Juan; in literature, 133, 148–49

Ponce Massacre, 12, 18; dramatization in literature, 147
Posmodernos, 101, 102
"Proclama de Panamá, La," 39

Quebec, 183n1
Quintana, Hilda E., 185n3
Quiñones, Ernesto, 86

Ramos Collado, Lilliana, 103, 115
Ramos Méndez, Mario, 14–15
Religious organizations, 26: Catholic, 26, 83; Pentecostal, 26, 185n18
Renan, Ernst, 18, 139
Ríos Cordero, Hugo, 121
Rivera, Ángel Israel, 25, 28
Rivera, Juan Pablo, 153; "Vida y obra de Marta la Diabla," 108
Rivera-Batíz, Francisco L., 158
Rivera de Álvarez, Josefina, 48, 185n3
Rivera Ruiz, Álvaro M., 136
Rivera Santana, José E., 17
Rodó, José Enrique, 61
Rodríguez de Tió, Lola, 21, 30, 36, 48, 57, 62; "Carta a mis amigas de la vuelta abajo," 58
Rodríguez-Frese, Marcos, 107
Rodríguez Juliá, Edgardo, 4, 22, 23, 56, 83, 98–101, 103, 107, 127, 146; *Caribeños*, 101; *entierro de Cortijo, El*, 75, 99, 100, 126; *noche oscura del Niño Avilés, La*, 100, 101, 143–45; *renuncia del héroe Baltasar, La*, 100, 101, 143; statehood, stance on, 98–99; *Tribulaciones de Jonás, Las*, 184n9, 185n24
Rodríguez, Jr., Abraham, 121
Rodríguez León, Mario A., 38
Rodríguez Vázquez, José R., 5, 14, 61, 132, 136
Romero, Ivette, 184n7
Rosado, José Ángel, 31
Rosas Cintrón, Olga I., 28
Roy-Féquière, 22
Ruiz Belvis, Segundo, 33
Ruiz Ruiz, Carlos, 127

Saba, 38
Sanabria Santaliz, Edgardo, 72
Sánchez, Luis Rafael, 10, 22, 38, 44, 48, 68; "guagua aérea, La," 47, 65–66, 123; *guaracha del Macho Camacho, La*, 46–47, 76, 122–23; *pasión según Antígona Pérez, La*, 47
Sandoval, Arturo, 160
Santiago, Esmeralda, 12, 21, 162, 170; *América's Dream*, 164–66; "Como se come una guayaba," 75, 164; comparison with Judith Ortiz Cofer, 170–75 passim; *Conquistadora*, 133, 162, 165, 169–70; *When I was Puerto Rican*, 162, 163–64, 170
Santiago (Negrón), María de Lourdes, 7, 29
Santos Febres, Mayra, 41, 68–69, 108, 185n3; "Act of Faith," 104; "Dilcia M.," 104; "Dulce pesadilla, Abnel," 125–26; *Mal(ha)b(l)ar*, 104; *Nuestra señora de la noche*, 152–53; "Oso Blanco," 126; *Sirena Selena vestida de pena*, 78
Scotland, 1, 20, 183n1
Shame, sense of, 2, 16, 18, 135, 177
Somaliland, 19
Soto, Pedro Juan, 48, 49, 50, 51, 71, 81
Sotomayor, Aurea María, 41
Sotomayor, Sonia, 113, 163, 175
South Sudan, 32
Sovereignty, 1, 15, 52; Caribbean context 37; soberanía, 27
Soviet Union, 20, 37
Spain, 34; cultural legacy in Puerto Rico, 61, 132; iniquities in rule of Puerto Rico, 30, 137, 169. *See also* Colonial condition; Hispanophilia
Spanish, centrality of, 66–68, 160
Sri Lanka, 1, 183n1
St. Eustatius, 38
St. Maarten, 38
Statehood, 14–15, 33; assimilation as cultural anathema, 22; estadidad jíbara, 15; in literature, 106; radical, 37, 185n23
Sued Badillo, Jalil, 134

Taínos, 16, 133. *See also* Agüeybaná
Tapia y Rivera, Alejandro, 112
Thomas, Piri, 21, 157
Torres, Daniel, 105; *Cabronerías o historias de tres cuerpos*, 123
Torres Caballero, Benjamin, 115, 120
Torres-Saillant, Silvio, 37–38, 132

United States, 1898 invasion of Puerto Rico, 30, 136; assimilation to, 16, 22;

citizenship, 23; cultural influence of, 81; discontent with, 30; political alliance to, 26. *See also* Colonial condition
University of Puerto Rico, Río Piedras campus, 17, 29, 50, 52, 80, 105

Vargas, Tomás L., 42
Vargas-Ramos, Carlos, x, 24
Varo, Carlos, 77, 186n7
Vega, Ana Lydia, 39, 48, 111, 120, 154; "Cuento en camino," 123–24; Ferré controversy, 2, 96–97; "Letra para salsa y tres soneos por encargo," 71; "Sobre héroes y tumbas," 12–13; "Un domingo de Lilliane," 26
Vega, Bernardo, 74–75, 156
Vega, José Luis, 101

Vélez, Diana L., 129
Vicioso, Sherezada, 116
Vientós Gastón, Nilita, 22, 48, 51; "Los 'puertorriqueñistas' y los 'occidentalistas,'" 96
Vieques, 17–18, 20, 42; as symbolic locale, 167–68
Villanueva Collado, Alfredo, 59, 108
Voting in Puerto Rico, 3, 23–28, 31–32; voter turnout, 27

Western Sahara, 19

Young Lords, x, 158, 162

Zeno Gandía, Manuel, 21, 30; "El negocio," 75

About the Author

Born and raised in Cabo Rojo, **María Acosta Cruz** received a B.A. from the University of Puerto Rico at Mayagüez, and an M.A. and Ph.D. in comparative literature from SUNY–Binghamton. She is associate professor of Spanish at Clark University in Massachusetts.